AUTHOR	CLASS
SMITH, D. M.	M
TITLE	No
North West	08465772

Lancashire County Council

Industrial Britain

THE NORTH WEST

Industrial Britain

THE NORTH WEST
David M. Smith

 David & Charles : Newton Abbot

08465772

Printed in Great Britain by
Clarke Doble & Brendon Limited Plymouth
for David & Charles (Publishers) Limited
South Devon House Railway Station
Newton Abbot Devon

Contents

List of Illustrations

Plates

Figures in Text

Preface

THIS IS ONE of the first of a new series of industrial studies of the major regions of Britain. The aim is to draw attention to recent changes in the structure and location of industry, and to examine some of the economic and social problems which have arisen in the process. Since the war the pace of change in some areas has been so rapid as to leave their economy almost unrecognisable, and existing published accounts of the industrial structure and geography of the regions are often out of date. By offering a contemporary view of industrial Britain, based on the latest available information, it is hoped that this series will help to provide the much-needed factual background against which wider regional problems and planning policies can better be understood.

The North West is a region of very great interest from an industrial point of view. As the home of the Lancashire cotton industry, it became one of the first of the highly-specialised manufacturing regions created by the Industrial Revolution. The subsequent decline of the cotton industry has brought a loss of 0·5 million jobs in the last fifty years, and the region has been desperately trying to find a new economic identity, particularly during the period since the Second World War. The way in which the regional economy is adjusting to changing circumstances, and how far the process can be assisted by regional planning, are matters of concern to similar regions elsewhere in Britain. The outcome is also relevant to parts of other advanced industrial nations which are experiencing the same difficulties, or can expect to face similar problems sooner or later.

The research on which this book is based was supported in part by grants from the Penrose Fund of the American Philosophical Society, to whom the author is very grateful. Other acknowledgments appear on pp 237–8.

1

An Introduction to the North West

THE NORTH WEST occupies an interesting position in Britain's regional make-up. With the bleak Pennine moors on the one side and the rich farmland of the Cheshire plain and western Lancashire on the other, it straddles the margins between upland and lowland Britain. Its sprawling industrial conurbations, with their great suburban extrusions, belong to modern metropolitan England, while the agricultural villages, small market towns, and isolated hill farms still evoke the pre-industrial era. The regional economy contains similar contrasts, with successful modern growth industries typical of the more prosperous regions of the Midlands and the South side by side with the mills and collieries which until recently epitomised the industrial North.

North West England comprises the counties of Lancashire and Cheshire, together with the High Peak area of Derbyshire. This definition is certainly not perfect, but for the present purposes it has the advantage of government blessing. Ever since Britain was divided into standard regions for various official purposes, the North West as defined above has remained unchanged, and in 1965 it was designated one of the country's economic planning regions. Like the other regions, the North West is defined largely by ancient county boundaries, so its precise limits owe more to historical accident and official expediency than to modern economic considerations. But it is for this area that an increasing number of regional statistics are being compiled, and it is within this framework that regional economic and land-use planning problems have been discussed for the past few years. In any case, the main industrial districts of south-east Lancashire and Merseyside fall clearly within the officially-defined North West, and the exact boundary line in most of the peripheral areas is not particularly important.

The North West is the most populous of the economic planning regions, with the exception of the South East. The present population is about 6·75 million, with the Greater Manchester and Merseyside conurbations accounting for more than half this figure. The North

13

West thus contains one in eight of Britain's inhabitants, on only slightly more than one-thirtieth of the land area, giving an overall population density not exceeded by any other region, and almost four times that of the nation as a whole. Nearly 30 per cent of the surface area is classed as urban, compared with 10 per cent in all England and Wales.

With a little over 3 million of Britain's 24 million workers, the North West makes a substantial contribution to the national economy. The region is the home of many prominent firms, including some of the country's major exporters, and accounts for about one-sixth by value of Britain's output of manufactured goods.

Some Basic Geographical Features[1]

From the physical point of view, the North West divides readily into two areas of sharply contrasting landscapes. On the western side are relatively flat lowlands, forming a northward continuation of the plains of the Midlands, while to the east are the Pennine uplands and their foothills (Fig 1). The lowland zone is widest in the south, in the Cheshire plain, where it extends up to thirty miles east to west. It narrows suddenly where Rossendale protrudes westwards from the main mass of the Pennines, and almost disappears north of the Fylde in the narrow coastal strips which separate Morecambe Bay from the Forest of Bowland to the east and the Lake District to the north.

The upland scene is entirely different from that of lowland Lancashire and Cheshire. In place of the gently undulating landscape of the plains are steep-sided valleys and elevated plateau surfaces, reaching over 2,000 ft on Bleaklow Hill and Kinder Scout in the Peak District. In place of the meadows, woods and fertile fields are the gritstone moors with their peat bogs and the green and grey limestone landscape of upland pastures and drystone walls. In place of the red-brick farmhouses, villages, market towns, and industrial cities are the scattered stone-built homes of the hill farmers, hamlets lying in the hollows, and valley mill-towns round the edges of the uplands.

It is the combined resources of these two contrasting zones which have helped man to make the region what it is today. The uplands, which receive most of the rainfall, act as a great water-storage area, and their swift streams have been an important source of power. The limestone areas provide a rock which has many and varied industrial uses, and the pastures of the plateaus nourished the sheep whose fleeces gave the first local weavers the yarn for their looms. Today Rossendale and the Peak District perform an important additional

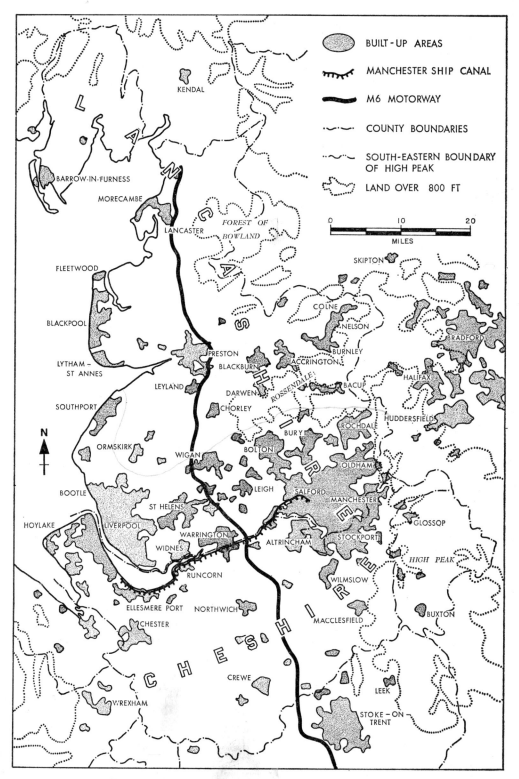

Fig 1. Major geographical features of North West England.

function as recreation areas for the population of the great industrial cities which fringe the Pennines.

The lowlands have the extensive areas of flat land needed for houses, factories, railway yards, shopping centres and all the other land-use requirements of a modern urban-industrial society. They provide easy land communications, and penetration from the sea is aided by estuaries, in particular the Mersey. The fertile soils support the crops and livestock which help to supply the huge urban markets, and the coast, as well as assisting the growth of trading and fishing, has provided ideal locations for seaside resorts and retirement towns.

But the most important of the lowland's natural resources, and the one which has done most to promote the region's economic development, is the Lancashire coalfield. For centuries this has provided a source of heat for the home and fuel and power for industry, and, despite reduced production in recent years, the field is still important to the region, which accounts for one-fifth of the national industrial and domestic consumption of coal. Of the region's other mineral resources, the most significant economically is the saltfield which underlies a large part of central Cheshire. It is a major source of rocksalt and brine, and has had an important bearing on the growth of the chemical industry.

The region's settlement pattern is dominated by the two major cities and their satellite towns (Fig 1). The South East Lancashire conurbation, as officially defined by the Registrar General, has a total population of about 2·5 million, and is thus the largest conurbation in Britain except for Greater London. The southern (Cheshire) side, apart from Stockport, is mainly suburban residential, but the northern side comprises a semi-circle of industrial towns and cities which flank the edge of the Manchester embayment and penetrate into the foothills, including Bolton, Bury, Rochdale and Oldham. On the northern side of the conurbation Rossendale interrupts the urban development which, had it not been for these upland fells, would doubtless have extended continuously to Blackburn and Burnley. As it is, houses and factories are squeezed into almost every valley, to give the Rossendale towns a population of about 50,000. When the valleys broaden out again to form the Blackburn–Burnley lowland, another string of industrial towns and cities appears, with about 370,000 people living in the area from Blackburn and Darwen in the west to Nelson and Colne in the east. To the west, Preston is the northernmost of the series of industrial towns which occupy the lowlands of central Lancashire. To the south, Wigan, St Helens, Leigh, Widnes and

The Tame valley west of Stalybridge. This is the landscape of nineteenth-century industrialisation, with mills, other factories and houses crowded together along the valley. In the distance are the Pennine moors.

Page 17: THE LANDSCAPE OF THE LAST CENTURY

Essex Street, Colne. These terrace rows are typical of the urban environment created by the rapid growth of the cotton towns during the last century.

Gateway House, Manchester. This glass and concrete office complex has recently been completed adjoining Picadilly Station. It symbolises the new city landscape which is gradually replacing the old.

Page 18: The NEW LANDSCAPE OF THE NORTH WEST

Spath Lane estate at Handforth, Wilmslow. One of the estates built for Manchester overspill outside the city, this is representative of the new environment being created for the region's industrial workers.

Warrington are the largest places in a dense but discontinuous urban-industrial belt connecting the two conurbations. The Merseyside conurbation, to the west, is divided into two by the estuary: the larger (eastern) part is dominated by Liverpool, and houses a total population of over 1 million, while west of the Mersey 350,000 people live in what has now become a virtually continuous built-up strip from Wallasey to Ellesmere Port.

Outside the main urban-industrial axis of Greater Manchester to Merseyside, and the lesser east-west belt from Colne to Preston, settlement is relatively thinly distributed. In northern Lancashire the big exceptions are Barrow-in-Furness, Lancaster and Morecambe, and the Fylde coast. In most of Cheshire the pattern is one of isolated industrial and service towns separated by predominantly rural areas.

Three major features of the region's communications—the Manchester Ship Canal, the M6 Motorway, and the sea—are shown on Fig 1. The Ship Canal, together with the heavily-used East Lancashire Road (Manchester to Liverpool), emphasises the traditional and continuing importance of east–west movement between the two conurbations. The motorway, which gives rapid access to the Midlands and the South as well as improving intra-regional movement, stresses what may become an important north–south development axis. The region's economy has for a long time been heavily dependent on sea trading, the major ports being Liverpool (the second port in Britain in terms of tonnage) and Manchester. Liverpool handles about 25 million tons of foreign trade and 5 million coastwise, while for the Port of Manchester, which includes all the installations along the Ship Canal, the figures are about 10 million and 4·5 million respectively. The secondary ports are Heysham, Preston and Garston. Mention must also be made of the region's rail connections, with freightliner services and the electrification of the main line to London helping to improve the vital links with the major growth regions to the south.

An Outline Economic History[2]

The present pattern of urban-industrial development is largely a product of the past two centuries. Most of the region's settlements were already in existence in medieval times, but it was the Industrial Revolution and its aftermath which determined the location of the major urban and industrial growth, selecting those places which were suitable for new economic functions and those which were to remain agricultural villages or small market towns.

The key to the economic development of the North West was, of

B

course, the rise of textile manufacturing. For hundreds of years, as in
other parts of the country, yarn had been spun and cloth woven to
satisfy local demand, but during the sixteenth and seventeenth
centuries the production of linen and woollen fabrics began to take on
special importance in Lancashire. Hand-loom weaving was practised
on an increasing scale in the towns, as well as on the Pennine flanks
where it was combined with agriculture. During the seventeenth
century the use of cotton yarn was introduced in Lancashire, and the
making of fustian spread rapidly. The first three-quarters of the
eighteenth century saw a five-fold increase in imports of raw cotton,
and by the end of this period there were 30,000 people in and around
Manchester working in cotton manufacturing.[3]

Until the latter part of the eighteenth century the Lancashire textile
trade remained a domestic industry, with hand-operated looms and
spinning wheels. Two developments were of special importance in
changing this: the mechanisation of cotton spinning, and the adoption
of the factory system based on water power. The various attempts to
produce yarn of a consistently high quality on a machine more
elaborate than the spinning wheel culminated in the inventions of
James Hargreaves and Richard Arkwright in the 1760s. The water-
powered factory, as a means of larger-scale production, was already
available by this time; it had been pioneered in silk throwing half a
century earlier, and there were already silk mills in the region at
Congleton, Macclesfield and Stockport. The first successful water-
powered cotton-spinning mills were built in the Derwent valley in
Derbyshire and not in the North West, but the new system was quickly
adopted in Lancashire. The search for water-power sites took cotton
mills into the recesses of many of the Pennine valleys, as well as to
almost every possible location around the edge of the Manchester
embayment where the swift-flowing steams emerge from the uplands.[4]

It was not long before steam power was applied to spinning
machinery, and the first Boulton & Watt engine to be installed in a
Lancashire cotton mill was put to work in 1789. The local coal now
proved an enormous advantage to the Lancashire industry, which
fortuitously found itself practically on top of one of Britain's major
coalfields. During the first half of the nineteenth century steam power
rapidly replaced the waterwheel in cotton spinning, and also in weaving
which was quickly mechanised after the development of efficient
power looms, so that, with the dual advantage of cheap local power
and access to materials and world markets via Liverpool, Lancashire's
future as Britain's major cotton-manufacturing region was assured.

The development of coal mining was of critical importance to

Lancashire's textile trade, as well as to other emerging industrial activities, and it was coal that had to provide fuel for fires in the countless terrace rows of workers' cottages which housed the region's rapidly growing labour force. Almost every part of the exposed coalfield was grubbed up in primitive fashion and its valuable contents hauled away. By the middle of the nineteenth century annual production had reached 10 million tons, and mining extended from the St Helens area in the west to the edge of the Pennines in the east, and from Colne in the north to almost as far south as Macclesfield in Cheshire.

Another important contributor to regional economic growth was the improvement of communications. Until the pace of industrial development began to quicken during the eighteenth century the internal movement of goods was accomplished satisfactorily, if laboriously, along rivers and the primitive roads. But this system soon proved inadequate as a lubricant for the new regional economy. The first improvement was the creation of the turnpike roads; by the middle of the eighteenth century most of the major regional routes had been turnpiked, and others followed, notably in the emergent manufacturing and mining districts.[5] Among other things, these roads helped to maintain the smooth flow of traffic between the ports and the industrial towns which were growing up well inland.

The first improvements in water transportation involved the creation of 'navigations' out of existing rivers. These included the Mersey & Irwell, and the Weaver which served the mid-Cheshire saltfield and agricultural areas. The first true canals were a direct result of the need for a more efficient way to move coal; the Sankey Navigation, opened in 1757, connected the River Mersey with mines to the north, and Brindley's famous Bridgewater Canal a few years later gave the Worsley mines access to the Manchester market. The opening of the Trent & Mersey Canal in the late 1770s gave the North West its first means of efficient bulk transportation to the Midlands, and other canals soon provided a connection with the West Riding industrial region. By the middle of the nineteenth century few important industrial towns in Lancashire and Cheshire were without a link with the regional system of waterways, and locations beside the canals attracted many factories and warehouses. The canals were important for the distribution of coal outside the coalfield as well as within the main industrial areas, enabling steam-powered factories to be set up in places like Lancaster, Preston and Liverpool at no great disadvantage compared with locations nearer the mines. The last great act in the development of the region's waterways was the cutting of the

Manchester Ship Canal, opened in 1894, which turned a city thirty miles inland into a major port for ocean-going vessels.

Just as the canals had an important bearing on regional economic growth and the location of industrial activity, so did the railways. As well as greatly improving communications between the port facilities of Merseyside and the industrial complex of south-east Lancashire, the railways gave greater flexibility to inter-regional trade. Lines were soon crossing the Pennines, and providing fast transport to Birmingham and London. The network thickened as the nineteenth century progressed, connecting up the industrial towns, extending the markets for their products, and providing the first efficient commuter services from city centres to the growing residential suburbs. And when the railway companies set up their huge locomotive and wagon works, the building of 'railway towns', as exemplified by Crewe, Horwich and Newton-le-Willows, introduced a new element into the regional pattern of settlement.

With coal providing the energy and the new canals and railways the means of movement, the regional economy continued to grow. Lancashire's prosperity epitomised the new industrial Britain in the making. By the middle of the nineteenth century the basic location pattern of the cotton industry had been established,[6] but its capacity and employment went on increasing. However, the continuation of the old silk industries at Macclesfield and Congleton in Cheshire, and the survival of some woollen manufacturing on the Pennine flanks, prevented cotton from completely monopolising the textile scene. Coal mining expanded to keep up with demand, and its efficiency improved as better equipment and deep-mining methods were adopted. The manufacture of textile machinery and the beginning of other engineering activities brought some diversity to the cotton and coal regions, but many places continued to rely on one industry for their livelihood —sometimes on one mill or one mine. Other industries which were establishing their place in the regional economy included chemicals in north Cheshire, glass at St Helens, and clothing in the Manchester district. As the ports grew, the range of commodities handled increased as well as the volume of trade, and Liverpool and Manchester attracted important processing industries.

Some idea of the pace of regional economic development is given by population figures. During the first half of the nineteenth century the population of the North West trebled, to reach 2·5 million, and between 1851 and 1901 it more than doubled. The region's share of Britain's population rose from 8·2 per cent in 1801 to 14·1 per cent at the end of the nineteenth century.

Such population growth could not be achieved without a dramatic effect on the regional landscape. Small villages became prosperous colliery or cotton-mill towns within a few years, and in existing market towns new industrial quarters soon extended along the river or canal-side. At first the bright red brick of the factories and workers' terrace rows contrasted vividly with the green meadows they rapidly enveloped, but the effect was soon subdued by the output of the factory chimney. In most of the lowland areas there were few topographical features to prevent urban development taking whatever direction economic advantage dictated, but on the edge of the uplands it was a different matter. Here narrow valley floors often provided the only reasonable building sites, and when the mills monopolised these, to be near the streams, the workers' cottages were forced up the hillside, or had to straggle along the valley occupying any suitable plot of land.

The most obvious impact of industrialisation on the regional way of life was undoubtedly the urbanisation of the population. During the first half of the nineteenth century the number of town dwellers in Lancashire increased fourfold, to exceed 1 million. By 1851 two-thirds of the county's population lived in what the Census officially defined as towns, while in Cheshire the proportion had risen to about half. Between 1801 and 1851 Manchester grew from 75,000 to 303,000 inhabitants, neighbouring Salford from 18,000 to 85,000, Oldham from almost 22,000 to over 72,000, and Liverpool from 82,000 to 376,000. In some smaller towns the rate of growth was even more spectacular; Stalybridge, due to the success of its cotton mills, increased from less than 4,000 in 1801 to over 23,000 in 1851, and Birkenhead, with its new shipyards, increased from barely 300 in 1821 to 25,000 thirty years later. The second half of the century saw a continuation of this growth, but with a number of important new trends. One of these was the rise of the residential suburb as the cities grew outwards, assisted by the new rail services from the central business districts. Another was the growth of seaside resorts, as exemplified by Morecambe, Blackpool and Southport, where the growing urban proletariat could spend their annual week of relief from the drudgery of the mill.

The North West thus greeted the twentieth century as one of the most prosperous and rapidly expanding industrial areas of Britain. Something like three-quarters of the population lived in towns or cities, whose ornate Victorian town halls, paved streets and public parks symbolised the pride with which society viewed an era of unprecedented commercial success. What the nineteenth century had created seemed indestructible, and there appeared to be good cause to look to the new century as one of continuing opportunity and prosperity. But such

optimism turned out to be unjustified. The First World War interrupted
business activity, and although normal conditions reappeared for a
while afterwards, all was not well with textiles. Hit for the first time
by serious competition from other countries, the cotton trade began
the contraction which has subsequently cost the region 0·5 million jobs.
The coal-mining industry also went into decline, gradually removing
the second of the twin pillars which supported the livelihood of large
parts of Lancashire. Replacement industries have been found, but the
problem of economic readjustment is still far from being solved, as
will be explained at length in subsequent chapters. Population figures
provide some measure of the slackening rate of regional economic
growth. In the 1890s the population increase in the North West was
over 12 per cent, while in the 1920s it was less than 3 per cent, and in
the 1950s less than 2 per cent. The first seventy years of the twentieth
century will have seen an increase of about 1·5 million in the region's
population, compared with over 3·5 million in the previous seventy,
and the North West's share of Britain's population has fallen to 12·7
per cent from its peak of 14·1 at the turn of the century.

Despite the slackening pace of the last four decades, the past
hundred years have had an enormous impact on the regional landscape. In terms of bricks and mortar, there are now almost four times
the number of dwellings in the North West than there were at the
time of the 1861 Census. But urban development has not been evenly
distributed throughout the region; indeed it has become increasingly
selective in its location. During the present century the emphasis has
shifted away from the cotton towns and mining areas towards the
Manchester–Merseyside axis and the coasts, and away from inner-city
residential districts towards extensive new dormitories on the outer
fringes. The growth points of the nineteenth century have thus been
partially replaced by areas more conducive to the success of modern
industry, and more in keeping with the realisation of a middle-class
suburban way of life.

Some Socio-Economic Patterns

The process of development, as outlined above, has had a major
bearing on the emergence of the region's present economic and social
geography. This is not the place for a full discussion of demographic
characteristics, social structure, health and so on, and the region's
economic character is examined fully in subsequent chapters. But brief
comments on a few socio-economic patterns of special significance are
in order at this stage as part of the general introduction to the region.

The occupation of the resident population provides a convenient indication of an area's general social and economic character, and this is summarised in Fig 2. The proportion of economically-active males in manual occupations varies very considerably within the region, but it is not difficult to discern three broad zones. First there is the roughly-triangular area bounded by Merseyside, the industrial towns east of Manchester, and Nelson and Colne in the north. Throughout practically the whole of this zone at least half the working men are in manual occupations, and in some places, notably on the coalfield between Liverpool and Manchester, the proportion exceeds three-quarters. The old textile districts north of Manchester stand out as an almost solid block, with at least two-thirds manual workers. To the north and south of this central zone the proportion of manual workers falls. In the northern zone Barrow-in-Furness, Carnforth, Lancaster and Fleetwood are exceptions, but generally less than half the active males are in manual occupations. The third zone, covering most of Cheshire and the High Peak, is much the same; immediately south of Manchester and the county boundary residential-suburban areas replace the industrial towns and cities, and the proportion of manual workers seldom reaches half the occupied males.

The second map in Fig 2 shows areas with relatively high propor-tions in the professional occupations; farming has been added as another activity where residence tends not to be associated with an urban-industrial environment. The areas where professionals make up one-fifth or more of the working male population tend to be concen-trated in Cheshire, on the southern side of the two conurbations. In the east a belt of predominantly middle-class suburbs fringes Manchester and Stockport, and in much of this area more than one in three work in the professions. The proportion in the Merseyside suburbs is not as high as it is south of Manchester, but in a string of local-authority areas from Hoylake to Lymm it exceeds one-fifth. To the north, in Lancashire, the professional areas are much less extensive. Coastal towns like Crosby, Formby and Southport are commuter areas for Liverpool, and some business men even travel daily to Manchester. East of Liverpool the big suburban areas, like Kirkby and Huyton, are predominantly working class, and around the northern half of Manchester the growth of other industrial towns has left little room for high-quality residential development. To the north, the better residential areas around Blackburn and Burnley, and on the northern sides of Bolton and Preston, raise the proportion of professionals to over one in five in parts of predominantly-industrial north-east Lancashire.

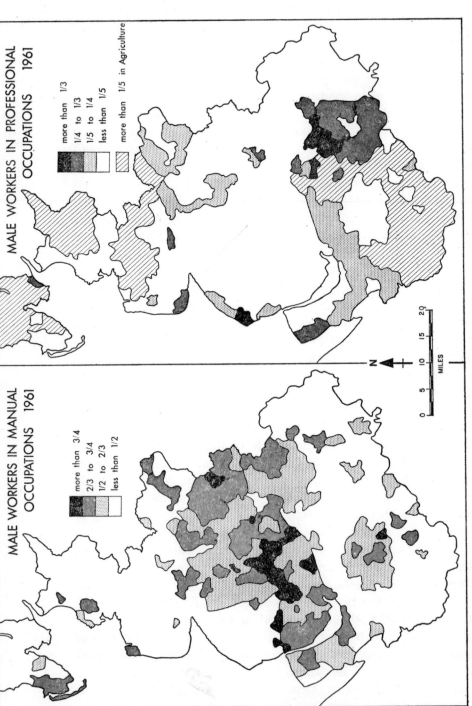

Fig 2. Socio-economic characteristics of the active male population. (Source: *Census of England and Wales 1961, Socio-Economic Group Tables*, 1966.) Professional occupations comprise Socio-Economic Groups 1–4 (as defined in the 1961 *Census*), manual occupations Groups 8–11, and farming Groups 13–15. The figures are based on a ten-per-cent sample, and are particularly liable to chance error in areas with small population (see Appendix A note 1). The 1961 figures are used here in preference to those from the *Sample Census* of 1966 because the distinction between professional and manual occupations was clearer in 1961.

Areas with a relatively high proportion in agricultural occupations are restricted to the northern and southern extremities of the region, and even here few areas of any extent have more than a quarter of active males engaged in farming. In the predominantly rural districts of the central part of the region, small industrial settlements, or the outward creep of suburbanisation, ensure that the farming element is greatly outnumbered by urban occupations.

The two maps in Fig 2 illustrate a very important feature of the social geography of the North West. It is sometimes said that the Mersey is a class boundary, separating predominantly working-class Lancashire from predominantly middle-class Cheshire. On the one side is industrial Lancashire, characterised on the mass media as the world of cloth caps and Coronation Street, the landscape dominated by grimy terrace rows, tall mills and factory chimneys, with perhaps a distant view of the moors. On the other side is the world of the business men on the commuter trains and the ladies who shop at a Wilmslow boutique, eating out at a Prestbury restaurant and owning a house on a tree-lined avenue or smart new estate. Many measures of class affiliation and social character could be used to support this distinction between the two counties: for example, Lancashire has almost twice the number of betting shops in relation to population as has Cheshire.[7]

This view exaggerates the situation of course, and is clearly an over-simplification. North Cheshire has its overspill estates of factory workers, just as most Lancashire towns have their middle-class suburbs. And there are large parts of western Lancashire which are more like rural Cheshire than the industrial districts to the east. But the distinction does serve to point out real internal differences in the way of life of the region's people. To some a cotton-mill closure or urban-renewal project can mean social disruption and economic hardship, and perhaps a move to another town; the nearest others may come to it is reading a paragraph in *The Guardian*. To some home is two-up-and-two-down and ten children, while to many others the reality of life in Ardwick or Chorlton-on-Medlock is a complete unknown. These differences in experience, outlook and values are of utmost importance in under-standing the region and its problems, and the attitudes to their solution. They help to explain why some people are reluctant to exchange a back-to-back in Moss Side for a neat semi-detached on an overspill estate in 'snobby' Cheshire. They help to explain the fierce protection of the green belt south of Manchester, and the reluctance of some Cheshire towns to accept overspill from the two congested conurbations. They have important repercussions in the local and regional political framework within which planning decisions are made.

One of the most important differences in way of life within the region is quality of housing. This is frequently measured by rateable value, with less than £30 taken as an indicator of a relatively poor dwelling. There are almost 0·5 million houses in this category in the North West, nearly a quarter of the regional total, and they are highly concentrated in the big cities and industrial towns. In much of north-east Lancashire, the coalfield, and many of the Pennine-fringe mill towns more than one-third of the houses are rated at less than £30. Outside the main industrial districts the proportion is generally low, often falling to less than 10 per cent in the suburban fringes of the conurbations. In some of the rural areas the proportion is raised by a residue of nineteenth-century agricultural labourers' cottages and the terrace rows of small industrial towns. In Liverpool, recent suburban development, mostly council houses, dilutes the local concentrations of poor housing to give a relatively low average, and the same is true of Manchester. But together these two cities have over 70,000 dwellings with a rateable value of less than £30.

Another indication of housing quality is access to certain amenities. In the North West the 1966 Sample Census showed almost one household in five without exclusive access to a fixed bath, which is roughly in line with the national average. The geographical pattern is illustrated in Fig 3. In many of the north-east Lancashire and Pennine-fringe industrial towns more than one in three households have no fixed bath, and the same is true of the western end of the coalfield. Liverpool housing looks worse by this measure than by rateable value, and Manchester only just fails to reach the 20 per cent category. The suburban areas of Cheshire, both to the south of Manchester and in the Wirral, stand out as well served with baths, as do some of the Liverpool suburbs and the Lancashire coastal retirement and resort towns.

There is a significant relationship between social structure, as indicated by occupational status, and the nature of the urban environment, as measured by quality of housing. (The statistical correlations between these and other socio-economic features are indicated in Appendix A note 2.) As might be expected, these characteristics also relate to the physical health of the population. For example, infant mortality tends to be almost twice as high in the industrial towns and cities as in the middle-class suburbs and dormitory towns, though its general relationship with other social characteristics is weak. The Registrar General's death-rate figures, adjusted to take into account areal differences in age and sex structure, reveal a similar distinction. Compared with a national index of 100, the death rate rises to over

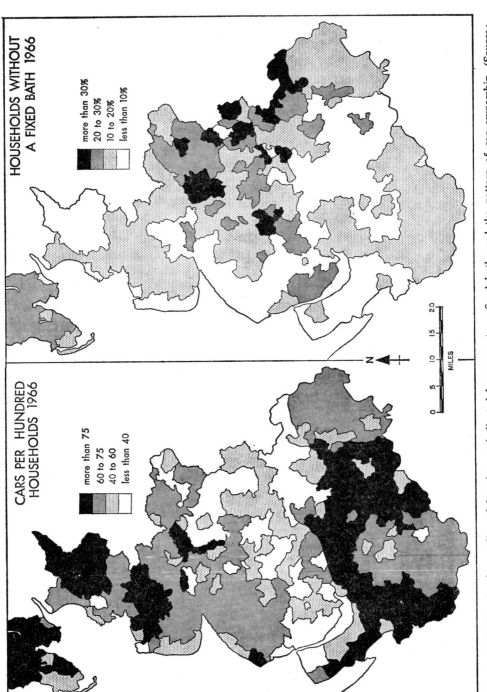

Fig 3. Variations in the quality of housing as indicated by access to a fixed bath, and the pattern of car ownership. (Source: *Sample Census of England and Wales 1966*.)

120 in most of the Merseyside–Manchester industrial belt, reaching
peaks in the mining areas and in many of the Pennine-fringe industrial
towns. But it falls below 100 in the north Cheshire commuter belt,
the Wirral suburbs, and some of the rural areas in the northern part
of Lancashire.[8] A further characteristic of the population which
correlates fairly closely with the other socio-economic features is the
level of education; in the main industrial districts of Lancashire
generally less than one in five people were educated beyond the age
of fifteen, according to the 1961 Census, while in the Cheshire suburban
belt the figure is over 40 per cent.

A useful indicator of material prosperity is car ownership, for which
detailed information by local-authority areas has been made available
for the first time in the 1966 Sample Census. Fig 3 shows that in much
of industrial Lancashire there are fewer than forty cars per hundred
households, while in the largely suburban belts of Cheshire the figure
generally exceeds seventy-five and it rises to over ninety in Hale,
Bowden, Wilmslow and around Macclesfield, where many of the
region's wealthiest citizens have their homes. Some of the rural
districts have twice the car ownership of the industrial towns; motor
transport is vital for many rural dwellers, while to the factory worker
living only walking distance from his job the lack of a car is no great
hardship. The proportion of households with two (or more) cars
provides a similar picture; in the central industrial zone two-car families
are fewer than 5 per cent of the total, whereas most places in rural
and suburban Cheshire, and Lancashire north of the Fylde, have over
10 per cent. Again, the 'best' of the suburbs south of Manchester top
the list, with over 20 per cent in Bowden and Hale, and only just
short of this in Macclesfield RD.

These important areal socio-economic differences find a reflection in
recent population trends, as sub-regional figures illustrated in Fig 4
show.[9] Between 1951 and 1964 the north-Cheshire suburbs south of
Manchester increased their population by something like 100,000,
and Merseyside (including the Southport area) added a similar number.
But there were decreases in some Lancashire industrial sub-regions.
The Manchester area and Oldham lost over 35,000, and in north-east
Lancashire, including the Blackburn–Burnley lowland and Rossendale,
the loss was almost 20,000.

Some of these differences are explained by the rate of natural
increase. For example, the rate in Merseyside was twice that of south-
east Lancashire, while in some of the older industrial districts there
was no natural increase, births being offset by deaths in the relatively
old population arising from generations of age-selective outward move-

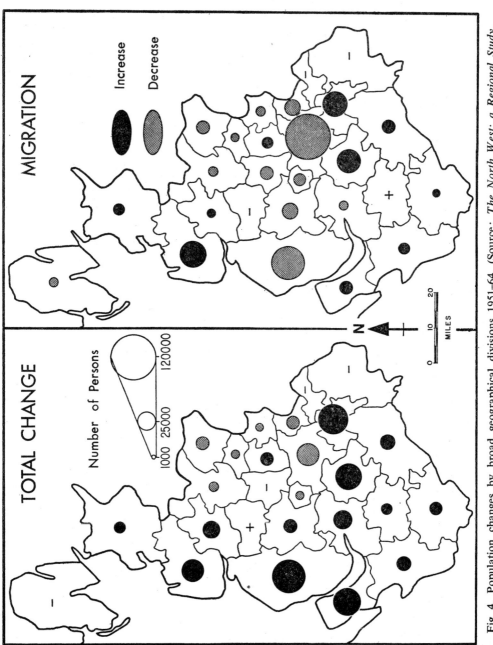

Fig 4. Population changes by broad geographical divisions 1951–64. (Source: *The North West: a Regional Study.* HMSO, 1965, pp 130–1.)

ments. But it is the pattern of migration which explains most of the region's population trends. Overall, the past decade and a half have seen a natural increase of 350,000 in the North West, but for every three of these, one person has left the region. The big losses in Merseyside north of the river (74,000), and in the Manchester sub-region (123,000), stand out clearly in Fig 4. With few exceptions, there has been net outward migration in the whole of the roughly triangular area with its corners represented by Liverpool, Nelson–Colne, and Manchester–Oldham. The large movement into the north Cheshire suburbs and the Fylde is in marked contrast. Some of the migration was over a relatively short distance—from central Liverpool or Manchester to nearby overspill towns for example—but on balance almost 10,000 people a year have moved away from the region altogether.

This movement from the industrial districts on which the region's earlier prosperity was based is largely a response to the limited economic opportunity and poor social environment these areas now offer. As each mill closes, some of those made redundant move to towns or regions with a better choice of jobs. To many the prospect of a small home in Cheshire suburbs, or in some prosperous town in the Midlands, is eventually strong enough to break old social and family ties in a declining textile town or mining community. As the younger and more enterprising move away, the air of depression and decay is perpetuated, in a way which seems to inhibit local economic regeneration. The textile districts north of Manchester do not have big unemployment problems, however, and there is little correlation between the local level of unemployment and population losses due to migration,[10] but it is not too much of a simplification to see the national distinction between expanding and highly prosperous regions and other less fortunate ones repeated on a local scale in the North West. The economic and social differences between the older industrial areas of eastern Lancashire, the coalfield and parts of Merseyside, on the one hand, and the more prosperous southern and western areas on the other, are at the root of many of the problems which face regional planning in North West England today. They are examined in greater depth in subsequent chapters.

The North West in a National Context

During the nineteenth century coal was the major sustainant of economic life in Britain. For most industries a location on or near a coalfield was virtually a necessity, for the cost of obtaining coal increased rapidly with distance from the pit-head. The great coalfields of South Staffordshire, Nottinghamshire and Derbyshire, Yorkshire, Lancashire, Northumberland and Durham, central Scotland and South Wales thus became the growth regions, each developing its own distinctive manufacturing specialisations. The only major industrial area well away from the coalfields was London, with the unique advantages of the metropolitan market, its status as a world commercial and trading centre, and access to coal by relatively cheap sea transport. But the present century has seen the gradual replacement of steam by electricity as the motive power in industry, lessening the attractions of a coalfield location, and this, coupled with other technological changes and increasing competition from overseas, has led to the decline of some of the most important coalfield industries. There has thus been a fundamental change in the comparative economic advantage of the major industrial regions, with many activities now preferring locations in the South or the Midlands.

A distinction is often made between the 'two nations' of Britain, or the 'fortunate' and the 'unfortunate' regions. Into the first category fall the rapidly expanding and prosperous areas of southern England and the east and west Midlands. The 'unfortunate' regions include the coalfield-based industrial areas of northern England, Wales and Scotland, and of course Northern Ireland. By almost any measure of economic growth and prosperity, the North West, taken as a whole, is one of the less fortunate regions of Britain.

Table 1 shows the difference between the 'fortunate' and 'unfortunate' regions in terms of recent population trends. The figures refer to the ten standard regions as redefined in 1965 to correspond with the new economic planning regions. The national population increase of 10·2 per cent for the period covered neatly splits the regions into two groups, the southern and midland regions having above average increases, and the northern regions, Wales and Scotland falling below the average. The North West's 5·8 per cent increase is lower than that of all the other regions in England. Changes attributed to migration also split the regions into two groups of five, and again the North West clearly belongs to the 'unfortunate' group. Although Yorkshire and Humberside and the Northern region, as well as Scotland, have rates of migrational loss greater than the North West, only Scotland has on balance lost a larger number of people. In natural increase (not included in the table) the North West's 6·1 per cent is exceeded in Scotland, the Northern region, and Yorkshire and Humberside, as well as in the southern and midland regions. Only Wales and the South West have lower rates of natural population growth.

Changes in employment in recent years show the same basic division of Britain as population trends with the national average growth rate again splitting the country into two. The North West falls clearly into the bottom half; only Scotland shows a lower growth rate. In manufacturing it is probably more accurate to split Britain into three,[11] so that southern England stands out on its own with over twice the

Table 1

REGIONAL CHANGES IN POPULATION 1951–67

Region	Total Change		Migrational Change	
	number (1000s)	per cent	number (1000s)	per cent
The 'fortunate' regions				
East Anglia	232	17·2	102	7·6
West Midland	671	15·3	106	2·4
South West	455	14·5	218	6·9
East Midland	411	14·3	86	3·0
South East	2,058	13·7	597	4·0
The 'unfortunate' regions				
Northern	220	7·0	−122	− 3·9
Yorkshire and Humberside	292	6·6	−110	− 2·5
North West	**371**	**5·8**	**−148**	**− 2·3**
Wales	130	5·1	− 45	− 1·8
Scotland	93	1·8	−522	−10·3
Great Britain	4,933	10·2	162	0·3

Source: Registrar General.

national employment increase, the two midland regions with Wales are marginally above average, while the rest falls well below the national figure. The North West and Scotland are the only regions to register a fall in manufacturing employment. In services the distinction between the 'fortunate' and 'unfortunate' regions clarifies itself again, and once more only Scotland has fared worse than the North West.

The unhappy performance of the North West, as measured by employment trends, is partially related to the structure of the economy. In 1965 *The National Plan* estimated that the North West had 22·3 per cent of its manufacturing employment in contracting industries— more than in any other region in Britain—with a correspondingly low proportion in expanding industries.[12] But another reason for the relatively slow rate of growth in manufacturing is that the region has been getting what some see as less than its 'fair share' of new industrial

Cotton mills in Oldham. Factories like these were the basis for the original prosperity of much of industrial Lancashire. Since the last war, hundreds of similar mills have closed, to be converted to other uses or demolished.

Page 35: THE TWIN SUPPORTS OF THE OLD ECONOMY

Howe Bridge Colliery, Atherton. Closed in 1959, this is typical of the many small pits which failed to survive the contraction of the coalmining industry during the past two decades.

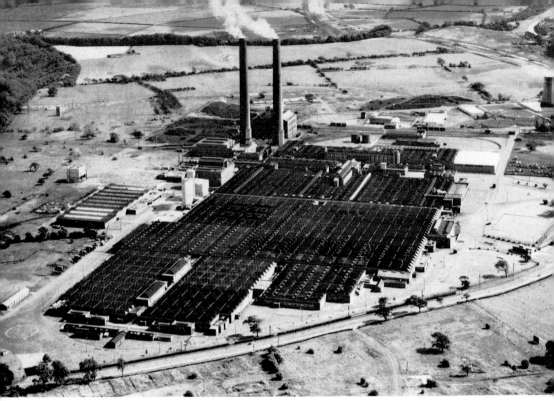

Courtaulds' Red Scar Works, Preston. This is the largest rayon yarn factory in the world, and typifies the region's new textile industry. Rayon produced here goes into the manufacture of clothing, fabrics and furnishings, and to the motor industry as tyre cord. The plant was established in 1935 and now employs 3,500 people.

Page 36: THE NEW INDUSTRIAL SCENE

The Ford motor factory at Halewood, Liverpool. The development of motor manufacturing during the 1960s has brought one of the big growth industries to Merseyside. The Ford factory provides work for more than 13,000 people, and is the largest single development in the region since the war.

development approved by the Board of Trade. The effect of government industrial-location policy will be examined in detail in subsequent chapters; it is sufficient here to point out that in 1967 the region had 11·3 million sq ft of floor space approved, representing 8·4 sq ft for each of the region's manufacturing workers compared with the national figure of 9·9. Only in the West Midlands and South East, where the Board of Trade is particularly tough in granting Industrial Development Certificates, was the square footage per worker lower than in the North West.[13]

In view of the recent performance of the regional economy as a job provider, it is not surprising to find the North West in 'unfortunate' Britain again when unemployment is considered. For the past two decades the regional rate has been consistently above the national average, though sometimes only slightly so. The three southern and two midland regions have generally fared better, but at times the South West has reached the North West's figure. Despite the very slow regional growth rate, unemployment in the North West has generally been the lowest in the 'unfortunate' regions, except for Yorkshire. Employment opportunity is an important factor in explaining population migration from the North West region as a whole.[14]

One of the most important indicators of a region's prosperity is the level of personal incomes. Figures compiled by the Commissioners of Inland Revenue show that the average annual income in the North West is about £20 less than for the United Kingdom as a whole, and that the North West ranks sixth among the regions, having a lower average income than the East and West Ridings and all the southern and midland regions except the South West. The average for London and the South East is £100 above the North West which has slightly more than the average number of people with incomes of over £500 a year, but where the proportion with over £1,000 is below the figure for the UK. In the £2,000 plus bracket, only the North Midlands region, the North and Wales had smaller proportions than the North West. In short, personal incomes in the region are below average, and there are a relatively large proportion of low income earners, with a correspondingly small share of high incomes.[15]

Earnings in specific occupational groups tell a similar story. In Autumn 1967 the average weekly earnings of adult male workers in manufacturing in the North West were almost 10s below the UK average, and in all occupations the differential was almost 7s. Nevertheless, only three regions have higher weekly earnings than the North West. There are big differences between individual industries; the shipbuilding and chemicals earnings in the North West are higher

C

than in any other region, but in engineering the North West ranks
sixth, and in both the textile and clothing industries it is as low as
ninth.[16] There is some evidence that wages in the North West have
risen relatively quickly in recent years; the average annual increase
in weekly earnings of manual workers in manufacturing was 5·8 per
cent between 1961 and 1965, which was better than in most of
'fortunate' Britain,[17] but it is clear that the average wage earner is still
worse off in the North West than in the nation as a whole.

Other measures of affluence are given by the *Family Expenditure
Surveys*, which show average weekly household incomes in the North
West to be below the national average. In 1964–6 average household
expenditure each week was about £20 4s compared with the UK figure
of £21 0s.[18] Ownership of a telephone, refrigerator, motor car and
central heating in the North West was below average. The North West
thus falls clearly within the underprivileged regions, its households
having generally less purchasing power and fewer of the material
trappings of an affluent society than those in the Midlands and most
of southern England. This impression is supported by the *Census of
Distribution and other Services, 1961*, which shows an annual retail
trade turnover of £164 per head in the North West compared with
the national figure of £175. Only Wales and the Northern region
as having a lower per capita turnover.

Some figures indicating the level of capital investment in the North
West are listed in Table 2, which again shows the region in an unfavourable position. When the total value of orders for new construction is expressed as a ratio of population, the North West is the lowest
of all regions, with an investment of more than 8s a head below the
British average. Only in the education categories and offices etc does
the region's figure slightly exceed the average. Figures for previous
years add weight to the view that the North West is getting less than
its 'fair share' of capital investment in housing, industry and the public
services. This is particularly disturbing in view of the extent of the
region's needs for the replacement of obsolete buildings of all kinds,
and is a matter to which the regional planning council has recently
drawn attention.[19]

This kind of comparison between the North West, other regions and
the national situation could be continued almost indefinitely. In
education, for example, 54·6 per cent of children in the North West
left school at the age of fifteen, compared with 50·7 in England and
Wales, and as few as 39·1 in the South Eastern region, according to
the Department of Education & Science figures for 1963-4. Only 14·8
went on to higher education compared with 15·6 in England and Wales

and 19·8 in the South East. The North West has a higher ratio of pupils to teachers than most other regions, and the number of doctors, dentists, social workers and so on per head of population generally shows the region to be less well-served than Britain as a whole. But the facts already presented are sufficient to act as an initial pointer to some of the major economic and social problems which the North West faces.

In the Industrial Revolution, and throughout the nineteenth century, the region played a leading role in Britain's conversion into an

Table 2

CAPITAL INVESTMENT 1966

Category	£s per head of population		Rank of North West (out of ten regions)
	North West Region	Great Britain	
Public Sector			
Dwellings	9·3	10·6	7
Schools	2·7	2·6	3
Universities	1·2	1·1	4
Health	0·7	2·2	10
Roads	2·6	3·0	5
Public corporations	2·0	3·5	9
Offices, shops, garages, etc	1·3	1·1	4
Miscellaneous	2·1	4·2	10
Private Sector			
Dwellings	9·6	11·1	8
Industrial	7·8	8·0	8
Other buildings	6·2	6·7	5
Total	45·5	54·1	10

Sources: Ministry of Public Building & Works. The figures refer to the value of orders for new construction received by private contractors.

industrial nation, and in return enjoyed a rapid rate of economic growth and considerable prosperity. But much of what was done in terms of industrial location, mineral extraction, urban development and so on was based on short-run profit considerations, with little regard to the long-run economic and social consequences. Now the region is paying the price for this. Many of the current problems can be viewed as the returns on an investment of two centuries of almost entirely unregulated capitalism, with no attempt at planning. The region has thus inherited an industrial structure predisposed towards a declining level of employment because of the type of industry. It has inherited a vast stock of houses which provided good-quality accommodation in the Victorian era but which are no longer adequate in a country with rapidly growing material standards and expectations. From decades of indiscriminate mineral exploitation and careless dumping of industrial waste the region has inherited an enormous derelict land problem: there are over 60 acres of derelict land for every 10,000 acres of its surface area—higher than in any other region. And it has inherited an economic and social geography which is characterised by very obvious local differences in economic growth, material prosperity, employment opportunity, social structure, housing conditions, and the general attractiveness of the environment.

In short, many people feel they are worse off living in the North West than they would be if they moved south. If outward migration is to be reduced, or even stabilised at the present level, more jobs have to be created more rapidly. The region also has to improve its capacity to generate the wealth needed to replace the slums, reconstruct the towns, and clear up the mess left by the last century, and to raise investment in social services and so on to levels comparable with the country's more prosperous regions. The nature, performance and prospects of the industrial economy are obviously critical considerations in all this, for if its contribution to national prosperity can be improved a rise in the level of public investment in the region is a reasonable expectation. It is to industry that this account now turns.

References to this chapter are on pages 239 and 240.

2

The Regional Pattern of Industrial Activity

WHAT KIND OF a region is the North West from an economic point of view? Which are its leading industries today, and how are they distributed? How far does the industrial structure vary from place to place, and to what extent do specialised towns or sub-regions still exist? It is important to answer these questions as accurately as possible, for since the Second World War, indeed during the present decade, the regional economy has changed to quite a remarkable extent. To many people industrial Lancashire remains virtually synonymous with cotton, and there are text-books which still portray the North West as essentially a textile-manufacturing region. But this is no longer true. As employment in cotton and some of the other traditional industries has fallen, other activities have taken their place, with the result that both the structure and location of industry have altered considerably within a relatively short period of time. This chapter attempts to set down the basic facts concerning the present industrial character of the region; the recent changes are examined in the next chapter.

This discussion is based largely on one source of information—the annual estimates of numbers of insured employees compiled by the Ministry of Labour. Most research requiring an up-to-date measure of industrial location and structure is now based on this material, but it is generally recognised as being far from perfect. It is derived from a sample, and does not purport to be highly accurate, particularly when relatively small numbers are involved (see Appendix A note 3). Although it is generally satisfactory for providing a broad indication of the distribution of employment in particular industries, it has to be used with care, and conclusions drawn from it must be treated with a certain amount of caution. In addition to the technical problems of using this material, the fact that it is presented by employment-exchange

41

areas is sometimes inconvenient. These vary greatly in size and shape
(which may be a serious problem in some statistical work), they are
not necessarily significant areas from an economic point of view, and
the employment figures cannot easily be compared with other data
compiled for local-authority areas. Finally, it must be stressed that
employment of labour is only one of a number of possible measures
of the importance of an industry in a given area. But despite these
difficulties, the Ministry of Labour figures are the best available,
indeed there is no practical alternative.

The Main Sectors of the Regional Economy

At the last count, the Ministry of Labour enumerated almost 3
million insured employees in the North West. Their allocation between
three major sectors of the economy is shown on Table 3, where a
comparison is made with the national structure. Mining and manufacturing (referred to in this book as the 'industrial' sector) are somewhat more important in the North West than in Britain as a whole,
while employment in the service sector is almost 5 per cent below
average. Agriculture, with forestry and fishing, is even less significant

Table 3

EMPLOYMENT IN THE MAIN SECTORS OF THE
REGIONAL ECONOMY 1967

Sector	Number of insured employees	Percentage of total		Index of concentration in the North West (a ÷ b)
		North West (a)	Great Britain (b)	
Agriculture, forestry and fishing (I)	20,000	0·7	1·9	0·37
Mining and manufacturing industry (II–XVI)	1,384,000	46·2	40·4	1·14
Service industries, trades and professions (XVII–XXIV)	1,585,000	53·1	57·7	0·92
Total	2,989,000	100·0	100·0	—

Source: Ministry of Labour. The figures are estimates only, and subject to the
reservations made in Appendix A note 3. In this and the next table, the Roman
numerals after the name of the industry indicate Orders of the Standard Industrial
Classification. The index of concentration measures the degree to which an employment group is more important (index greater than 1·0) or less important (less than
1·0) than in Britain as a whole.

in the region than it is in the nation when measured by the labour force.

In this book the emphasis is placed firmly on the industrial sector of the economy, in particular on manufacturing. It was as a major manufacturing area that the North West initially rose to prominence, and it is still more of a manufacturing region than almost any other in Britain. It is largely the manufacturing industries which give the region its distinctive economic character and differentiate one area from another; and it is the performance of the industrial sector which is mainly responsible for the region's current slow rate of economic growth, and for the major internal differences in prosperity. But before industry is examined in detail some comments on agriculture and the service sector are in order, to establish their place in the regional economic geography.

Employment in agriculture is greatly underestimated in the Ministry of Labour returns, as many of those engaged in it are self-employed. There are less than 18,000 insured employees in the North West, but the total farming labour force is probably more than double this figure; in 1965 it was estimated that there were about 50,000 full-time agricultural workers and 6,000 working seasonally or part-time.[1] In addition, 80,000 to 90,000 jobs are provided by the processing, packing and marketing of the region's farm products, and by the manufacture and maintenance of agricultural machinery.

Agriculture occupies a major proportion of the working population in few parts of the region. The Ministry of Labour figures show about 10 per cent in agriculture in most of Furness, part of the Fylde, the Ormskirk area, and around Nantwich in central Cheshire. These areas in fact probably have something like one in five employed in farming. Elsewhere the proportion may be 5 to 10 per cent in much of northern Lancashire and southern and central Cheshire, falling below 1 per cent in the region's main industrial districts.

About two-thirds of the surface area of the North West is agricultural land, compared with four-fifths in the country as a whole, the difference being largely explained by the extent of urban development in the region. Roughly half the agricultural area of almost 1,400,000 acres is under permanent pasture—twice the national average—while arable farming is correspondingly under-represented (420,000 acres). The remaining agricultural land, 280,000 acres, is classed as rough grazing, most of this being on the Pennine moors. The best land is in the south and west of the region.[2]

Forestry provides work for only about 300 men in the North West, divided between Furness and western Cheshire. Fishing is of major importance in only one town, Fleetwood, which, with about 1,300 employees, is the third most-important fishing port in England and Wales. The Fleetwood boats fish off Ireland, western Scotland and in the Irish Sea, and most of their catch, worth £4,000,000 a year, is processed in the port before being sent inland to market.

As employer of more than half the labour force, the service sector is very important to the North West. It has its own characteristics; employment in the distributive trades and in transport and communication is above the national average, reflecting the region's strongly urban-industrial character, while almost all the other major service groups are represented in smaller proportions in the North West than in Britain as a whole.

The main centres of service activity are, of course, Liverpool, with over 300,000 service employees and Manchester with 250,000. These are the leading regional centres for office employment and professional and public services, and have large populations of their own to cater for. Both are ports and focal points of commercial activity, and have the usual range of shipping offices, merchanting organisations, bankers, and so on, as well as the choice of personal services expected in a large city. The third service city in terms of employment is Preston, with 50,000 including the offices of Lancashire County Council. Then come Blackpool and Stockport, each with about 40,000, followed by Birkenhead, Bolton, Chester (with Cheshire county offices), Oldham and Salford, each with at least 30,000 employed in service.

The proportion of all local employment accounted for by the service sector varies considerably, from over 90 per cent in Hoylake in the Wirral at one extreme, to 18 per cent in the mill town of Shaw at the other. The proportion is relatively high in the major cities; in Manchester and Liverpool it is two-thirds, the same is true of Birkenhead and Wallasey, in Preston it is 60 per cent, and in Chester almost 70 per cent. In the coastal resort towns it is even higher; Southport, Morecambe and Grange-over-Sands all have at least three-quarters of their employment in services. High figures are also recorded in some suburban areas on the edge of the conurbations, for example Altrincham and Wilmslow. But in many of the smaller industrial towns and cities the proportion drops to round about a third, and in half-a-dozen places it is only about one in five.

The Industrial Sector

The industrial sector provides work for 1·4 million people. But it is also indirectly responsible for many service jobs, in construction, public utilities, transport and communication, and various professional services. In addition, employment in retail trade and personal services is ultimately dependent on industrial workers spending the money they have earned. The performance of the economy as a whole is thus highly dependent on the prosperity of the industrial sector, at both regional and local level.

The distribution of industrial employment is mapped by exchange areas in Fig 5. This emphasises the concentration in the central section of the region; in fact the roughly-triangular area with corners at Merseyside, Colne and the south-eastern edge of the Manchester conurbation contains almost 90 per cent of all industrial employment. The concentration is densest in the Manchester area, where the city itself has about 140,000 industrial workers, and the largest of the adjoining towns, Salford, Stretford, Oldham and Stockport, add another 175,000. Immediately to the north, Bolton, Bury and Rochdale between them have close on 100,000, then come the small Rossendale towns, and finally north-east Lancashire with about 110,000 industrial workers between Blackburn in the west and Colne in the east. At the western end of the main industrial belt is Merseyside, with almost 200,000 in Greater Liverpool and a further 60,000 in the Wallasey–Ellesmere Port strip on the opposite side of the estuary. The area separating the two conurbations has something over 150,000 industrial employees, depending on just how it is defined. To the south of the central concentration the leading industrial towns are Chester, Northwich, Crewe and Macclesfield. North of the Merseyside-Manchester-Colne triangle, only Preston and Barrow-in-Furness stand out, with industrial employment small in the populous coastal strip of the Fylde.

Fig 5 indicates the relative importance of the industrial sector to the economy of each area, measured by its share of total employment, and reveals a clear geographical pattern. In much of the main industrial concentration, excluding Merseyside, manufacturing with mining accounts for over 70 per cent of all employment compared with the regional average of 55 per cent. In Shaw, Leyland, Littleborough, Great Harwood, Horwich and Ramsbottom the proportion is over four-fifths. The highest proportions are generally found in the area west of Manchester, including the active coalfield, and in the old Pennine-fringe textile towns. In the larger towns employment in the industrial sector reaches 70 per cent only in Stretford, for the service sectors tend to be better developed than in the small mill or mining towns where many services are obtained outside. Both Manchester and Liverpool have only a little more than one-third of their employment in industry. None of the industrial towns around the Mersey estuary have a very

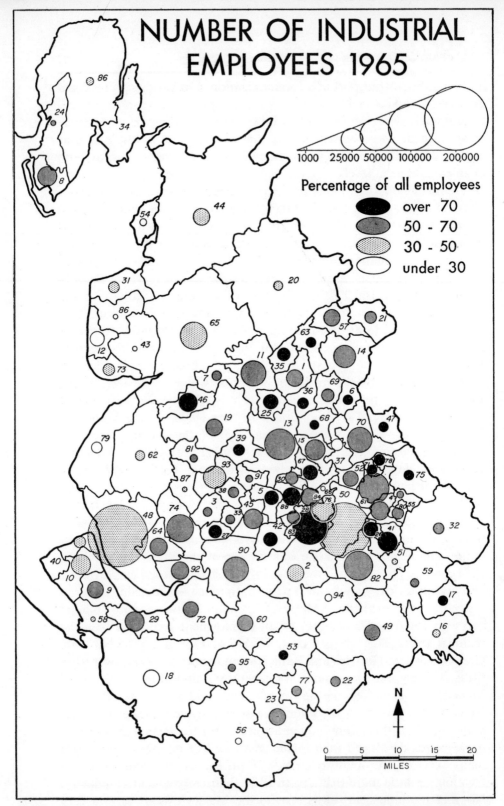

NUMBER OF INDUSTRIAL EMPLOYEES 1965

1000 25,000 50,000 100,000 200,000

Percentage of all employees
over 70
50 - 70
30 - 50
under 30

N

0   5   10   15   20
MILES

Fig 5. The distribution of industrial employment 1965. (Source: Ministry of Labour.) The circles are proportional in size to the number of insured employees, and are shaded in accordance with the percentage of total employment in the industrial sector. Figures are for Orders II-XVI of the SIC, and are plotted by employment-exchange areas (identified by numbers 1–95, and listed in Appendix B). Because employment-exchange areas do not generally correspond with local-authority areas, and sometimes cross county boundaries, the regional limits shown on this and most subsequent industrial maps differ slightly from those on maps in the previous chapter.

high proportion of industrial employment, though it is generally at least the regional average, and the same is true of most of the central Cheshire and Peak District industrial towns.

In order to examine the structure and location of industry in more detail six broad sectors are recognised, and their regional employment is listed in Table 4. The engineering, vehicles and metals group is the clear leader, with two-fifths of all industrial employment, and nearly

Table 4

EMPLOYMENT IN THE MAIN SECTORS OF THE
INDUSTRIAL ECONOMY 1967

Sector	Number of insured employees	Percentage of total industrial employment		Index of concentration in the North West (a ÷ b)	Exchange-area mean percentage	Standard deviation of exchange-area percentages
		North West (a)	Great Britain (b)			
Engineering, vehicles and metals (V–IX)	568,000	41·1	48·6	0·85	31·5	21·3
Textiles and clothing (X and XII)	289,000	20·9	13·0	1·61	30·2	23·0
Chemicals, glass and ceramics (IV and XIII)	166,000	12·0	9·3	1·29	12·9	18·1
Food, drink and tobacco (III)	130,000	9·4	8·9	1·06	8·1	10·8
Other manufacturing (XI, XIV–XVI)	197,000	14·1	14·3	0·99	—	—
Mining and quarrying (II)	34,000	2·5	5·9	0·42	4·9	10·5

Source: Ministry of Labour. The mean percentages and standard deviations for North West employment-exchange areas refer to 1965, and are thus not strictly comparable with the other figures.

twice as many workers as in textiles and clothing. The importance of some sectors differs considerably from the national industrial structure, as indicated by the percentage figures and indexes of concentration. The engineering group, despite its recent growth, is still under-represented in the North West, while employment in the textile group is well above the national average. The chemicals group is also more important regionally than nationally. The food and other-manu-facturing groups fall close to their national figures, while mining and quarrying is under-represented.

Table 4 includes the exchange-area mean percentages for each of the sectors, except the 'other' category for which it would have little meaning. These differ from the regional figure, because each exchange area is of equal importance in calculating the mean while the regional percentage is heavily weighted by the figures for Manchester and Liverpool, which account for almost one-sixth of all industrial employment. Also listed is the standard deviation of exchange-area percentages, to give a measure of the average departure from the mean. In each case the standard deviation is large, indicating that the importance of individual industrial groups varies very considerably from area to area.

The problem now is to identify those parts of the region in which particular activities are of special importance in terms of employment. To do this maps have been prepared showing areas with more than the exchange-area mean employment in certain industrial groups, with the differences from the mean expressed as so many standard deviations. The use of the standard deviations enables the degree to which the industry is concentrated in a given area to be related to the overall statistical distribution of exchange-area percentage values for that industry, and provides a sensible basis for inter-industry comparisons. It must be remembered that the figures throughout refer to proportion of industrial employment; the inclusion of services and agriculture in the total would reduce the percentages considerably.

Engineering, Vehicles and Metals

Employment in the region's leading industrial sector subdivides into a number of categories. Engineering employs 170,000 and covers the manufacture of various kinds of machinery and industrial plant, with textile machinery, paper-making machinery, food-processing plant and printing presses having particular importance. The electrical branch has 150,000 workers, including almost 60,000 in electrical machinery, 25,000 in insulated wires and cables (over one-third of the British total), and over 35,000 in domestic electrical appliances and advanced electronic equipment. Shipbuilding and marine engineering (30,000) is now overshadowed by vehicle manufacture, which includes over 60,000 in motor vehicles, over 40,000 in aircraft, and 13,000 in the production of railway locomotives, carriages and wagons. About 38,000 work in metal manufacturing, mainly iron and steel.

Fig 6 shows how the proportion employed in the engineering, vehicles and metals group varies within the region. Five areas stand out with at least three-quarters of all industrial employment (ie the mean plus two standard deviations): Barrow-in-Furness with its shipyards, Lytham St Anne's with its aero-engineering works, Altrincham

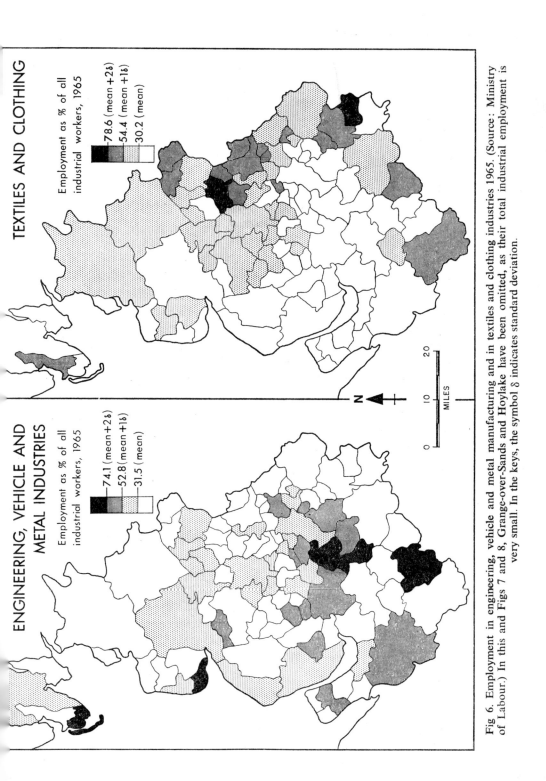

TEXTILES AND CLOTHING

Employment as % of all
industrial workers, 1965

78.6 (mean +2δ)
54.4 (mean +1δ)
30.2 (mean)

ENGINEERING, VEHICLE AND
METAL INDUSTRIES

Employment as % of all
industrial workers, 1965

74.1 (mean+2δ)
52.8 (mean+1δ)
31.5 (mean)

N

MILES

0   10   20

Fig 6. Employment in engineering, vehicle and metal manufacturing and in textiles and clothing industries 1965. (Source: Ministry of Labour.) In this and Figs 7 and 8, Grange-over-Sands and Hoylake have been omitted, as their total industrial employment is very small. In the keys, the symbol δ indicates standard deviation.

which has an important machine tool industry, Crewe with its railway works and Rolls-Royce plant, and Sandbach which has the Fodens and ERF truck factories. In general, the area to the south and west of Manchester has a high concentration on engineering and metals, which accounts for over half the industrial employment in most places. The engineering group is under-represented in much of central and eastern Cheshire, the High Peak, northern Lancashire except for Furness, and some of the old cotton and coal districts of central Lancashire.

When the various branches of this sector are examined, some localisation is apparent. The most obvious is in shipbuilding, with about 14,000 workers at Barrow, home of Vickers, and roughly the same number on Merseyside with the big Cammell Laird yards in Birkenhead. Barrow has two-thirds of its industrial employment in shipbuilding and marine engineering, and Birkenhead about half. The motor-vehicle industry was largely concentrated around Leyland, Crewe and Sandbach until the recent developments on Merseyside. Aero-engineering is more dispersed, with major factories in Bolton, Great Harwood, Oldham, Preston, St Anne's, Stockport, Warrington and near Chester. Railway engineering is highly concentrated, largely in Crewe, Horwich and Newton-le-Willows. The iron and steel industry has one major plant, at Irlam beside the Manchester Ship Canal, and a few smaller ones; just outside the region is the large integrated Shotton works on the west side of the Dee estuary. The main non-ferrous metal works are around Manchester, Merseyside and Warrington, and Bootle has the largest tin plant in Britain.

The engineering and electrical industries, taken as a whole, tend to be more evenly distributed than the metal industries. But there are still local specialisations, like textile machinery in some of the larger cotton towns, machine tools in the southern part of the Manchester conurbation, and electrical machinery on the Trafford Park industrial estate and in Liverpool. Engineering of all kinds occupies 50,000 employees in Liverpool, 40,000 in Manchester, 30,000 in Stretford, and at least 10,000 in each of Oldham, Blackburn and Stockport.

Textiles and Clothing

All textile manufacturing now employs just under 200,000 workers. The increasing use of artificial fibres makes it unrealistic to try to distinguish the old cotton industry as a separate entity. This was recognised in the 1958 revision of the Standard Industrial Classification, where cotton and man-made fibres—often used in the same factory, indeed on the same looms—were amalgamated for statistical purposes.

Even with the addition of man-made fibres and linen, cotton could claim less than 120,000 insured employees in 1967, and by the time this account is published it may well be less than 100,000. The mighty giant upon whose shoulders the North West became one of Britain's great industrial areas now employs less than one in twenty-five of all the region's workers.

The other textile industries include 24,000 in finishing, 10,000 in woollen and worsted, and almost as many in knitwear. The clothing industry employs 90,000, including 13,500 in footwear manufacturing. Even after the recent contraction the North West is still the leading region in Britain for textiles and clothing manufacture, with about one-fifth of the garment industry, one in seven of the footwear workers, and about 30 per cent of all textile employment.

The localisation of textiles and clothing forms a clearer geographical pattern than is the case with the engineering group (Fig 6). There is a very obvious distinction between central and western Cheshire, the southern part of Lancashire and the coastal strip, where employment is below the exchange-area mean, and the remainder of the region where these industries form an important, often dominant, element in the economy. The highest percentages employed in textiles and clothing occur in an almost continuous belt along the eastern edge of the region, from Nelson and Colne in the north to the Peak District in the south, where the proportion of all industrial workers generally exceeds 50 per cent. The highest figure is in Chapel-en-le-Frith, but this is an anomaly as it is almost entirely accounted for by the Ferodo brake-lining plant, asbestos being included in textiles in the Standard Industrial Classification. In two textile and clothing towns proper, Haslingden and Rawtenstall, the proportion exceeds 80 per cent, and nearby in Ramsbottom, Bacup, Royton and Shaw it is still over 70 per cent of all industrial employment. In southern Cheshire, Nantwich and Congleton have 60 per cent in textiles and clothing (mainly in garment manufacturing), and in Macclesfield the figure is almost half. A large part of northern Lancashire is shown in Fig 6 as having above-average employment in textiles and clothing, but this area is not important in terms of the actual number of workers. It is interesting to see Manchester and some of the adjoining towns below average for textiles and clothing. This is an indication both of the extent of recent industrial changes in the area, and of the fact that the city has not for a long time been dominated by textiles to the same extent as many of the smaller towns to the north and east.

The individual branches of the textile and clothing industries show different location patterns. The cotton industry (including man-made fibres) is concentrated in the area from Manchester to the Blackburn–Burnley lowland; its location and recent performance is discussed in detail in Chapter 5. Most of the woollen and worsted industry is on the extreme eastern side of the region, where it adjoins the West Riding textile district: Saddleworth and Mossley have about 2,500 workers between them. The leading knitwear centre is Liverpool, but this industry is also found in many of the larger textile towns such as Ashton-under-Lyne, Bolton, Oldham and Rochdale. In carpet manufacturing the leading towns are Blackburn, Chorley and Denton; in felts they are Rawtenstall, Bury, Colne and Bacup. The finishing trade is fairly widely distributed, in response to the demand for its services and, finally, Macclesfield and Congleton retain some remnants of the old silk industry.

Manchester and Salford account for almost 30,000 of the region's clothing workers. Manchester, with London's East End and Leeds, is one of the country's three leading garment production centres, and, appropriately enough, is first in terms of rainwear. More than a quarter of the nation's hatting industry is in the North West, strongly localised around Denton and Stockport. Most of the footwear factories are in and around Rossendale (where slippers are a major speciality), but there are also some in the Furness district.

Chemicals, Glass and Ceramics

Under this heading come a number of quite distinct industries without a common denominator of the kind that unifies the textile group. The chemicals industries themselves employ almost 120,000 workers, or a quarter of the national figure. The North West is the leading region for the manufacture of chemicals based on salt and soda, and has important petro-chemical, dyestuffs and pharmaceutical industries. The processing of vegetable and animal oils and the production of soaps, detergents and fats is also included in chemicals.

The 25,000 employed in the glass industry (almost one-third of the national employment) are largely in St Helens, home of Pilkington Brothers. Ceramic industries, including bricks, pottery and so on, are generally under-represented in the North West.

The chemicals, glass and ceramics group is even more highly localised within the region than textiles. Fig 7 shows a major concentration around the eastern end of the Mersey estuary, but the type of industry varies from town to town: in Bebbington it is largely vegetable oils and detergent, including Unilever at Port Sunlight, Ellesmere Port has the Shell refinery at Stanlow which is the basis of

Page 53: THE MODERN TEXTILE INDUSTRY

The production of tyre yarn at Courtaulds' Red Scar Works, Preston. In the picture rayon yarn is being threaded to a loom weaving tyre cord.

An English Electric locomotive. This is the first of fifty 2,700 hp diesel-electric loco-motives for British Rail, made by the English Electric Traction Division at Vulcan Foundry, Newton-le-Willows.

Page 54: THE ENGINEERING INDUSTRIES

The Hawker Siddeley Dynamics factory at Lostock, near Bolton. The Hawker Siddeley group, with a major share in the region's aero-engineering industry, work on missiles and space vehicles as well as civil aircraft. This picture shows the machine shop.

a big petro-chemical complex, and Runcorn and Widnes specialise in chlorine, caustic soda and acids. The chemicals district is extended south-east into the Cheshire saltfield, where the production of salt and soda-based chemicals under the leadership of ICI is concentrated in the Northwich area; to the north Warrington has a variety of chemical industries, and to the east is the large Shell plant at Carrington on the edge of Manchester. St Helens stands out largely on the strength of its glass industry, though it does have a chemicals tradition and 1,000 workers in the pharmaceutical and toilet-preparations branch. Although Liverpool does not have a big proportion of its labour force in chemicals there are 12,000 workers, with the processing of imported goods such as animal and vegetable oils as the main branch.

Taken as a whole, the chemicals district extending from Merseyside eastwards to Irlam and central Cheshire has well over 60,000 people working in these industries, not including glass. The chemicals, glass and ceramics group accounts for over half the industrial employment in much of this area, which is a distinctive specialised segment within the regional economic geography. Outside this area the group is a major component in the economy of only two other places, Fleetwood and Morecambe, both with ICI plants. Elsewhere much of the chemicals industry is concerned with making dyes for textiles and other markets, the leading centres being Manchester and Stretford with over 17,000 workers between them.

Food, Drink and Tobacco

Bread and flour confectionery is the leading employer in the food industry. Its 26,000 workers include over 14,000 in biscuit manufacturing—about one-quarter of the national figure. Other important food industries are meat processing, chocolate and sugar confectionery, fruit and vegetable products and sugar refining. Brewing accounts for two-thirds of the 16,000 employed in drink industries, and a further 5,500 work in tobacco factories.

The leading food-manufacturing centre is Liverpool, where the labour force of 40,000 workers represents one-fifth of all industrial employment. The city has a long tradition of importing bulk commodities for processing, and most of its food industries have grown up in this way. Across the estuary, food industries are also important in Wallasey, Birkenhead and Bebbington, with a combined employment of 9,000. Merseyside has the largest flour-milling industry in Europe, a major sugar refinery, big biscuit factories, oil processing for fat and margarine, and a wide variety of other food industries.

D

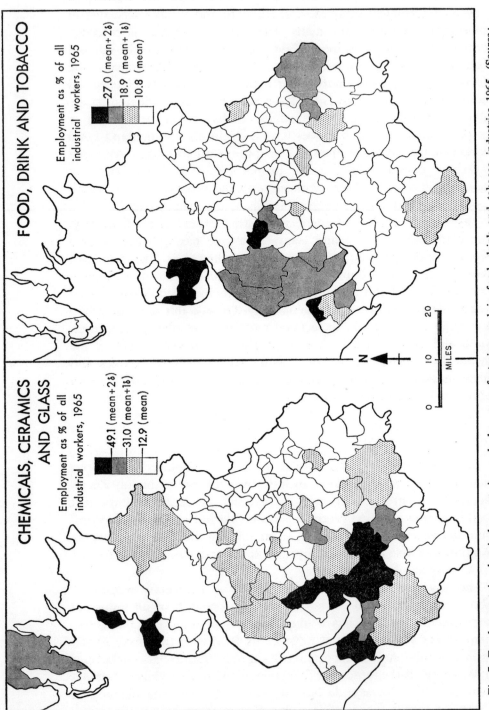

Fig 7. Employment in chemicals, ceramics and glass manufacturing, and in food, drink and tobacco industries 1965. (Source: Ministry of Labour.)

Second to Liverpool is Manchester, with nearly 11,000 employees, and almost as many again if Stretford and Stockport are included. As on Merseyside, the processing of imports explains a lot of this, with industries such as grain milling and the big Kelloggs cereals plant around the docks and in Trafford Park. Food industries account for 10 per cent of industrial employment in Stretford and Stockport, and only a little less in Manchester.

Fig 7 shows that in a number of places away from Merseyside and Manchester the food industries occupy an important place in the local economy. North of Merseyside, they account for about one-fifth of industrial employment in Southport and there is a large Heinz factory on the edge of Wigan. Blackpool has almost 4,000 food workers, making up more than one-third of the industrial employment, which is partly explained by the demands of the holiday trade. East of Manchester, Hyde has 2,500 workers in food, and almost 1,300 in the tobacco industry, which is also found nearby in Ashton-under-Lyne and Middleton as well as on Merseyside. Like Hyde, Glossop has about one-fifth of its industrial employment in the food group, in this case in pickle-making. Food manufacturing of one kind or another is found in every town and city of the region, in some cases employing many hundreds of people, but in few places does this make up more than about 5 per cent of all industrial employment.

Other Manufacturing Industries

The largest industry in this residual sector is the manufacture of paper and cardboard. The North West is second only to the South East as a paper-manufacturing region, and the 50,000 employees represent one-fifth of the national total. This is an old industry in Lancashire, and its products are varied. About 17,000 are employed making paper and board proper, slightly less are in box and carton manufacturing, which is often found in association with clothing and footwear industries; many of the remainder work in wallpaper factories. Printing and publishing, with 40,000 employees, is less important in a national context than is the paper industry, but it still has a considerable number of workers in some of the larger towns and cities.

Employment in the paper and printing groups combined is illustrated in Fig 8. The town with the biggest proportion of its employees in this group is Darwen, where paper manufacturing, including wallpaper, occupies about a quarter of all industrial workers. About one in five work in paper and board in Radcliffe and Saddleworth, and almost as many in New Mills. However, the highest employment in paper

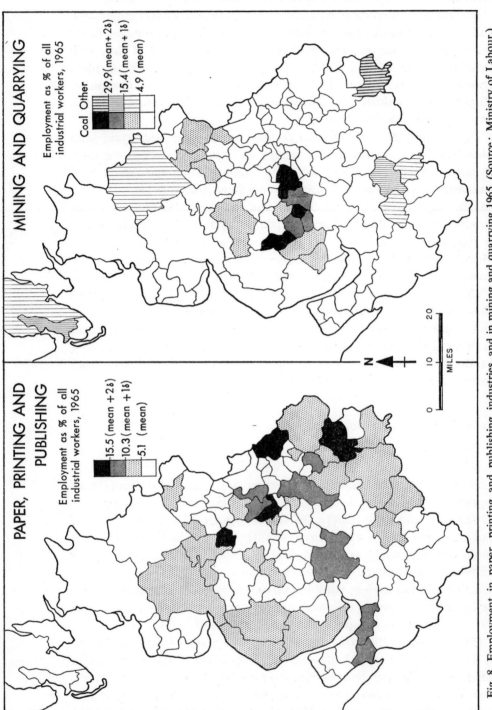

Fig 8. Employment in paper, printing and publishing industries, and in mining and quarrying 1965. (Source: Ministry of Labour.) In the mining and quarrying map the figures refer to all employment in this group; the two types of shading indicate dominant activity.

and board in numerical terms is in the big cities; Manchester has almost 6,000, Liverpool 5,000. Warrington over 3,000, and Blackburn, Bury, Hyde and Radcliffe all have about 2,000. Paper manufacturing is largely concentrated in the Pennine-fringe textile districts, but there is some on Merseyside, notably the big Bowater plant at Ellesmere Port (where over 3,000 are employed in paper and board), and at Barrow-in-Furness. Printing and publishing is mainly a big-city activity, with 16,000 employed in Manchester and the Stockport area and 8,000 in Liverpool accounting for over half the region's employment.

The 30,000 employed in rubber manufacturing in the North West represent over one-fifth of this industry nationally. The Manchester area has about half the region's rubber workers, with 6,000 in the city itself, over 2,000 in both Salford and Middleton, and other important factories in Ashton-under-Lyne, Hyde, Oldham and Radcliffe. Merseyside comes second, with 7,000 in Liverpool. The influence of the motor industry can be seen in the production of tyres; in Leyland over 3,500 work in the rubber industry, and Michelin has a plant in Burnley. Hindley is also important for rubber manufacturing, and Dunlop have added a new factory at Skelmersdale New Town to those in Manchester and Liverpool.

Of the region's other industries, leather is worth mentioning as the 10,000 employed account for almost one-fifth of the national total. The main locations are Manchester, Liverpool, Bolton and Oldham. About 12,000 people work in plastics and 6,000 in the production of linoleum, oilcloth and related products.

Mining and Quarrying

Most of the region's employment in mining and quarrying is in coal, which provides about 28,000 jobs. Stone quarrying (mainly limestone), salt mining, and the extraction of clay, sand and gravel account for a further 5,000.

Fig 8 shows the areas in which mining and quarrying are a relatively large component in local employment. Most of the collieries are in a belt between the two conurbations, and the high proportions employed in mining in this compact area stand out on the map. The coal-mining industry is considered in more detail in Chapter 5.

Limestone quarrying is very highly localised in the southern part of the Peak District in Derbyshire. Here the quarries south and east of Buxton employ almost 2,000, in what is one of the largest concentrations of its kind in Britain. Almost all the other workers in stone quarrying are in northern Lancashire. Most of the operations for clay, sand and gravel are around Macclesfield, Congleton and Northwich in the south and the Lancaster area in the north. The saltfield of mid-Cheshire stands out clearly in Fig 8; the four exchange areas of Middlewich, Sandbach, Northwich and Winsford together have about 1,500 employed in the salt industry. It accounts for almost 20 per cent of all industrial employees in Middlewich, but overall there is nothing like the dependence on mining which exists in the coal district of central Lancashire.

Industrial Concentration and Local Specialisation

The areal concentration of certain industrial groups, and the high degree of dependence on one activity in some places, are matters of great practical significance. The performance of some industries will clearly have a wider regional impact than others; developments in textiles and engineering can be expected to have an effect on a large proportion of towns in the North West (though the effect may be greater in some than in others), whilst what happens to shipbuilding and coal mining, for example, will have a much more local impact. Similarly, the prosperity of some highly-specialised towns or districts is closely tied to the way in which one particular industry performs, whereas places with more varied structures would be affected less dramatically by, say, a sharp recession in textiles or the rapid growth of electronics. Industrial concentration and specialisation may usefully be examined in a little more detail.

In Table 5 the industrial sector is divided into thirteen branches, which are listed in order of their degree of geographical concentration. This is measured by a coefficient of localisation, which simply indicates how far the areal distribution of the industry in question differs from the distribution of total industrial employment. The coefficient varies between 0 and 100: a high one indicates a high degree of concentration, and a low one shows rough accordance with the distribution of all industry. (For particulars of the calculation see Appendix A note 4.)

The most highly-localised industry is shipbuilding, with Birkenhead and Barrow-in-Furness accounting for over two-thirds of its regional employment. Second comes mining and quarrying, then the bricks, pottery and glass group where the high coefficient is explained mainly by the concentration of glass-making in St Helens. The vehicle industries, including aircraft, are fourth, the biggest proportions of industrial employees being in Crewe, Leyland, Sandbach and St Anne's. The leather industry, insignificant in terms of regional employment, comes next, followed by textiles, with a coefficient which still indicates

considerable localisation. The chemicals industries are only slightly
less localised than textiles. Both the metal and clothing industries, with
coefficients of 38·8 and 38·0 respectively, are perhaps more evenly
distributed than might have been expected; some recent dispersal has
in fact reduced the figure for metal manufacturing from 45·5 in 1953
and that for clothing from 42·5. The final four industries can be

Table 5

INDUSTRIAL CONCENTRATION AND SPECIALISATION

Industry	Number of insured employees 1967	Coefficient of localisation	Exchange-area mean percentage	Standard deviation of percentage values
Shipbuilding	32,000	77·8	1·6	8·7
Mining and quarrying	34,000	73·2	4·9	10·5
Bricks, pottery, glass etc	48,000	57·3	3·8	8·7
Vehicles	118,000	50·5	7·9	15·6
Leather	10,000	45·4	0·7	1·7
Textiles	199,000	45·3	22·8	22·6
Chemicals	118,000	42·4	9·1	15·5
Metal manufacture	38,000	38·8	2·5	5·5
Clothing	89,000	38·0	7·4	12·0
Food, drink and tobacco	130,000	34·8	8·1	10·8
Paper, printing and publishing	91,000	29·5	5·1	5·2
Timber and furniture	35,000	27·4	2·4	2·9
Engineering, electrical and other metal goods	380,000	22·7	19·5	15·3

Source: Ministry of Labour. The industries are as defined by Orders of the SIC,
except engineering etc, which is a combination of Orders VI and IX. In all but
the first column, the figures refer to mid-1965.

regarded as fairly evenly distributed in relation to all employment,
but each has a few highly-specialised towns.

In some places the degree of specialisation is such that it is tempting
to term them 'one industry' towns and many of the mining and cotton
towns are often referred to casually in this way. There are others where
the presence of two predominant activities, perhaps coal and chemicals
or engineering and textiles, might warrant the label of 'two industry'
town. In how many cases, however, is the local economy really
specialised enough to justify these descriptions today, in view of recent
diversification? One objective method of answering this has been
applied to employment figures for the broad industrial sectors used
in the previous section. Places have thus been classified as either 'one
industry' or 'two industry' towns, specifying whether the industry or
industries in question are textiles (and clothing), engineering (including
vehicles and metals), chemicals (with ceramics etc), or coal mining. All

areas not so classified have varied or diversified structures. (The precise method used is described in Appendix A note 5.)

The results set out in Fig 9 (left-hand map) thus provide one possible view of the geography of industrial specialisation in the North West. The pattern revealed is interesting, for in addition to the areas of specialisation which might be expected in the old textile districts, a number of 'one industry' areas appear in Cheshire. In four of these, Chester, Crewe, Sandbach and Altrincham, the specialisation is in the engineering, vehicles and metals group, with the remaining one, Nantwich, in chemicals. A number of nearby areas, including Runcorn, Irlam and Stretford, fall into the 'two industry' category with engineering etc and chemicals. At the western end of the coalfield, St Helens combines coal and the chemicals group (ie glass); adjoining Ashton-in-Makerfield combines coal with engineering. But no area falls into the 'one industry' category as a mining town: coal mining no longer dominates local employment structures to the extent that it used to.

In north-eastern and central Lancashire a number of places are classified as 'one industry' textile (and clothing) towns. These include Nelson, the Rossendale towns, and to the south Prestwich, Royton and Mossley. But there are fewer than might have been expected—some indication of the gradual diversification in the textile districts. In fact a number of towns in this part of the region show up as textiles and engineering in the 'two industry' category. Other 'one industry' towns include Barrow (engineering, ie shipbuilding) and Dalton-in-Furness (textiles including clothing), emphasising the dependence of the Furness area on a narrow range of industries. Lytham St Anne's appears as an engineering town, largely on the basis of the aero-engineering works.

Another method which is often used to measure the degree of local specialisation is illustrated in the second map in Fig 9. The coefficient of specialisation compares the local structure with the regional structure, which can be taken to represent diversification. Like the coefficient of localisation, this index varies between 0 and 100, with a relatively high figure indicating a big departure from the regional structure and hence a high degree of specialisation (see Appendix A note 6).

High coefficients are found in the old Pennine-fringe textile districts, but there are also large areas of specialisation in the north-western and south-western parts of the region. The northern area is not particularly important, as the number of industrial workers here is relatively small, but the southern one, with coefficients of over 50 in

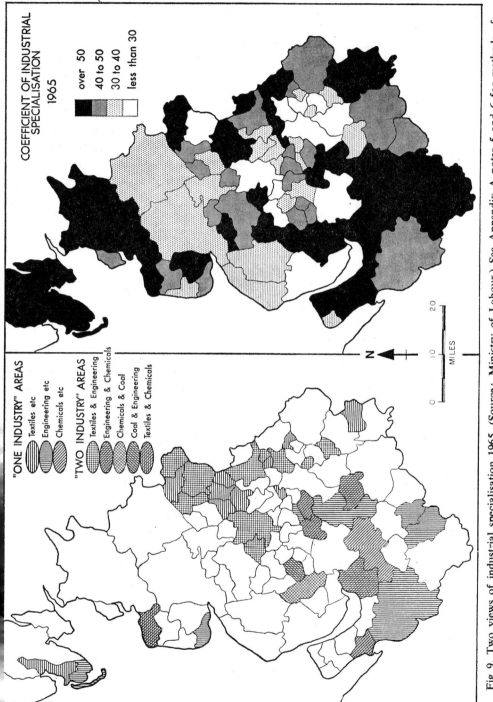

Fig 9. Two views of industrial specialisation 1965. (Source: Ministry of Labour.) See Appendix A notes 5 and 6 for methods of calculation.

many exchange areas, contains most of the Merseyside and its periphery with the exception of Liverpool, as well as almost all the central Cheshire industrial towns. The difference between this area and the Pennine-fringe is, of course, that the specialisation here is mainly in growth industries, whereas the towns of north-east Lancashire, Rossendale and the eastern side of the Manchester conurbation are greatly dependent on the contracting textile trade.

The biggest departures from the regional industrial structure produce specialisation coefficients of 70 and over. Nantwich, Crewe and Sandbach in southern Cheshire all fall into this category, as do Chapel-en-le-Frith with the Ferodo plant, Irlam with its iron and steel and chemical works, Leyland, and in the Furness area Barrow and Dalton. In none of the textile towns is such intensive specialisation found today—in fact few have a coefficient of over 60—and the only place in the coalfield with over 70 is the mining town of Upholland. The lowest coefficients, indicating diversified structures, are, as might be expected, in the larger cities.

The two maps in Fig 9 clearly give no more than a broad indication of the geography of industrial specialisation. This is a difficult thing to measure, since whatever method is used the results tend to be sensitive to the kind of industrial classification and areal subdivisions adopted. The more detailed the classification, the greater the likelihood of high coefficients of specialisation, other things being equal. The smaller the areas for which data are compiled, the larger the observed specialisation might be. For example, the four Rossendale textile and footwear towns each have high coefficients of specialisation, but this would be somewhat reduced if they were combined into one unit for statistical purposes. Similarly, highly specialised districts within the big cities are hidden by the generally low coefficients. Until industrial statistics are compiled and made available on a more rational system of areal units these problems will remain. But the maps do help to emphasise that intensive specialisation, with its restriction on the range of local employment opportunity, is not confined to the older industrial areas of Lancashire. Many parts of Cheshire and some coastal towns have an equal or greater degree of specialisation, and are highly dependent on a few large firms. This specialisation is generally in what are at present growth industries, but this was true of the coal and cotton towns sixty years ago.

Industrial Sub-Regions

The best way to summarise the present industrial geography of the North West is through the identification of sub-regions. Various divisions have been proposed by government departments for purposes of economic analysis, but as a summary of regional industrial character the most useful is the classification adopted by the Lancashire and Merseyside Industrial Development Association for a series of studies in the early 1950s. The region's main industrial districts were divided into five: the Weaving Area (north-east Lancashire and Rossendale), the Spinning Area extending from the Pennines to Preston, South-East Lancashire (Greater Manchester, including parts of north-east Cheshire), the Coal/Chemicals Area stretching from the Wigan district in the north to Runcorn and Warrington in the south, and finally Merseyside.[3] In a later modification the area from Preston to Wigan was recognised as a mixed textile and engineering region.[4]

The speed with which the regional economy has changed in recent years has prompted a fresh look at industrial sub-regional delimitation. Upheaval in the textile trade has blurred the distinction between the spinning and weaving zones, and fewer places can now justify the simple description of textile towns. The expansion of engineering and metal industries and the contraction of coal mining have further modified the traditional sub-regional specialisation pattern. A new summary view of the regional industrial geography is therefore proposed in Fig 10, and Table 6 summarises the employment structure of each of the sub-regions recognised. (See Appendix A note 7 for the method of delimitation used.)

The main industrial districts of the North West divide up into eight sub-regions. In the north there are two textile and engineering regions— Central Lancashire and North East Lancashire. The engineering and textile groups are of roughly equal importance in both sub-regions, together making up at least 70 per cent of all industrial employment. The only places here where textiles retain their traditional dominance are Bamber Bridge, Chorley, Standish, Nelson and Colne; in many areas the engineering and metal industries are now bigger employers than textiles. It must be noted that, in Fig 10, sub-region 4 extends further north than it realistically should, because the large Preston exchange area incorporates territory which would otherwise have been included in the North Lancashire sub-region.

Despite recent industrial diversification, two textile-manufacturing regions are still identified. The northern one (East Central Lancashire) comprises Rossendale and the Bury–Rochdale area, where the textile and clothing group (including the Rossendale footwear industry) still employs almost 60 per cent of all industrial workers, three times as many as in engineering and metals. Most towns have well over half their industrial employees in textiles, and Heywood is the only place with more engineering workers than mill hands. The second textile region, South Pennine and Peak Fringe, is less specialised than East Central Lancashire, with just under half its industrial employment in

Table 6

EMPLOYMENT STRUCTURE IN THE MAJOR INDUSTRIAL
SUB-REGIONS

Sub-region	Total employees (approx)	Service activities (percentage of total)	Industrial activities (percentage of total)	Proportion of industrial employees in main structural subdivisions (per cent)				
				Engineering, vehicles and metals	Textiles and clothing	Chemicals glass and ceramics	Other manufacturing	Mining and quarrying
1	43,000	44	53	71	10	7	10	2
2	58,000	61	36	11	41	14	31	3
3	141,000	70	27	36	12	16	36	—
4	326,000	45	54	37	33	7	22	1
5	188,000	37	63	39	37	4	17	3
6	171,000	33	66	20	58	2	20	—
7	182,000	34	66	27	16	26	9	22
8	920,000	52	48	48	19	10	22	1
9	112,000	36	63	17	48	9	22	4
10	137,000	40	60	24	2	56	17	1
11	640,000	63	37	48	7	8	36	1
12	103,000	57	39	67	12	8	11	2

Source: Ministry of Labour. The figures on which the percentages are based were obtained by the addition of 1965 employment statistics for individual exchange areas, which somewhat underestimate the actual number of persons employed. Figures in the total employees column have been adjusted to add up to the North West regional total. The sub-regions are defined in Fig 10.

textiles and clothing. It extends into south-eastern Cheshire to take in Macclesfield and Congleton. As in the other two Pennine-fringe regions, industrial activity accounts for about two-thirds of all employment, which is substantially more than in any of the other sub-regions except the Coalfield and North Cheshire.

The southern part of central Lancashire comprises the Coalfield and Greater Manchester sub-regions. Although in the former employment in mining is slightly less than in the chemical group (see Table 6), the Coalfield description is preferred to the old Coal/Chemicals label on the grounds that employment in coal here is almost ten times the regional percentage, while in chemicals it is only twice the regional figure. In any case, most of the chemicals group employment is in the

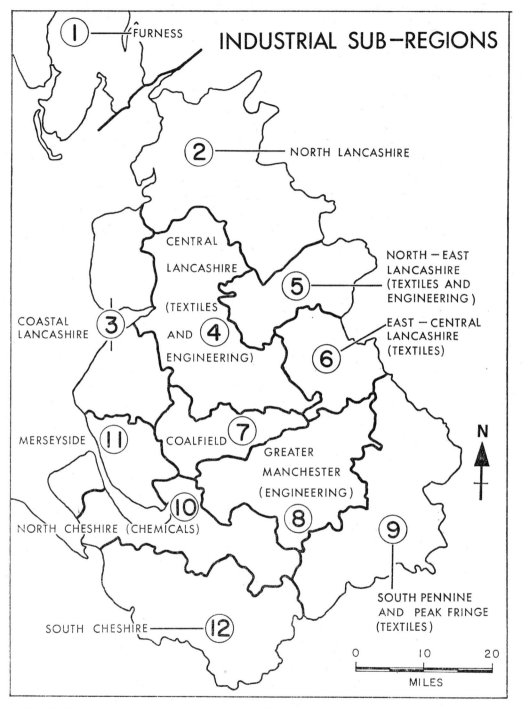

INDUSTRIAL SUB-REGIONS

1 — FURNESS

2 — NORTH LANCASHIRE

CENTRAL LANCASHIRE (TEXTILES AND ENGINEERING) 4

NORTH—EAST LANCASHIRE (TEXTILES AND ENGINEERING) 5

COASTAL LANCASHIRE 3

EAST—CENTRAL LANCASHIRE (TEXTILES) 6

MERSEYSIDE 11

COALFIELD 7

GREATER MANCHESTER (ENGINEERING) 8

N

NORTH CHESHIRE (CHEMICALS) 10

SOUTH PENNINE AND PEAK FRINGE (TEXTILES) 9

SOUTH CHESHIRE — 12

0   10   20
MILES

Fig 10. The industrial sub-regions of the North West. This map is based on a statistical analysis of the Ministry of Labour employment estimates for 1965, as outlined in Appendix A note 7.

glass industry in St Helens, a town which falls less certainly within
the Coalfield sub-region than the other places included. The Greater
Manchester sub-region extends from Oldham in the north-east as far
as Warrington in the west. Although this is designated an engineering
region, there is in fact considerable industrial variety. Textiles and
clothing provide only one in five of industrial jobs in this sub-region
today, while the engineering group accounts for half.

The south-western part of the main industrial concentration falls
into the sub-regions of Merseyside and North Cheshire. Merseyside, as
here defined, has almost half its industrial employment in the engineering and metals group, but the variety of its activities is indicated by the
high proportion in other manufacturing in Table 6. The North Cheshire
sub-region extends from Bebbington in the west to Middlewich in the
east, and has over half its industrial employment in the chemicals
group.

The four remaining sub-regions are less industrialised than those
already considered. Furness is the only one with more than 40 per
cent of its workers in industrial activity. North Lancashire is mainly
rural in character, with manufacturing largely confined to Lancaster,
Morecambe and Clitheroe. Coastal Lancashire, with its resort towns,
has 70 per cent of its workers in the service sector, but manufacturing
is growing in both volume and variety. In South Cheshire the local
importance of railway engineering, aircraft and motor manufacturing
raises employment in the engineering, vehicles and metals group to
two-thirds of all industrial workers.

While this system of sub-regions adequately summarises the regional
industrial geography, it must be recognised as a simplification of
reality. Certain core areas of intensive specialisation are easy to
identify, but there are few abrupt changes in local industrial structure
today; the general trend is towards less local specialisation and thus
less internal differentiation of industrial character. The questions of sub-
regional delimitation will be returned to in the broader context of
general economic well-being in Chapter 6.

The Regional Labour Market

So far this chapter has been concerned with types of industrial activity
as it varies within the region. Another important dimension of
industrial character is the geography of labour supply and demand,
including the daily movement to and from work, the local sex structure
of the labour force, and levels of unemployment.

The daily journey to and from work is an important dynamic

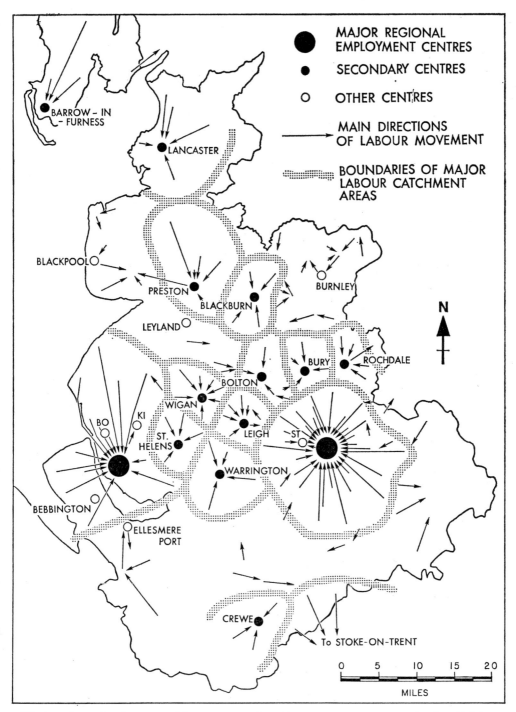

Fig 11. The regional pattern of journey to work 1966. (Source: *Census of England and Wales, 1961, Workplace Tables*, 1966.) 'Secondary employment centres' are defined as places with at least 30,000 employed, a net inward movement of workers, and a fairly clear catchment area of more than local extent. The 'other centres' all have over 20,000 employed and a net inward movement. The arrows indicate the direction of the largest movement from every local-authority area, except where this is exceeded by the movement in the opposite direction, in which case no arrow is shown. The following abbreviations are used: BO = Bootle, KI = Kirkby, ST = Stretford.

element in the spatial structure of the economy. The patterns of movement in the North West are illustrated in Fig 11, which shows the main direction of travel to work from each local-authority area, the main focal points, and tentative boundaries between the catchment areas of the more important centres of employment. In the interests of clarity, much information on direction and volume of movements has been left off the map, which makes no attempt to reveal all the details of local labour interchange.

Two major regional employment centres are identified—Manchester and Liverpool. The city of Manchester, with 330,000 resident workers, has a net inward movement of over 100,000 each day. Most of the influx comes from neighbouring towns and cities with their own industries, such as Salford, Stockport, Stretford and Middleton, and from the southern suburbs. The only place in the immediate vicinity which takes more workers from the city than it exports is Stretford, with the Trafford Park industrial estate. Manchester's labour catchment area is fairly symmetrical, and extends at least ten miles in most directions. It is somewhat elongated to the south to take in the outer-suburban belt around Knutsford, Alderley Edge and Macclesfield, while to the north and west the presence of other important employment centres restricts Manchester's pull. The edge of the city's catchment area is less distinct on the east; Oldham appears to fall within it, but Mossley's biggest outflow is across the county boundary into Saddleworth, and some of the other Pennine-fringe mill towns have more exchange with their neighbours than with Manchester. In the Peak District, Whaley Bridge and New Mills, like Buxton, have their main outflow into Chapel-en-le-Frith RD, where stone quarries and the Ferodo factory are important employers.

Liverpool has 350,000 resident workers, and a net daily inflow of 50,000. Its catchment area is much less regular in shape than Manchester's, extending fifteen miles to the north, and taking in the whole of the Wirral to the south, but much more tightly restricted to the east. St Helens is an employment centre in its own right, and Kirkby, with its big industrial estate, attracts more workers from Liverpool than go the other way. South of the Mersey, more Bebbington residents go to Birkenhead than Liverpool, and the Vauxhall motor factory near Ellesmere Port is attracting an increasing number of workers, including many from Liverpool.

The industrial districts between the two conurbations contain four secondary employment centres, and there are another three north of Manchester. All provide at least 30,000 jobs and have a net daily inflow of workers. In the west, St Helens draws from the southern

Page 71: THE MODERN COALMINING INDUSTRY

Parkside Colliery, Newton-le-Willows. This is one of the two new collieries constructed in the Lancashire coalfield. The shaft was sunk in 1957 and production, which started in 1964, is planned to be 900,000 tons a year. The modern winder towers contrast with the appearance of the traditional headgear.

The Shell works at Carrington, near Manchester. This is the largest of the Shell petro-chemicals plants in Britain. A wide range of petroleum-based chemical products are manufactured. The raw material is naphtha pumped by pipeline from the Shell refinery at Stanlow twenty-three miles away.

Page 72: THE PETRO-CHEMICALS INDUSTRY

The industrial chemicals plants at Carrington. On the left is the propylane oxide unit and on the right the ethylene glycol plant.

part of the coalmining district, but the main focus for labour movement in the western end of the coalfield is Wigan. To the east is Leigh, and to the south Warrington which draws substantial numbers from south of the Mersey. North of Manchester is the familiar triumvirate of Bolton, Bury and Rochdale, each with a quite distinct catchment area discernible within a complex pattern of local labour interchanges. These catchment areas are terminated in the north by Rossendale, where no clear focus is evident. North of this, labour movements appear to be so localised that not even Burnley can be designated a secondary employment centre, but to the west Blackburn and Preston are focal points at the same sort of level as the places mentioned above.

In northern Lancashire, Lancaster is the only industrial town with a net inward movement of workers, and in central and southern Cheshire Crewe is the only place with secondary-centre status. In neither case can a catchment area be clearly defined.

In addition to the main and secondary employment centres shown in Fig 11, a number of places are designated 'other employment centres', all having a labour force of at least 20,000 and a net daily inward movement. In some cases, for example Stretford, Bootle and Kirkby, they are well within the areas dominated by a main centre, but nevertheless attract many workers themselves. Also in this category are Blackpool, and Leyland where the motor plant attracts workers from the surrounding rural districts as well as from Preston.

The regional pattern in the North West is one of relatively short journeys to work, as Fig 11 clearly shows. In fact, most people still work in the town in which they live, and are not included in the movements on the map. Things have changed since each mill and each mine virtually had its own local catchment area, but old habits and customs die hard. The modern kind of commuting over distances up to ten or more miles is in any case difficult in areas where car-owners are a minority, public transport is often slow, and the out-dated road system is quite unsuitable for heavy peak-period motor traffic. These facts are important, because if industry is to develop where it can operate most efficiently instead of perpetuating less suitable nineteenth-century locations in the older industrial towns, greater daily mobility of labour is needed. This has recently been stressed by the North West Economic Planning Council,[5] and some of the implications will be considered in Chapter 8.

One of the reasons for the relatively short journey to work in many parts of the North West is the large proportion of women employed. This varies from less than 10 per cent of the industrial labour force

E

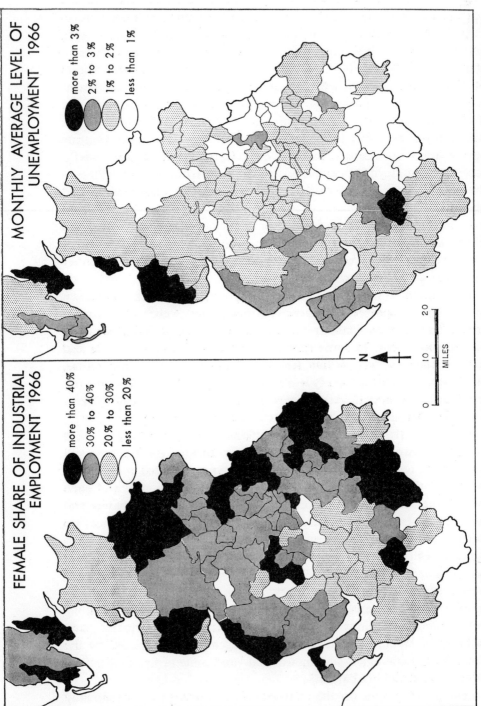

Fig 12. Two aspects of employment opportunity: female employment, and average monthly unemployment. (Source: Ministry of Labour.)

in some places to more than 50 per cent in others, with the higher proportions generally in the eastern part of the region, and the lower ones in central Cheshire and adjoining parts of Lancashire (Fig 12). In many of the Pennine-fringe textile towns over 40 per cent of the industrial jobs are held by women, the highest proportions being in Bacup, Royton, Shaw, Glossop and Congleton. Comparable figures are found in some coastal towns, part of central Lancashire, and Winsford in central Cheshire. The lowest female employment is in some of the specialised engineering and metal-manufacturing towns: Barrow-in-Furness and Birkenhead dominated by their shipyards, Leyland, Ellesmere Port and Sandbach with their motor works, St Helens with the predominantly male-employing glass industry, Irlam with its iron and steel works, the railway engineering centres of Crewe and Earlstown, and Stretford with its big engineering industry.

The pattern of female employment is largely a reflection of the local industrial structure. Just over half the workers in textiles are women compared with the average of 30 per cent in all manufacturing, and if a town also has a clothing industry, where roughly four jobs in five are taken up by women and girls, there will generally be plenty of opportunities for employment. Other major industries with over one-third of their workers females are the food, drink and tobacco group and paper, printing and publishing. But there may also be other economic and social factors influencing female employment; some families have less need for a second income than others, and there are some mining communities where the wife's place is by custom very firmly in the home and not in the nearby mill.

In many places where there is a shortage of jobs for women in industry, this is compensated for by the service sector. Females in fact make up round about 40 per cent of the total labour force of most of the larger towns in the region, with their well-developed service sectors, making them roughly comparable with the small textile towns, where there are plenty of jobs for women in the factories but less in services. Female employment also rises to a figure comparable with the regional average in some of the heavy industrial towns such as Crewe and St Helens when the service sector is added, though in others the proportion remains relatively small.

Finally, some comments on the general level of local employment are in order. The average of the exchange-area monthly unemployment figures in 1966 (mapped in Fig 12) show some perhaps unexpected features. The Pennine-fringe textile towns, where relatively high unemployment might have been anticipated, look no worse than most other parts of the region. In fact, some of them appear to compete

with areas in central Cheshire for the distinction of having the lowest
average rates of unemployment in the region. The highest proportions
are largely concentrated on the western coastal strip, where the Merseyside conurbation averages about 2·5 unemployed per 100 insured
employees, and most of the resort towns, Grange-over-Sands, Morecambe and the Fylde coast from Blackpool to Fleetwood, have even
higher figures.

How is it that the eastern edge of the region, with its rapidly
contracting textile industry, has such a low apparent level of unemployment? There are two fairly obvious reasons. First, it is well-known
that many women will seek work only when it is readily available, and
when a mill closes and puts them out of a job they will not necessarily
register at the employment exchange as would a man. Thus there may
be hidden female unemployment not reflected in official statistics.
Figures for the 1954–64 period show that the proportion of females
at work has remained steady at round about 42·0 per cent in the North
West, compared with an increase from 36·4 to 39·2 in Britain as a
whole;[6] at a regional level the lost jobs in textiles have been barely
replaced, while employment opportunity for women at a national level
has increased. The second reason is that the number of unemployed
has been kept down by substantial outward population migration. If
a redundant worker sees some prospects of getting another job he may
stay where he is and register as unemployed, but if the prospects are
hopeless he is more likely to move away. So the anomalous situation
of towns with better prospects having higher statistical unemployment
than places with few vacancies can easily arise in industrial Lancashire.
There are a number of ways in which more realistic unemployment
rates could be calculated, taking into account outward migration; one
recently used by David Eversley produced a figure of 5·0 per cent for
the Yorkshire and Humberside region in 1966, compared with the
official 1·5 per cent.[7] If the same kind of calculation could be applied
to the exchange areas of the North West, the unemployment figures
in many of the old textile towns with substantial outward migration
would no doubt rise to alarming levels.

Unemployment may also be measured by its variability. The ratio
of largest to smallest monthly unemployment has been calculated for
1966, which caught the regional economy on a downswing, with an
increase from 1·5 per cent unemployed in January to 2·1 per cent in
December. The geographical pattern of unemployment variability
reveals a concentration of high ratios in the eastern part of the region,
indicating a rapid increase in unemployment as the textile trade reacted
quickly to the general recession which was building up. By the end of

1966 many of the textile towns had unemployment above the regional average, while in the early part of the year they had little more than 1 per cent. The rise in unemployment was too quick to be immediately diluted by outward migration, and provided a reminder of the continuing sensitivity of these places to any slight reversal of regional or national economic fortunes.

References to this chapter are on page 240.

3

Recent Changes in the Regional Pattern of Industry

Two PERIODS HAVE been particularly important in moulding the regional pattern of industry. The first was the Industrial Revolution of the late-eighteenth and early-ninteenth centuries, which gave Lancashire its factory cotton industry and saw the rise of other major regional activities such as coal mining and chemicals manufacturing. The geographical pattern which resulted was a simple one, dominated by a vast textile-manufacturing district with local areas of product or process specialisation. There was little diversification, and even the major regional cities remained largely dependent on the narrow range of products which had been the basis for their initial growth. The second major period of change is the one in which the region finds itself at present. The decline of the traditional industries, in particular textiles, and their gradual replacement by new ones, has brought a second industrial revolution which, when it has run its full course, may well have changed the industrial structure and geography of the North West as dramatically as did the first.

This chapter attempts to identify the more important changes in the regional pattern of industrial activity during the post-war years. As in the previous chapter, the emphasis is on industrial location and on the different experiences of different parts of the region. Again, much of the information is derived from the Ministry of Labour employment estimates, in the absence of a suitable alternative, and the general problems involved in using these figures are added to by the need to make year-to-year comparisons. For this reason, no systematic attempts are made to identify changes in employment in individual industries at exchange-area level. The Ministry figures are used simply as indicators of broad trends in the location of the industrial sector as a whole, or to illustrate structural changes at a regional level. (See Appendix A note 8.)

Changes in the Main Sectors of the Economy

The Ministry of Labour estimates indicate an increase of about 50,000 in the number of insured employees in the region between mid-1953 and mid-1967. However, too much significance cannot be attached to this figure because of the margin of error of the estimates and the effect of short-run fluctuations in the level of economic activity. The year ending June 1967 was a bad one, with regional employment falling by 45,000; the 1953–66 increase was thus almost 100,000. But however it is calculated, the regional growth rate is very much lower than the national rate; 1·5 per cent against over 11 per cent for 1953–67. Figures for 1953–63 in *The North West Study* give a similar result: the number of employees at work in the region rose by 51,000, an increase of 1·8 per cent compared with 9·1 per cent for Britain as a whole.[1]

The overall growth of employment has been the balance between a loss of about 150,000 jobs in agriculture, mining and manufacturing and an increase of about 200,000 in the service sector. The continued build-up of employment in services has been very important to the North West in the post-war period, but, even so, the growth rate of 13 per cent in 1953–67 was well below the national figure of 22 per cent. In mining and manufacturing the loss of jobs was almost 9 per cent of the 1953 total, compared with a rise of more than 2 per cent in Britain as a whole. As the region's traditional strength is in its industrial sector, with less than the national average employed in services, its basic economic structure has given it a predisposition towards a relatively slow rate of overall employment growth in recent years, for nationally employment in services has risen almost ten times as fast as employment in industry.

There have been sharp internal differences in the volume and rate of change in employment within the North West region. In *The North West Study*, trends over the 1953 63 period were examined for twelve broad sub-regions, revealing a marked contrast between the Manchester and Merseyside conurbations with their substantial volume of new employment, and the areas to the north of Manchester with decreases in total employment.[2] But a sub-regional analysis of this kind inevitably overlooks important local trends and, at the risk of introducing some of the statistical inaccuracies which are bound to arise at a more detailed level, an examination of changes by individual exchange areas is presented here. While the general pattern of change revealed in this way can be accepted as a reasonably accurate reflection of what has actually taken place, the reservations about the reliability of the

Ministry of Labour figures, as set out in Appendix A, must be borne in mind throughout.

Changes in total employment by exchange areas are illustrated in Fig 13. The left-hand map shows the volume of increase or decrease; the other illustrates rate of change. Decreases are almost entirely confined to a roughly-triangular area with its corners represented by Ashton-in-Makerfield and Standish in the west, Nelson and Colne in the north, and Glossop in the south-east. Almost every area within this 'triangle of decline' has registered a net loss of insured employees since the early 1950s, the main exception being some of the towns around Manchester. The cities of Manchester and Salford show the largest decreases, having together lost almost 1,000 jobs a year since 1953. The northern part of industrial Lancashire, including the Blackburn–Burnley lowland and Rossendale, constitutes an almost uninterrupted zone of decrease, with Padiham near Burnley as the only exception. The decrease in employment in most of the coalmining district is somewhat relieved by growth at Westhoughton and Wigan, and in some places to the south.

Much of the net increase in employment is concentrated in an east–west zone straddling the Lancashire–Cheshire boundary from the south-western part of the Manchester conurbation across to Liverpool and corresponding broadly with the valley of the Mersey. The largest growth has taken place on Merseyside, with almost 45,000 additional jobs in Liverpool, Crosby, Bootle, Kirkby, Garston and Prescot, and about 16,000 on the opposite side of the estuary in Wallasey, Bebbington and Ellesmere Port. Birkenhead stands out as the only area with a loss of employment, explained by a big decrease in shipbuilding. The area of substantial increase extends eastwards to include Wigan, Runcorn, Warrington and Leigh, with Stretford, Altrincham and Stockport as the major growth points on the southern and eastern sides of the Manchester conurbation. Outside the triangle of decline and the Mersey growth zone most places show a modest employment increase, but Preston and part of the Fylde stand out in the northern half of Lancashire.

The map of rates of change helps to highlight the places where the most rapid growth or decline is taking place. This map should be read with the first one to get the rates in perspective; a rapid change where only a small volume is involved could be attributed to the fortunes of one concern, the closure of a mill or mine, or the building of a single new factory or office block, and is in any case subject to a fairly wide margin of error. But a large percentage change coupled with a big volume of employment increase or decrease may be a pointer to more

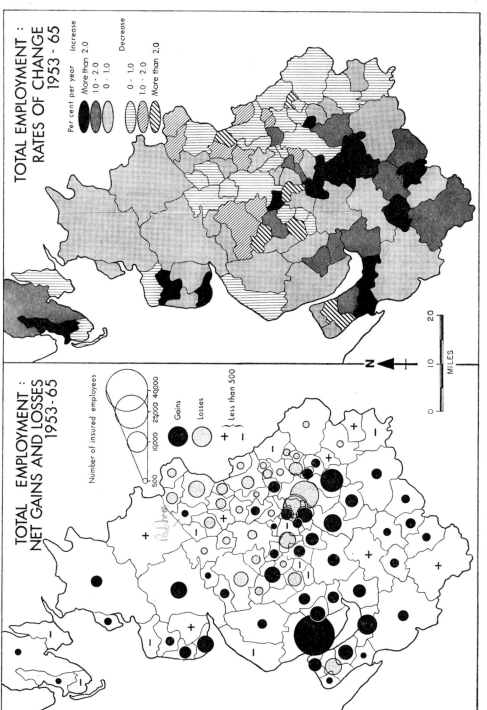

Fig 13. Changes in total employment 1953–65. (Source : Ministry of Labour.)

fundamental strength or weakness in an area's economy. Broadly, two sets of areas with relatively high rates of decrease can be identified in industrial Lancashire. In the east there are a number of the old textile towns, including Nelson and Colne, the Rossendale towns (except Haslingden), and to the south Littleborough, Royton, Shaw and Mossley. In the west is the old coal and cotton sub-region, with especially large percentage decreases in Ashton-in-Makerfield, Atherton and Standish. The most rapid increases are on the south-western side of the Manchester conurbation, in some central Cheshire towns, and in parts of the Fylde. Large percentage gains are recorded in the Furness area outside Barrow, but the numerical increases here are relatively small.

It is largely the performance of the industrial sector which has been responsible for the pattern of change illustrated in Fig 13. There is a very high positive correlation between percentage changes in total employment and industrial employment in the 1953–65 period (correlation coefficient $r = 0.844$), while the correlation between total employment and the service-sector changes is much smaller ($r = 0.457$). In statistical terms, the pattern of change in industrial employment 'explains' just over 70 per cent of the changes in total employment, while the changes in the service sector explain little more than 20 per cent.

Before the industrial sector is examined in detail some brief comments on services are in order, as growth in employment here has done so much to replace jobs lost in the factories. The largest increases have been in the professional services and the distributive trades, with a total of over 200,000 additional jobs since the early 1950s. Only the transport and communication branch has registered a substantial loss, amounting to almost 40,000 employees. But the service sector as a whole has not done as well in the North West as in all Britain, as was indicated above. The region is unfortunate in having a particularly prominent transport branch, as this is the only part of the service sector to have declined nationally, while the leading national growth section, professional services, is slightly under-represented. The North West has thus had a structurally-induced tendency towards a relatively slow rate of overall employment growth in services, accentuated by unfavourable change rates in almost all its major branches when compared with national trends. The same conclusion was arrived at in *The North West Study* for the period up to 1963.[3]

The geographical pattern of employment changes in the service sector (Fig 14) makes an interesting comparison with total employment. There are none of the big losses shown in Fig 13; although

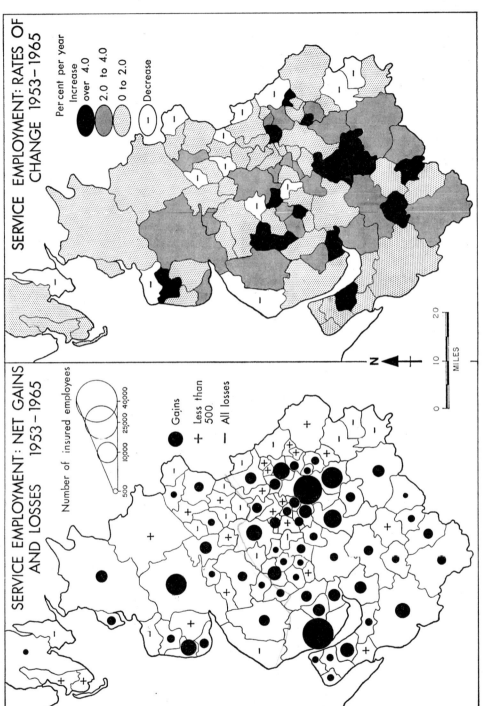

SERVICE EMPLOYMENT: NET GAINS AND LOSSES 1953–1965

Number of insured employees

500   10,000   25,000   40,000

● Gains
+ Less than 500
— All losses

SERVICE EMPLOYMENT: RATES OF CHANGE 1953–1965

Per cent per year
Increase
over 4.0
2.0 to 4.0
0 to 2.0
— Decrease

N

MILES
0   10   20

Fig 14. Changes in employment in the service sector 1953–65. (Source: Ministry of Labour.)

about a dozen exchange areas did have a decrease in service employment most were very small and only in Bacup did the figure exceed
500. The losses and smallest gains are noticeably concentrated in the
Pennine-fringe industrial zone along the eastern edge of the region,
where the unhappy performance of the service sector can be related
to the general contraction of industrial employment and decreases in
population. In a few places the service sector has grown significantly
despite the decline in manufacturing, but it is nevertheless clear that
in a large part of industrial Lancashire the services have not adequately
compensated for the loss of jobs in other sectors.

The most substantial growth of service employment has been in the
bigger cities, as might be expected. Since the early 1950s Manchester and
Liverpool have each added over 20,000 service workers, Stockport and
Preston 10,000, and places like Bolton and Oldham over 5,000. The
most rapid growth in percentage terms has been on the southern side
of the Manchester conurbation, in central Cheshire, some of the fringes
of Merseyside, and, surprisingly perhaps, in parts of the Lancashire
coalfield. However, some of these increases are not large in terms of
the volume of new jobs.

The Performance of the Industrial Sector

The remainder of this chapter attempts to answer two fundamental
questions. Firstly, why has the industrial sector of the economy
performed less satisfactorily in recent years in the North West than in
almost all the other regions in Britain? This will be considered only
briefly, as a full discussion would involve detailed comparisons with
the performance of other regions. The second question, or set of
questions, relates to internal differences in the performance of the
industrial sector: which are the major growth areas; where has industrial
employment declined to the greatest extent; how far have industrial-
location patterns changed; how far has diversification proceeded; and
where have the major new industrial developments taken place? These
are critical matters, for the answers should help us to understand
those broader issues of regional and local economic well-being which
have an important bearing on the evolution of a regional planning
strategy. In Chapter 4 attempts will be made to explain the internal
differences observed in industrial development.

The performance of the industrial sector as a whole, with its loss of
over 130,000 jobs since the early 1950s, is related to two major factors.
One is the existing industrial structure, the other is the rate of growth
or contraction of its individual components. The importance of both

these explanations has been stressed a number of times in the informative reports of the Lancashire and Merseyside Industrial Development Association (LAMIDA)[4] as well as in other published work.[5] The significance of the distinction between the two was clearly set out in *The North West Study* as follows:

> First it might have been the case that a majority of the individual firms in the region increased their demand for labour less rapidly than firms engaged in comparable types of production in other parts of the country. Since there is no evidence of a particularly rapid rise in labour productivity generally in the North West, it would follow on this hypothesis that firms in the region were tending to be less successful than their competitors elsewhere, and it would appear that the region must suffer from some peculiar handicap which adversely affected most forms of industrial activity there. Alternatively, the North West's main disadvantage may have been in the structure of its manufacturing employment. In other words, individual firms in the North West may have been growing just as rapidly as firms producing the same sort of goods elsewhere, but they may have tended to specialise in types of production which have nationally given rise to slower employment growth. Slow growing and declining sections of manufacturing may have made up a large part of the North West's particular 'mix' of industries than they have nationally.[6]

In *The North West Study* this second explanation was found the most acceptable. The conclusion was that the evidence available suggested that weaknesses in the structure of the manufacturing sector were by far the more important cause of the region's slow employment growth. The notion that the North West suffered from some 'peculiar handicap' which prevented industry from performing as well there as in other regions was largely rejected. If such handicaps had been found, in the form of unfavourable economic circumstances such as high production costs, bad access to markets, inefficient labour and so on, it would have raised the question of whether the economic revival of the region is a practical possibility. If economic factors tend to inhibit industrial growth and repel new development, a substantial increase in the economic growth rate would be very difficult to achieve without massive subsidies. As it is, acceptance of the bad-structure hypothesis implies that if this can be improved by bringing in growth industries, the problem of generating adequate new employment will soon be solved.

But can the structural explanation really be accepted with such confidence? The available evidence upon which such a judgment can be made is to be found in comparison between the industrial structures of the North West and those of Britain as a whole, and between

regional and national growth rates in the various branches of manufacturing. The high proportion employed in the declining textile and
clothing industries in the North West, and the under-representation of
the expanding engineering, vehicles and metals group, was indicated
in a previous chapter. It remains to examine the growth rates.

Table 7

CHANGES IN EMPLOYMENT IN THE INDUSTRIAL SECTOR 1953–67

Industry	Increase or decrease (−) in insured employees	Average annual change (per cent)	
		North West	Great Britain
The Growth Industries			
Motors and aircraft	35,000	3·6	1·3
Paper, printing and publishing	19,000	1·9	1·8
Engineering and metal goods	72,000	1·7	2·3
Other manufacturing	8,000	1·0	2·2
Glass, bricks etc	4,000	0·7	0·4
The Stable Industries			
Food, drink and tobacco	5,500	0·3	0·2
Chemicals	2,700	0·2	0·5
Timber and furniture	− 1,000	−0·1	−0·3
Metal manufacture	− 6,000	−0·9	0·0
Footwear	− 2,200	−1·0	−1·0
The Declining Industries			
Shipbuilding	− 12,000	−1·9	−2·2
Garments	− 29,000	−2·0	−1·4
Leather	− 4,300	−2·7	−1·6
Textiles	−176,000	−3·3	−1·9
Mining and quarrying	− 33,000	−3·5	−2·6
Railway engineering	− 17,000	−4·0	−4·0

Source: Ministry of Labour. The figures are approximate, and subject to the
reservations made in Appendix A note 8.

In Table 7 the industrial sector is divided up into sixteen branches,
and changes in employment between 1953 and 1967 are shown. The
branches are those used for various purposes in the previous chapter
(ie Orders of the SIC, with VI and IX combined), except that vehicles
and clothing have been split, to enable the expanding motor-vehicle and
aircraft industries to be separated from the declining railway engineering, and footwear to be separated from the more rapidly contracting
garment trade. The industries are listed in order of their rate of growth,
which splits them into three fairly distinct categories. Two of the
leading growth industries come as no great surprise: motors and
aircraft with the fastest rate of growth, and the engineering and metal
goods group with the biggest number of new jobs. Textiles show

the largest actual fall in employment, but the rate of decline was greater in both railway engineering and mining. Substantial losses have taken place in employment in shipbuilding and in the garment industry, but these are dwarfed by the figure for textiles.

Table 7 shows how the rates of change in the North West compare with Britain as a whole. In the growth industries the big Merseyside motor factories have given the first branch more than double the national growth rate, and in the paper group the rates are almost the same. But in the critically-important engineering and metal industries the region has failed to maintain the national rate of growth; had it been able to do so an additional 25,000 jobs would have been created. In the declining industries, only shipbuilding and railway engineering have not lost jobs at a faster rate in the North West than in Britain as a whole. It is especially significant that in both textiles and mining, once the lynch pins of the regional economy, the decline of employment has been at a much more rapid rate than nationally. Of the sixteen industries listed, only six have better rates of change in the North West than in Britain, and those which compare unfavourably with the national rates include both the largest contributor to new employment and the one with the largest loss.

Returning to the problem of explaining the poor performance of the region's industrial sector, the effect of these rates of change may now be compared with the effect of the region's industrial structure. Between 1953 and 1967 there was a net loss of about 130,000 jobs in the industrial sector, but if the North West had achieved the national industrial-employment growth rate there would have been an increase of 35,000 jobs. So the region's comparative loss in relation to national trends is 165,000, or the sum of the actual loss and what would have been gained if the region had kept up with the national growth. The amount of this loss which can be attributed to the region's poor industrial structure is calculated by applying national rates of change to the region's 1953 structure, to show what increase or decrease would have taken place if every industry had performed the same in the North West as in Britain. The result is that the actual loss of employment in the region would have been about 50,000, giving a comparative loss of 85,000 (50,000 plus the 35,000 which the region would have gained if the industrial sector as a whole had performed as well as it did nationally). The difference between the 85,000 and the true comparative loss of 165,000, ie 80,000, must be explained by the generally-unfavourable change rates of individual industrial groups in the North West compared with national rates. So a little more than half the difference between the performance of the industrial sector in the

North West and in Britain as a whole can be attributed to an unfavourable industrial structure, the rest resulting from the unsatisfactory performance of individual industries. However, it must be stressed that this result is influenced by the industrial subdivisions used; a more detailed subdivision would pick out further structural weaknesses within the sixteen branches, which would add more weight to the structural explanation.

The conclusion is, then, that *The North West Study* and other observers have probably been right to stress weaknesses in the existing structure in explaining the poor performance of the region's industrial sector; but to say that they have been by far the most important cause seems too strong. It would be dangerous to minimise the fact that many industries are not doing as well in the North West as nationally, and the clear implication is that the region possesses certain economic disadvantages compared with some other regions as a location for some kinds of new industrial development. It would be dangerous also to assume that industrial diversification alone could speed up economic growth to rates comparable with those of the Midlands and southern England. What this means in terms of the future economic development of the region and the viability of its component parts will be the subject of further comment and speculation in later chapters.

The Geographical Pattern of Changes in the Industrial Sector

It is now time to look inside the region and try to identify the main areas of industrial growth and decline. The pattern of net gains and losses in industrial employment, revealed by Fig 15, is similar in certain respects to that shown by total employment (Fig 13). In particular the Mersey growth zone and the triangle of decline are faithfully reproduced.

In the main industrial districts of central and eastern Lancashire there are hardly any places where industrial employment has risen. In the immediate vicinity of Manchester very small increases have been registered in Swinton and Middleton, but these are overshadowed by losses of over 40,000 in Manchester, almost 14,000 in Salford, 8,000 in Oldham, and 5,000 in Ashton-under-Lyne. To the north big losses are shown in Bolton and Rochdale, and industrial employment has gone down by 5,000 in the Rossendale towns and in Burnley, Nelson and Colne by over 10,000. In central Lancashire the only place between Warrington and Leyland to show an increase is Wigan. The areas with substantial increases in industrial employment are few and most are in the belt from Merseyside to the south side of the Manchester

Cadbury's factory at Moreton in the Wirral. Cadburys came here in the early 1950s, and employment has subsequently risen to 4,000. The factory buildings received a Civic Trust award for the quality of their architecture.

Page 89: TWO NEW FOOD FACTORIES

The Heinz canning factory at Kitt Green, near Wigan. This was opened in 1959 as the largest food-processing factory in Britain. It was one of the major successes in attracting new employment to the former South Lancashire Development Area, with its declining coal industry.

The Shell oil refinery at Stanlow, near Ellesmere Port. This is one of the largest and most comprehensive refineries in Europe, and feeds an adjoining petro-chemical works as well as the Shell plant at Carrington. Ship Canal docking facilities for tankers are in the foreground.

Page 90: BULK PROCESSING INDUSTRIES BESIDE THE SHIP CANAL

The Bowater paper mill at Ellesmere Port. This complex includes a groundwood pulp mill and plants making paper sacks, corrugated cases and other paper products. The Ship Canal is on the far side of the factory, and the large volumes of raw material are stored on the right.

conurbation. Liverpool, Prescot, St Helens, Runcorn, Wallasey and Ellesmere Port have together gained about 30,000 employees. To the east, increases of about 2,500 are shown in Warrington and Irlam, and there have generally been net increases around the southern fringe of Manchester in a roughly-semicircular area from Stretford to Denton.

The map of rates of change emphasises the speed with which jobs have been lost in central Lancashire and parts of the active coalfield. Here the rate is over or near 3 per cent a year, which at the extreme, in the Standish, Upholland and Ashton-in-Makerfield area, amounts to a loss of half their original industrial employment during the twelve-year period. Most of the old textile district on the eastern side of the region has lost employment in manufacturing at the rate of at least 1 per cent a year, with the highest rates in Bacup, Royton and Mossley. Big growth rates are confined to a few places on Merseyside, the edges of the Manchester conurbation, the Fylde and Furness.

If the pattern of change illustrated in Fig 15 can be regarded as broadly representative of the past two decades, the picture is not altogether encouraging. Certainly the recent growth has made Mersey-side job prospects look better than they have for a long time, and in some other areas the establishment of new industries has helped to absorb redundant mill workers. But in much of the coalfield and the old textile districts the loss of employment in the traditional activities has been far too large to replace. Even the expansion of employment in services has been unable to compensate for the loss of jobs in the industrial sector in most of what has been termed the triangle of decline. In much of this area the only consolation at present is that employment in textiles and mining cannot be reduced at the present rate indefinitely, because the losses of the past twenty years, if they occurred again, would remove these industries completely.

Because of the way different industries have performed, there have been important changes in the employment structure of many parts of the region. Generally, these can be regarded as changes for the good, representing diversification and the shift of employment from declining industries to those with higher productivity and earnings, and better growth prospects. The extent of these changes can be measured by an index similar to those used to measure localisation and specialisation in the previous chapter (see Appendix A note 6), which compares the structure at some base year (1953) with what it is like at some subsequent date (1965). This index of structural change (sometimes referred to as an index of diversification') has been calculated for each exchange area at the Order level of the SIC, and can be anything between 0,

F

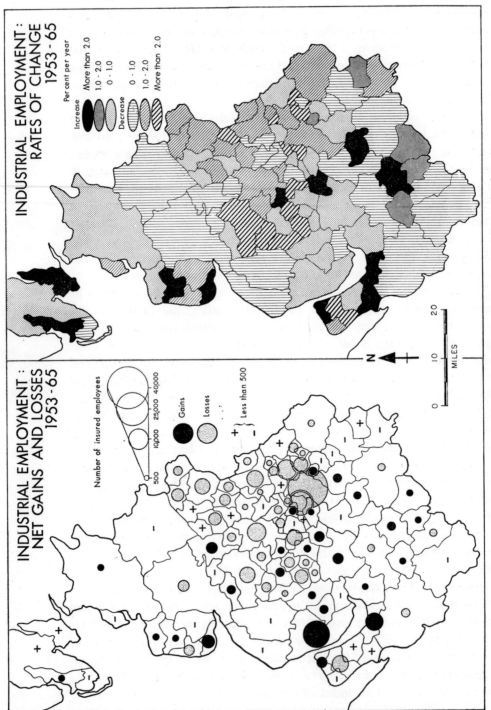

Fig 15. Changes in industrial employment 1953–65. (Source: Ministry of Labour.)

indicating no change, and 100, indicating a complete reversal of the original structure. The results are mapped in Fig 16.

Areas with indexes of over 30 have experienced very considerable structural changes considering the brevity of the period under review. Some of the changes are more important than others, however, because of the number of jobs and type of industry involved. For example, the biggest structural changes in the Wirral, at Hoylake and Neston, are relatively insignificant as neither place has much industry, whereas adjoining Wallasey and Ellesmere Port, with indexes of almost 30 in both cases, have seen very important developments. At Wallasey the large Cadbury factory has contributed to a 3,000 increase in employment in the food industry, which now accounts for two-thirds of the town's industrial workers. The arrival of the motor industry and expansion of paper manufacturing have been the main contributors to change in Ellesmere Port. In the rest of Cheshire, Winsford and Wilmslow stand out with big indexes of change. Winsford has gained a number of new industries, including clothing, engineering and a computer-assembly plant, as part of its town-expansion scheme connected with the reception of Merseyside overspill. In Wilmslow engineering has added about 800 workers. The lowest index in Cheshire is at Crewe, where what diversification has taken place appears to have had little effect on the dominant position of the railway engineering and vehicle industries.

In Lancashire, big structural changes are indicated in the Fylde and Furness. Those in Furness are less significant than they look on the map; the small manufacturing centres have attracted new employment, mainly in clothing (Dalton) and engineering (Ulverston), but diversification in Barrow (index of 12) has been less marked, despite some important recent developments. In the Fylde the structural changes in the Thornton and Kirkham exchange areas involve sectoral shifts of only a few hundred workers. But in Lytham St Anne's, with an index of 40, the changes have been more substantial; 1,000 workers have been added in engineering and almost 3,000 in other metal goods.

It is in central and eastern Lancashire that the extent of structural change, as it varies from place to place, becomes especially interesting and revealing. High indexes appear in the main coalmining area in central Lancashire suggesting considerable diversification. But much of this is explained by the contraction of the major industries of coal, textiles (in Wigan) and railway engineering (Earlstown), though the expansion of engineering and the construction of food, paper and asbestos factories in the Wigan area have brought some diversification. A zone of relatively high indexes extends from the eastern end of the

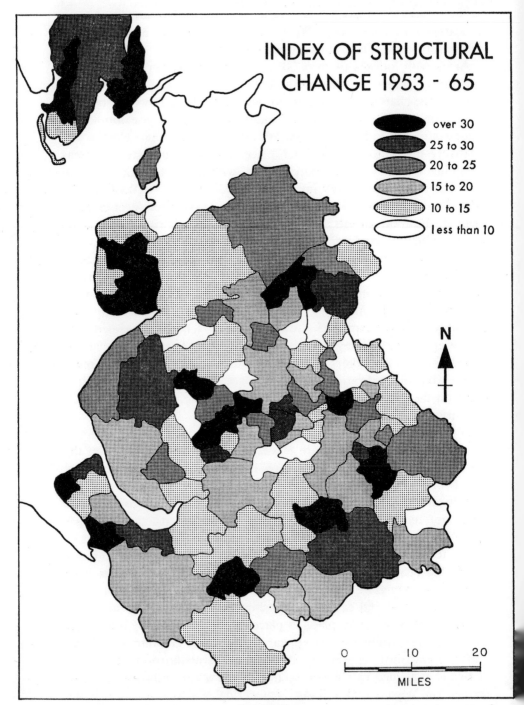

Fig 16. Changes in industrial structure 1953–65. (Source: Ministry of Labour.) The measure used is sometimes referred to as an index of diversification. The calculation of this index is described in Appendix A note 6.

main coalmining area to the northern side of Manchester. Here the biggest index is in Middleton, where the rapid growth of British Vita, the foam-rubber manufacturers, has made up for a large proportion of the loss of 3,500 jobs in textiles since 1953. In Oldham employment in textiles has gone down by almost 15,000 and the number working in the industrial sector was reduced by 8,000 between 1953 and 1959, but in the first half of the 1960s new jobs kept pace with redundancies. Much of the growth has been in engineering, with the Ferranti plants as a major contributor.

In the core of the Manchester conurbation—the city and adjoining Salford and Stockport—the indexes of change are smaller, but this can partly be attributed to the size of the places involved. Because of the way the measure is calculated a big employment centre needs very large shifts in employment from one industry to another to get a high index, whereas this can be produced in very small places by a shift of a few hundred. When this is taken into account the indexes of 18 in Manchester and 16 in Stockport can be seen to represent substantial changes in industrial structure. In Manchester it is largely the result of rapid contraction of certain activities, including 30,000 employees lost in textiles and clothing, and 10,000 in vehicles (including railway engineering), with a rise of 5,000 in engineering as the only real compensation. In Stockport about 6,000 jobs in textiles and clothing have been replaced by a similar number in metal manufacturing, engineering and metal goods, and vehicles.

Of the smaller towns east of Manchester, Hyde and Marple (both with indexes of over 30) and Denton, show the biggest structural changes. Hyde has been particularly fortunate in attracting replacement industries for jobs lost in textiles and metal manufacturing, the empty mills now housing tobacco, chemicals, and a variety of other industries. On the fringe of the Peak District, Glossop has almost been able to replace the 1,500 jobs lost in textiles, with the Maconachie pickle factory making the largest contribution. To the south Macclesfield has diversified considerably, with the 3,500 jobs lost in textiles and clothing partly compensated for by a rise of 2,000 in the pharmaceutical industry as a result of new developments by Glaxo and ICI.

The industrial districts to the north of Manchester show an interesting contrast in terms of structural change. In north-east Lancashire, Great Harwood, with an index of almost 50, has gained 3,000 jobs in the vehicles group, mainly in aircraft, to replace losses of 2,000 in textiles and 1,500 in engineering (mainly in the textile-machinery branch). Padiham has been able to gain more jobs in engineering than it has lost in textiles. Even Burnley, despite its size, has registered an index of 28; again, this is the result of a big shift from textiles to engineering, the former having lost almost 8,000 while the latter gained over 4,000. Colne has diversified less successfully than other places in the Blackburn–Burnley lowland, but the big contrast is with the area to the south. The small towns of Haslingden, Rawtenstall, Bacup and Ramsbottom all have indexes of less than 12, and the same is true of Rochdale and Littleborough. Although employment in textiles has declined here, to the extent of 5,000 jobs in Rochdale and about 1,000 each in all the other places except Haslingden, there has not been enough development of replacement industries to produce a big structural shift in employment. Only in Rawtenstall has the engineering branch provided additional work for more than a couple of hundred, and in Rochdale, with its textile-machinery industry, hundreds of jobs have been lost in engineering.

The relatively low indexes of structural change in parts of the Merseyside to Manchester belt cause less concern, as much more employment is in growth industries. The failure of Stretford (index of only 4) to diversify, and even the persistence of the high degree of specialisation in Irlam with its steel and chemical works, is obviously no problem as long as these industries remain prosperous and continue to provide new employment.

The differential rates of growth and contraction of individual industries in different parts of the region have brought about some important changes in industrial location. The centre of gravity of all industrial employment has shifted in a west-south-westerly direction, away from the old textile districts towards Merseyside.[8]

A comparison between coefficients of localisation in 1953 and 1965 shows that four major industries have become noticeably more dispersed, while three are now more concentrated than before. The largest reduction in localisation has been in metal manufacturing, which has been growing on a small scale in a number of the old textile towns, such as Rochdale, Oldham, Bury and Bamber Bridge, while in a few of the traditional centres between Manchester and Merseyside, noticeably in Warrington, employment has fallen. There has also been some dispersal of the clothing industry, including about 1,000 new jobs in the Furness area, but the reduced coefficient of localisation is mainly explained by the large drop in employment in the Manchester garment trade. The third industry to become less localised is chemicals, where important developments have occurred outside the traditional north-Cheshire concentration at such places as Preston, Hyde and Macclesfield. The fourth is engineering, which has increased its employment substantially in many parts of the region as the major replacement for the declining textile industry, though continuing growth in the traditional centres, in particular around the southern fringes of the Manchester conurbation, has been enough to pull the centre of gravity of engineering employment to the south of where it was in 1953.

The three industries with significant increases in geographical concentration are textiles, food and vehicles. What remains of the cotton industry has become more highly localised in the areas north of Manchester, and the centre of gravity of textiles has moved northwards, contrary to the general trend. The increased localisation of the vehicle group is explained by the different experiences of its two major components: the decline in railway engineering has resulted in a fall in employment in a number of places, including Manchester, while the extensive recent developments in motor manufacturing on Merseyside have produced a new vehicles concentration to rival those in central Lancashire and southern Cheshire. In the third industry, food, new developments have strengthened the existing concentration in and around Merseyside.

One major conclusion can be drawn from this section. The belt extending from Merseyside to the fringes of the Manchester conurbation is clearly the region's main growth zone. It is the only area of any size with general and substantial increases in industrial employment, and appears to be in a good position to attract new jobs and new industrial concerns with good growth prospects. The shift in emphasis towards this belt as the major focus of industrial growth, at the expense of the other industrial areas to the north and east, is a matter of fundamental importance to the future economic development of the region and the way this is planned. However much it may seem desirable to disperse new industrial growth into the old mill towns of the Pennine fringes and restrict it in the Manchester to Merseyside belt, this is contrary to what appears at present to be the region's 'natural' course of spatial economic development. Whatever pattern of population and industrial distribution the regional planner finally decides upon for the North West it must have regard to the very strong attractions of the Mersey growth zone as a location for industrial development, a matter which is returned to in the final chapter.

The Location of New Industrial Development

So far this section has been confined to a discussion of trends in employment. But employment is not the only possible measure of industrial development, and in some industries, particularly those which are capital intensive, the amount of new plant constructed may be a better indicator of the favoured areas for expansion. The Board of Trade keeps detailed records of new industrial buildings completed, but they do not cover the reoccupation and conversion of existing premises. This is a particularly serious omission in the North West because of the large amount of new industry which has developed in old cotton mills (see Chapter 4). The amount of industrial floor space provided by the conversion of existing premises has in some years exceeded the amount constructed as newly-built factories; in 1964 the figures were about 6 million sq ft in conversions compared with 4·5 million in new development, in 1965 it was 8·25 million against 5·5 million.[9] The pattern of new building is nevertheless of great interest as an indicator of where major investment in new plant has taken place.

The first geographical analysis of the Board of Trade data was undertaken a few years ago by H. B. Rodgers, who examined the location of new projects and major extensions completed up to 1959.[10] The concentration of new development in the Manchester–Merseyside belt was made clear, with the highest new square footage per insured employee found in south Merseyside, north-central Cheshire, and south-central Lancashire. Rodgers summarised his observations as follows:

> . . . the main mass of new industrial development in the North West has sought sites along the two major axes of communications which traverse the region, the east–west axis of the Ship Canal and the East Lancashire Road and the north–south line of direct road and rail communications to the threshold of the industrial Midlands, now improved by the completion of the M6 motorway. Along the first of these axes the growth of industry has been much faster at the western than at the eastern end: in Manchester industrial expansion has been sluggish, particularly when put in *per capita* terms, and it has largely been confined to the southern and western margins of the conurbation. In contrast, all the sub-regions which cluster about the Mersey estuary have made spectacular economic progress which cannot be explained entirely as an achievement of the government's policies of industrial guidance, for growth has been fastest outside the boundaries of the old Development Areas.[11]

Rodgers' illuminating study has been updated by an examination of industrial building during the six-year period from the beginning of 1960 to the end of 1965. During this time there were 1,372 new projects or extensions completed, involving over 35 million sq ft of floor space and an estimated additional employment of over 66,000. The location of new building (Fig 17) clearly shows the importance of

Merseyside, with more than 11,000 sq ft built in the Liverpool exchange areas and on the south shore of the estuary. The inclusion of St Helens, Prescot, Widnes and Runcorn adds a further 3,000 sq ft, giving a total of over one-third of the North West's new industrial building within ten miles of Liverpool's city centre. The happy position of Merseyside and its immediate surroundings is emphasised in the second map, which shows very high ratios of floor space completed to the number of industrial workers. Most of the development on Merseyside was in motor-vehicle manufacture and engineering, which accounted for 5·5 million sq ft in Liverpool, and well over half the new building in the conurbation and its immediate surroundings. But also making a big contribution were food (Wallasey), paper (Ellesmere Port), chemicals including oil refining (Ellesmere Port and Bebbington) and glass (St Helens).

Moving inland, Warrington stands out prominently as a growth centre, as do Irlam with the expansion of its chemical and steel works, and Stretford with new development in chemicals and engineering. But in Manchester less than 2 million sq ft of new industrial building has been constructed, and the area per worker in much of the Manchester district is very low. Even the southern fringe, including Altrincham and Stockport exchange areas, makes a poor comparison with Merseyside. On the eastern side of the city the only places with more than 20 sq ft per worker are Denton and Hyde.

To the north of Manchester the volume of new development in the old textile districts looks encouraging. Bolton, Bury, Rochdale and Oldham together attracted almost 2·5 million sq ft, mainly in engineering, and about the same amount was built in the Blackburn–Burnley lowland, including Nelson and Colne. But the ratios of floor space to employees are less satisfactory. The only really high ratios are found in Burnley and Padiham, which attracted some government-assisted industry in the 1950s, and Darwen with its important wallpaper plants. The inclusion of converted cotton-mill space would make the situation look better in many of the textile towns, but the reoccupation of a mill represents replacement of industry previously lost, rather than a new addition to the local economy.

Outside the major industrial areas, most new development has been in the Fylde and in southern Cheshire. In the Fylde, chemicals, aircraft and engineering industries created a total of almost 800,000 sq ft, with a very high ratio of area to workers. Electronics and other engineering at Winsford, clothing at Crewe, and pharmaceuticals in Macclesfield and district, are among the main contributors to the 1,200,000 or so sq ft built in south-central Cheshire.

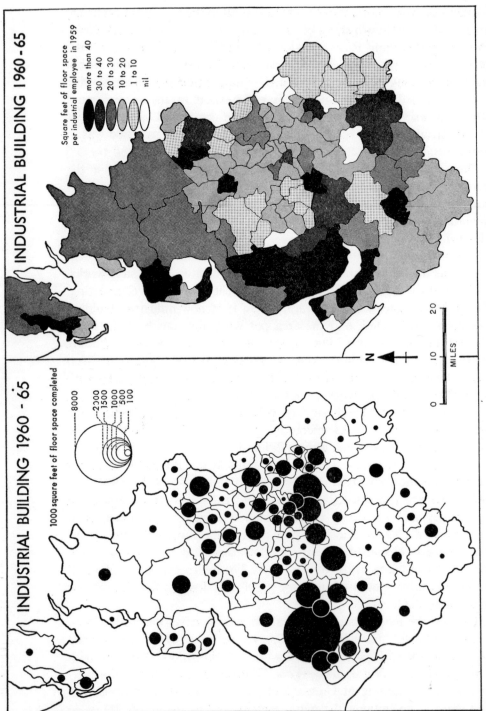

Fig 17. The location of new industrial building completed in the period January 1960 to December 1965. (Source: Board of Trade.)

The pattern of new development makes an interesting comparison with that of change in industrial employment, as shown in Fig 15. They both portray the same general picture of the Merseyside conurbation and its immediate hinterland as the region's major growth zone, tailing off in the direction of Manchester. But the old textile districts north of Manchester look a lot healthier in Fig 17 than in Fig 15, in terms of new development if not in the ratio of floor area to the existing working population. And there are also many local differences. In fact, the correlation between percentage changes in employment in the mid-1959 to mid-1965 period and the amount of new industrial development per worker is relatively low (r = 0·370).

One of the most important features of new industrial developments in recent years is the major contribution made by a small number of very large projects. In 1960-5 forty-eight projects of 100,000 or more sq ft, or about one in twenty-eight of all projects completed, accounted for as much as one-third of the new industrial floor space constructed. It is probably fair to assume that they also provided something like one-third of the 66,000 new jobs. The inclusion of eighty more projects of between 50,000 and 100,000 sq ft raises the proportion of new floor space to half the total.

If major projects like these are accounting for such a disproportionately large share of new development, their location is of very great importance. In the six years under review the area within a radius of ten miles from Liverpool city centre accounted for over one-third of new floor space, but attracted very nearly half the projects of over 50,000 sq ft, and exactly half those over 100,000. Compared with this, the Manchester area did not do anything like as well; the 50,000 to 100,000 category greatly outnumbered the larger projects, which were almost entirely confined to locations on the upper reaches of the Ship Canal.

The location of the larger projects is shown in Fig 18. The new motor factories, Ford at Halewood, Standard Triumph nearby at Speke, and Vauxhall near Ellesmere Port, accounted for something like one-eighth of new floor space constructed in the region in the first half of the 1960s. Among other major developments shown in the northern part of Merseyside were a big extension for the Metal Box Company at Speke, the British Enka man-made fibres plant, and a 250,000 sq ft replacement of existing premises for R. Silcock & Sons, manufacturers of animal feed. Big developments at Kirkby include a large factory for Fisher & Ludlow's domestic electrical-appliance production, the former Tubewright's steel depot (now being developed by the Bootle tin-smelting concern of Williams, Harvey & Co), and plants for

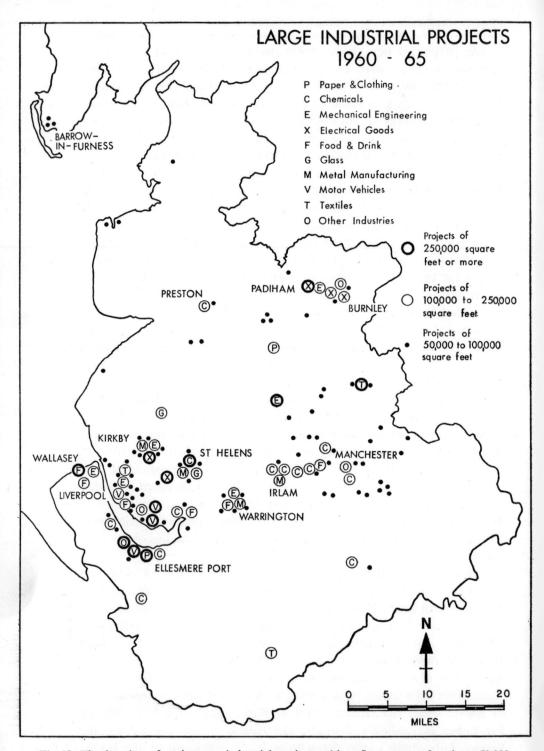

Fig 18. The location of major new industrial projects with a floor space of at least 50,000 sq ft completed during the period January 1960 to December 1965. (Source: Board of Trade.)

AC-Delco and Otis Elevators. The most spectacular growth on the southern side of the Mersey estuary has been in and around Ellesmere Port; as well as the Vauxhall factory, the map shows a large project in paper by the Bowater organisation, the Metal Box Company's plastics plant at Bromborough Port industrial estate, and further expansion in oil refining at Stanlow. The second major growth point in the Wirral is Wallasey, with one major development in marine engineering and two additions to the Cadbury plant at Moreton.

To the east of the Merseyside conurbation, St Helens was the location for three projects of over 100,000 sq ft, that of the Delta Metal Company producing copper alloys and brass forgings, and two projects in the glass industry. Another glass works has been built by United Glass Industries at Skelmersdale New Town to the north. The largest projects in Warrington were in brewing and industrial plant, and an extension to the Lancashire Steel Corporation mill.

In the Manchester conurbation most of the projects of over 100,000 sq ft were in the chemical industries, mainly in the chemicals and dyes branch, but also including the extension to the Colgate-Palmolive soap factory in Salford. It is clear that the western side of the conurbation, with access to Manchester's docks and the Ship Canal, has been the favoured area for big new development, to the east the largest projects were all in the 50,000 to 100,000 category.

The only area outside Manchester in the old textile districts which has attracted large new industrial-building projects in recent years is in the former North-East Lancashire Development Area. The projects of over 100,000 sq ft shown in Fig 18 in the Burnley area are extensions to the Michelin rubber factory on Heasandford industrial estate, the Joseph Lucas plant on Eastern Avenue, the Burco electrical canteen-equipment works at Rosegrove, Mullards at Simonstone, and the new Main Morley gas-appliance works at Padiham. The concentration of large projects in the Burnley–Padiham district emphasises the failure of much of eastern and central Lancashire to attract new plants of a substantial size. The emptiness of the coalmining area and Rossendale is particularly obvious in Fig 18, but again the conversion of cotton mills must be mentioned as creating industrial space not revealed by the records of new buildings.

It is clear that an important distinction can be made between the scale of new development in the Mersey growth zone on the one hand, and the rest of industrial Lancashire and northern Cheshire on the other. In and around Merseyside new projects in the 1960–5 period averaged over 40,000 sq ft, while elsewhere the figure seldom exceeded 20,000. This is very important because big projects tend to have a disproportionately large impact on the economy and employment of the areas in which they are located, through the attraction and stimulation of component suppliers and other ancillary activities. The setting-up of one large plant can often do far more for a town's economic revival in the long run than a number of small projects.

Table 8

THE INDUSTRIAL DISTRIBUTION OF NEW BUILDINGS COMPLETED
15 JANUARY 1960 TO 31 DECEMBER 1965

Industry	Floor area (sq ft)	Sq ft per employee at mid-1959
Engineering and metal goods	9,510	29
Chemicals	4,250	32
Vehicles	3,900	38
Food, drink and tobacco	3,850	30
Paper, printing and publishing	3,180	39
Bricks, glass and ceramics	2,450	53
Textiles	1,740	5
Metal manufacturing	1,650	39
Clothing	770	7
Timber, furniture etc	763	25
Shipbuilding	500	11
Leather	90	8
Other manufacturing	2,210	39

Source: Board of Trade.

One more item of interest can be learned from details of new industrial building, namely, how it has been distributed between the major industries (Table 8). This provides a check on the growth characteristics identified earlier in this chapter on the basis of employment trends (Table 7), and confirms the importance of the engineering and metal goods group and vehicle manufacturing as major growth industries. But two of the 'stable' industries in terms of employment, chemicals and the food group, have expanded their plant considerably. Chemical manufacturing is highly capitalised, with a small ratio of workers to floor area, and the new large-scale developments in food are doubtless less labour intensive than most of the older firms in this trade. The expansion of the chemical industry's capacity in recent years makes it one of the region's major growth industries, a status which is further emphasised by the fact that chemicals consistently comes third (to engineering and electrical, and miscellaneous manufacturing) in the number of development enquiries dealt with by

LAMIDA.[12] The remainder of Table 8 broadly agrees with Table 7, even if there are variations in the ranking of individual industries. In terms of floor area completed and square footage per worker, textiles, clothing, shipbuilding and leather all fall into the bottom half of the growth league, just as they do in terms of employment trends.

References to this chapter are on pages 240 and 241.

4

Explaining Recent Trends

THE EXPLANATION OF changes in industrial location and areal differences in growth rates is not any easy matter. The various factors affecting plant location are well-known, but it is often very difficult to determine their relative importance in specific instances, and it is quite impossible to put all the factors together into some kind of mathematical model which could adequately predict the trends which have been observed.[1] All that can be attempted here is to examine each of the main influences in turn, in the hope of arriving at some reasonably sound, if rather imprecise, interpretation of post-war trends.

It is clear that the local industrial structure has had an important bearing on the performance of different parts of the North West. Much industrial development simply involves the expansion of existing plants and is pre-determined in its location. But other factors are involved in deciding where new developments take place, not least of which are national industrial-location policy and various local planning constraints. Among the economic considerations are the availability and cost of land and premises, the supply and quality of labour, and access to materials and market. A manufacturer looking for somewhere to build a new factory has to weigh all these in the balance before deciding whether to locate in the North West in the first place, and again, before selecting from the alternative sites which may be available.

The Structural Element[2]

In the previous chapter it was shown that industrial structure has been partly responsible for the relatively slow rate of employment growth in the North West region as a whole. This might also be expected to apply to some places within the region, for it will be clear from the earlier discussions of local specialisation that some areas are heavily dependent on a narrow range of declining industries, while others

106

Astmoor Industrial Estate, Runcorn New Town. Standard factory units are being constructed by the Development Corporation to provide 950,000 square feet of industrial floor space. The estate should eventually employ almost 6,000 people.

Page 107: MODERN FACTORIES IN THE NEW TOWNS

Gillibrands Industrial Estate, Skelmersdale New Town. The spacious layout, modern architecture and attractive forecourt treatment contrast with the drab industrial landscape of the older towns. By 1968 almost one million square feet of factory space had been constructed on this estate.

Telephone cable machines at the Prescot works of BICC. These high-speed twinning machines, designed by British Insulated Callender's Cables Ltd, perform part of the process of manufacturing insulated telephone cables.

Page 108: REGIONAL INDUSTRIAL INNOVATIONS

Pilkington's float glass process. This revolutionary method of producing glass was invented by Pilkington at St Helens in 1959. A continuous ribbon of molten glass is floated on a bath of molten tin, where the glass conforms to the perfectly flat surface of the metal.

have more activities with growth potential. To attempt to understand how far intra-regional variations in rates of employment change since the early 1950s might be attributed to differences in industrial structure it is necessary to see just what the structure was like at the beginning of the period under review.

Fig 19 shows the proportion employed in the growth and declining sectors in 1953. The growth industries are engineering, electrical and metal goods, motor vehicles and aircraft, bricks and glass etc, paper, printing and publishing, and the other manufacturing group. The declining industries are mining, shipbuilding, textiles, railway engineering, leather and garments. Fig 19 shows high proportions in the growth industries in most of the Merseyside to Manchester belt, and in much of the western part of the region; there was a much smaller growth component in central and eastern Lancashire and in eastern Cheshire, where the big declining industries of cotton and coal mining are concentrated. The very high proportion employed in declining industries in the coalfield and many of the textile towns emphasises the extent of the problem which these areas were faced with in the early 1950s; four-fifths employed in coal mines, cotton mills, railway works or garment factories was hardly a basis for industrial expansion.

The pre-existing local industrial structure has built into it a predisposition towards expansion or contraction of employment, quite irrespective of what new industry may be attracted into the area, and a comparison between Figs 19 and 15 suggests a fair degree of correspondence between structural features and local industrial growth rates.[3] But how far does structure really explain the pattern of employment change? This question was posed in the last chapter in relation to the region as a whole, and it was found that the structural element, important though it is, can be exaggerated. The same may be true at a more local level: it is easy to assume that the poor performance of the coal and cotton towns can be entirely attributed to their existing industrial mix, but too often this hypothesis is accepted without adequate testing. In *The North West Study* the influence of structure was considered on a regional scale, but there was virtually no attempt to take this question down to the local or sub-regional level.[4]

Some attempt to evaluate the structural explanation is particularly important, in view of the planning implications involved. The argument is similar to that put forward in the previous chapter when the performance of the region as a whole was under review. If the unhappy experiences of the declining parts of the region can be attributed entirely, or very largely, to the unfortunate industrial structure which they have inherited, the development of new industries can soon alter

G

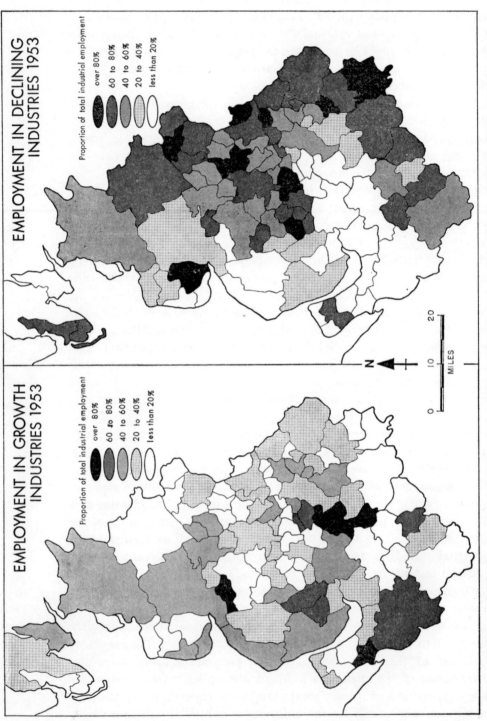

Fig 19. Employment in the growth and declining sectors of the industrial economy 1953. (Source: Ministry of Labour.) The growth industries are Orders VI, VIII other than railway engineering, IX, XIII, XV and XVI; the declining industries are Orders II, VII, XII (also mining in part), X, XI and VII other than footwear. The definitions are on the revised SIC.

this to produce a diversified structure with more growth potential. Achieving this objective then boils down to the problem of how to get new industry. But if something other than structure seems to be exerting an important influence on the rate of economic growth (or decline), the problem takes on a different form. If the poor performance of parts of the region can also be attributed to their general unattractiveness to new industry, this raises the question of how they can be made more attractive, and ultimately whether their economic revival is a practical possibility at all.

Testing the structural hypothesis requires a means of predicting the geographical pattern of employment change that would have occurred if industrial structure had been the only cause, and comparing the result with what actually happened. If the two correspond closely, the structural explanation is upheld. If they do not, then the importance of factors other than structure is suggested. The way this can be done was discussed in the previous chapter. For each area the 'comparative' change is identified—how the area performed compared with the regional average; then the 'compositional' change is extracted, ie that which can be attributed to structure; finally, the difference between comparative and compositional change gives 'competitive' change— that which must be explained by features other than structure. The method of calculation is set down fully in Appendix A note 9.

If this approach is to yield anything useful, it must be based on a detailed structural breakdown of each area's industry. For the test described here industrial employment is divided into nineteen categories (see Appendix A note 9), which is just about as detailed a classification as the 1958 change in the SIC permits.

The compositional change for each area is calculated by applying the regional rates of increase or decrease over a given period (in this case 1953–64) to each of the nineteen structural components. In other words, local rates of change are held constant in order to observe the effect of structure alone. When the changes predicted in each component are added the result is the change in total industrial employment which can be attributed to the local structure. The difference between comparative and compositional changes is the change which would have occurred in a given area if it had the same industrial mix as the regional average, but with its own local rates of change; in other words, it is the change which cannot be attributed to local structure.

The geographical pattern of compositional change (Fig 20) illustrates the predisposition towards increase or decrease in employment arising from the original (1953) industrial structure. It shows what would have happened in each exchange area given no geographical variations in the rates of change in individual industries. The pattern revealed is an interesting one, and clearly bears some resemblance to what did take place, as comparison with the left-hand map in Fig 15 will show. The triangle of decline identified in the previous chapter is repeated, and the increases in employment in the belt from Liverpool towards Manchester are paralleled by substantial compositional gains. But there are some important differences. The second map in Fig 20 indicates the extent to which structure, as measured by the nineteen subdivisions chosen, fails to predict what actually happened, ie, the differences between compositional change and comparative change. A competitive gain indicates that the area has done better than its 1953 structure would suggest, while a loss indicates a decrease in employment greater than might be expected on the basis of structure. Although some of the competitive changes are explained by structural features hidden by the industrial classification used, they must in many cases be attributed to local differences in the experiences of individual industries. In some parts of the region the growth industries have done better than in others, just as in some of the declining industries the rate of loss of employment has varied from place to place.

Much can be learned from the map of competitive changes. The triangle of decline has disappeared, and many of the old textile towns seem to have done better (or less badly) than their structure would suggest—some indication of the development of replacement industries. But parts of Rossendale and much of the coalmining area have done even worse than expected, and Manchester, Salford and a number of neighbouring towns have suffered very large competitive losses indeed. The poor performance of the Manchester area, explained by the shortage of land for development, relocation of industry in the process of urban renewal, and the restrictions of government industrial-location policy, provides another indication of the area's rather slow rate of economic readjustment, particularly when compared with Merseyside. The positive competitive changes in Liverpool, Ellesmere Port, and most places immediately to the east, indicate much better growth than predicted on the basis of structure. This emphasises the importance of the Mersey growth zone as an area with attractions to new industry which appear not to be shared by most other parts of the region.

How close is the relationship between changes attributable to structure and actual change? The correlation coefficient between compositional and comparative change ($r = 0.44$) indicated some correspondence but not a very close one.[5] In fact the competitive changes explain (statistically) much more of the variations in actual

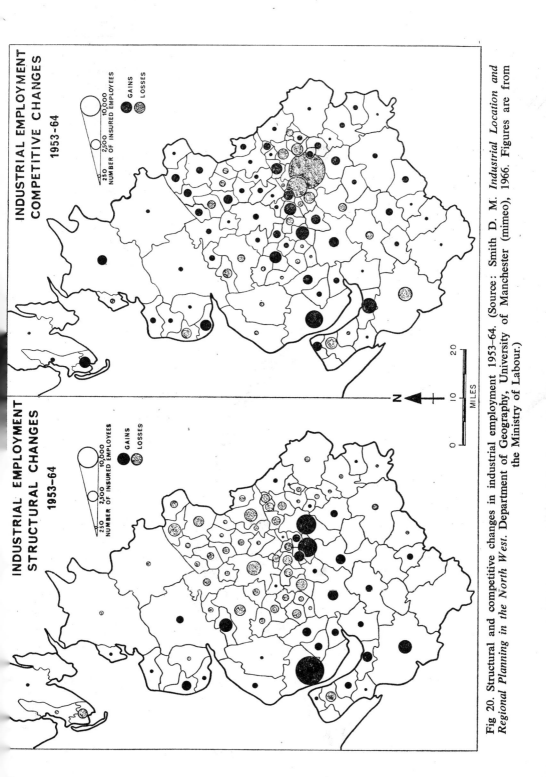

Fig 20. Structural and competitive changes in industrial employment 1953–64. (Source: Smith D. M. *Industrial Location and Regional Planning in the North West*. Department of Geography, University of Manchester (mimeo), 1966. Figures are from the Ministry of Labour.)

change than is accounted for by structure. But it would be a mistake
to conclude on the basis of this test alone that local growth rates are
so much more important than the pre-existing structure as a cause of
the geography of industrial-employment changes. The method used
here is sensitive to the level of industrial aggregation; the more detailed
the classification the more structural features will be revealed, and the
closer will the calculated compositional change correspond with actual
change. Similarly, a less detailed subdivision will produce less correspondence: a test conducted for the 1953–65 period at the Order level
of the SIC (fourteen divisions) produced a lower correlation coefficient
$(r = 0·39)$ than was found at the nineteen subdivisions level. Clearly,
if it were possible to divide up the major industries further, particularly
engineering and textiles, a better structural explanation would be dis-
covered, for different branches have had different rates of change. The
application of the regional growth rate in all engineering, for example,
to a town with a big textile-machinery industry, will obviously produce
an over-optimistic prediction of employment change on the basis of
structure. And some comparative gains in the cotton towns can be
attributed to local specialisation in less severely contracting branches
of the trade. The Minimum List Heading level of classification would
provide a much more detailed structural subdivision, but the change
in the SIC means that it would have to be based on 1959, which gives
too short a period to be confident that rates of change have long-term
significance.

But despite these technical reservations this test helps to put the
structural hypothesis in perspective. Although the effect of variations
in local industrial structure cannot be rejected as insignificant, it is
unwise to accept this as virtually the sole cause of the post-war
geographical pattern of employment change. Even when allowance is
made for structural features hidden by the industrial classification used
here, it is clear that important differences in growth potential do exist
within the region, reflected in the competitive changes. The Liverpool-
Manchester growth zone has attracted much new industry, admittedly
with government help in Merseyside, and the expanding industries
seem to be capable of more rapid growth here than in most other
areas. At the same time certain of the cotton and coal towns have been
almost entirely immune to the attempts which have been made to
attract new industry to them. Their ills cannot be attributed to structure
alone, and repetition of the structural explanation without major
reservations only serves to obscure the more fundamental problem of
whether they have a long-run future as viable locations for industrial
activity.

Government Policy

Government policy has clearly been an important determinant of the location of industrial development in the North West in recent years. By witholding an Industrial Development Certificate (IDC), the Board of Trade can prevent new building projects considered inconsistent with the 'proper distribution of industry', and by offering financial inducements new industry can be enticed into areas where it is judged to be needed. By 1968 these inducements had become so attractive that, according to LAMIDA, the question facing firms considering expansion was no longer whether they can obtain an IDC, but whether they can afford to forego the financial benefits offered in the development areas.[6] Government policy has thus become probably the most important single factor affecting plant location at a sub-regional level within the North West.

Post-war industrial-location policy began with the Distribution of Industry Act of 1945, under which areas with high unemployment could be designated as development areas and financially assisted. No part of the North West was included initially, but in 1946 the South Lancashire Development Area was established in the southern part of the coal mining district. In 1949 Merseyside was scheduled in recognition of persistently high unemployment, and North-East Lancashire was added in 1953 as rapid contraction of employment in the cotton industry followed the collapse of a brief post-war boom. These development areas are defined in Fig 21. In 1958 the Distribution of Industry (Industrial Finance) Act enabled assistance to be given to certain places outside the development areas, including Furness, and, in 1959, Oldham and some of its neighbouring cotton towns.

Under the Local Employment Act of 1960 the development areas were replaced by a large number of relatively small development districts. Of the three previously scheduled areas in the North West, only a slightly extended Merseyside was now thought to need government help. In March 1963 Widnes was added to Merseyside, and two months later the Furness Development District was created.

The only other part of the region scheduled under the 1960 Act was Blackpool, the treatment of which indicates some of the weakness of this legislation. Qualification for government assistance was dependent on a place reaching an arbitrarily-chosen level of unemployment, and in April 1960 Blackpool was made a development district on the strength of 4·5 per cent out of work. But the figure dropped during the summer, and the town was de-scheduled in July 1961 when unemployment was 1·4 per cent, despite the fact that no industrial

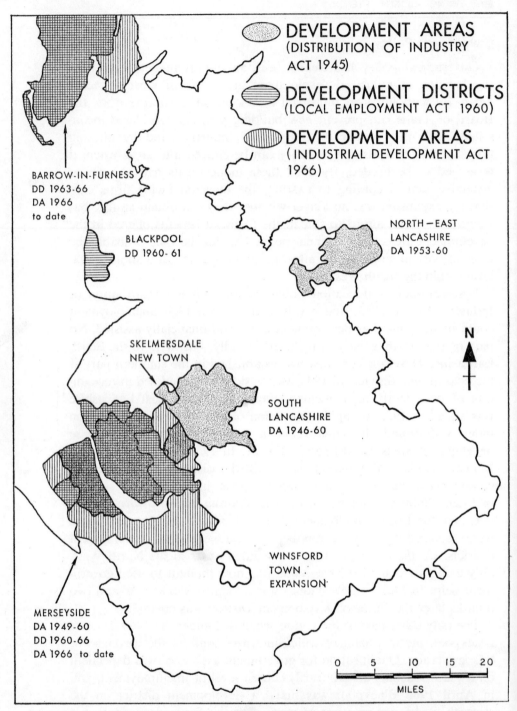

Fig 21. Areas assisted by post-war government industrial-location policy. (Source: Board of Trade.) Note: The North-East Lancashire Development Area extended across the county boundary to include a small part of Yorkshire.

development involving more than a hundred new jobs had been attracted since 1960.[7] By April 1963 unemployment had risen again, to 6·1 per cent. The small development districts were ill-designed to deal with the seasonal unemployment of coastal resorts like Blackpool, and other towns where the proportion out of work hovered around what was deemed to be the critical level.

In 1966 an attempt was made to meet these and other criticisms of previous legislation. Under the Industrial Development Act the development districts were abandoned in favour of much more broadly defined development areas, which were supposed to be selected on the basis of population change, migration and the objectives of regional policies, as well as on unemployment.[8] In the North West a Merseyside Development Area was designated, comprising the old development district with the addition of St Helens and a more extensive area on the southern side of the estuary (Fig 21). The former Furness Development District and Grange-over-Sands became part of the large Northern Development Area. In addition, Winsford and Skelmersdale New Town qualify for development-area grants under the 1966 Act, as overspill reception areas for Liverpool. The Industrial Development Act, like the 1960 Act, ignored the claims of the former development areas of South Lancashire and North-East Lancashire, both seriously affected by the continuing decline of the coal and cotton industries, but lacking high statistical unemployment.

The financial assistance available to firms setting up in the development areas or districts has varied from Act to Act. But throughout the post-war period it has largely taken the form of loans or grants towards the initial capital costs of development. At present (late-1968) the main financial benefits are grants of up to 35 per cent towards the cost of building new factories or extensions, and 45 per cent (compared with 25 per cent outside the development areas) towards the cost of new plant and machinery. One possible criticism of this kind of assistance is that it favours capital-intensive industry, whereas areas of high unemployment are perhaps in greater need of labour-intensive activities. But the introduction of regional and selective employment premiums has added assistance related to number of workers; firms in the development areas now receive a subsidy of 37s 6d a week for each male employee, with lesser rates for females and juveniles. Other instruments of government industrial-location policy are the acquisition of land for industrial estates, and the building of premises to encourage firms to set up in particular areas.[9]

How far has government policy influenced the location of industrial development within the region since the war? How far has it assisted the general economic revival of the North West? Unfortunately it is impossible to answer either of these vital questions precisely. The difficulty arises from the fact that all industrial projects in the development areas cannot automatically be attributed to the financial assistance available; some of them would have occurred anyway. But some general inferences can be made, on the basis of the limited information which the Board of Trade makes available.

The amount of industrial building approved by the Board of Trade in recent years and the anticipated additional employment, at a broad

Table 9

INDUSTRIAL BUILDING APPROVED BY THE BOARD OF TRADE
1956–66

Subdivision	Floor area (millions of sq ft)	Estimated additional employment		Employment in 1956 as percentage of regional total
		number of jobs	percentage of regional total	
Merseyside	34·9	101,410	55	28
Manchester	25·5	29,460	16	40
South Lancashire	9·9	14,860	8	8
North-East Lancashire	6·3	12,840	7	8
South Cheshire/High Peak	6·1	12,470	7	6
Mid-Lancashire	3·9	4,450	2	5
Fylde	2·1	5,050	3	3
Furness	1·3	6,390	3	1
Lancaster	0·9	1,380	1	1

Source: Board of Trade. The figures include all industrial building projects, some of which are not in manufacturing. The subdivisions are the nine groups of exchange areas used by the Board of Trade and Ministry of Labour for statistical purposes. Only Furness corresponds exactly with present or former development areas.

sub-regional level, gives some idea of how government policy has been applied (Table 9). A comparison between the figures for Manchester and Merseyside is particularly revealing; the Manchester subdivision, with 40 per cent of the North West's workers in the mid-1950's, had only 16 per cent of the estimated employment between 1956 and 1966, while Merseyside approvals involved new jobs equivalent to twice its 1956 share of regional employment. Most of the development in the Merseyside subdivision has been financially assisted, while in Greater Manchester, without development-area status, IDCs are frequently refused. The next two areas listed, both including development areas up to 1960, had development approved roughly in proportion to their shares of regional employment. The slightly lower figure in North-East

Lancashire appears to reflect a tougher IDC policy since de-scheduling, and the much smaller amount of building approved before the creation of the development area in 1953. Of the other subdivisions, Mid-Lancashire (including Preston and Leyland–Chorley) had less approved development than might have been expected, while in Furness the beneficial effect of new projects in the early 1960s shows up clearly. It must be stressed that approval of a project is no guarantee of its eventual completion, but Board of Trade figures for developments completed, available since 1960, generally confirm the sub-regional allocation suggested by Table 9.

Table 10

INDUSTRIAL DEVELOPMENT APPROVED IN THE ASSISTED AREAS
1945–68

Area	Floor area (millions of sq ft	Percentage of regional total
Development Areas, 1945–March 1960		
Merseyside (scheduled 1959)	29·7	25·1
South Lancashire (scheduled 1946)	7·5	6·5
North-East Lancashire (scheduled 1953)	3·9	3·3
Total	41·1	34·9
Development Districts, April 1960–June 1966	11·3	23·8
Merseyside Development Area, July 1966–March 1968	4·6	33·5

Source: Board of Trade. Separate figures for the Furness part of the Northern Development Area since 1963 are not available. The figures for the development areas 1945–60 include the whole of this period irrespective of the date of scheduling.

Table 10 isolates the area of building approved within the development areas or districts themselves. The proportion of all regional development in assisted areas under the 1945 and 1966 Acts is shown to have been a little over one-third of the total, but fell to less than a quarter under the 1960 Act. The Merseyside Development Area's share of approved building has increased since 1966, but so has the area covered. Projects outside the development areas still account for almost two-thirds of the floor space of all approvals, which could be taken as evidence that the Board of Trade's treatment of the non-scheduled areas as a whole is not quite as tough as some observers have suggested.

Much industrial expansion in the existing and former development areas would clearly not have taken place there, or elsewhere in the

North West, without the attraction of government grants or refusal of IDCs in more attractive locations. This includes such major developments as the motor factories on Merseyside, electrical equipment and tyres in North-East Lancashire, and some recent projects in the Furness area. In this respect government policy has certainly assisted in the general economic revival of the region as well as of selected areas. But against this is the fact that the North West's share of all new development approved by the Board of Trade in recent years has been small in relation to the size of the region's labour force. During each of the last five years the amount of new floor space approved, expressed as a ratio of workers in manufacturing, was lower in the North West than in any other region except the South East and West Midlands, a fact to which LAMIDA has repeatedly drawn attention as evidence of 'unfair' treatment of the region.[10]

One reason for this is that the major part of the region's industrial districts are outside the development areas. This means that Manchester and the old coal and cotton towns can be treated in just the same way as Birmingham and London in terms of refusal of IDCs. The Board of Trade of course claims to be sympathetic towards the plight of problem areas not qualifying for financial assistance, and between 1961 and 1967 approved 800 projects in the cotton belt, with an estimated eventual employment of 25,000.[11] But during the same period the loss of jobs in the cotton industry alone was over 70,000. And there are instances of the refusal of an IDC in towns badly needing new employment; the objection to Marley Tile's proposal to build a factory in Haslingden in the Rossendale Valley is a frequently cited example.[12]

It is inevitable that the encouragement of growth in the development areas will operate to the disadvantage of other places. The greater the financial incentives, the more likely the choice of a development area as against other locations in the region. The grants in effect at present represent a very important cost reduction, for example a £3,000,000 paper mill employing 300 workers could save something like £1,000,000 on its initial investment in buildings and plant and 7 per cent of its annual wage bill of about £375,000. Faced with the possibility of this kind of saving, many firms now feel that they have no choice but to go to a development area. The charge that current policy is stifling industrial development in the non-scheduled areas is being made forcibly by LAMIDA,[13] who claim that several companies outside the development areas are considering moving into them, and that others anticipate difficulty competing with firms getting generous government subsidies.[14] On the government side it is claimed that

72,000 of the 93,000 jobs created by firms moving into Merseyside between 1945 and 1965 have been diverted from the South East and West Midlands, compared with only 15,000 from the rest of the North West, so that Merseyside's new prosperity is not at the expense of other parts of the North West.[15] But there is a growing feeling that current policy may involve robbing Peter, in the form of the old coal and cotton districts, to pay Paul, the development districts. The setting up of the Hunt Committee in 1967 to look into the problems of the intermediate or 'grey' areas represented official recognition that a fundamental policy review was required.

Government policy has clearly acted as both a positive and a negative influence on the pace of local industrial development. It has helped Merseyside to become an important growth area, it has assisted diversification in Barrow-in-Furness, and it has attracted some new industries to the former North-East Lancashire and South Lancashire Development Areas. At the same time, growth has been restricted in other parts of the region, both by the refusal of IDCs and by the creation of circumstances which now make it difficult for many firms not to choose a development-area location. The precise effect of all this on the growth rate in Manchester and the cotton towns is impossible to measure. Further comments on these matters are reserved for the final chapter.

Industrial Land[16]

The national government policy implemented by the Board of Trade is by no means the only official constraint imposed on manufacturers' freedom of locational choice. Substantial areas around the fringe of the major conurbations are incorporated in green belts, which include many attractive industrial sites in the Mersey growth zone, and the development control exercised by local planning authorities restricts industry to selected areas of every town and city. Industrial land is thus very much scarcer than a casual glance at a map of undeveloped areas within the region would suggest, and the availability, cost and quality of land is an important determinant of both the general location and exact siting of new industry. Scarcity is aggravated by the general trend for less employment to be provided on a given area of land, as industry becomes more capital intensive.

The cost of land for industrial development varies very considerably. A poorly sited plot in one of the Pennine-fringe mill towns might be obtained for as little as £1,000 an acre, while one of the few remaining areas near the centre of Liverpool or Manchester might be thirty times

as much. The cost of land is thus likely to have some bearing on the
location of any plant, and will be a major factor in cases where the
initial cost of land or the rental makes up a relatively large share of
total production costs. Variation from place to place in the cost of
land should thus help to explain something of the geographical
pattern of recent development. But they are also of interest in another
respect—as an indication of the supply of industrial land in different
parts of the region, and the pressure of demand for it.

In Fig 22 an attempt has been made to map the broad pattern of
areal variations in land costs. This has been built up from information
on representative sites in all parts of the region, and involves much
generalisation. The cost isolines, or contours, may suggest that land is
available at the price indicated in every part of the region, but this is
not so under the present conditions of planning restrictions. In areas
zoned for non-industrial uses or as green belt the cost of land for
industry is in theory infinitely high.

The main feature indicated by the land-cost surface is a ridge
between Manchester and Merseyside, with the central parts of the two
cities represented by peaks of very high values. The isolines stop at
£15,000, but small parcels of land zoned for industry around central
Manchester and acquired by the city between 1963 and 1968 averaged
almost £20,000 per acre,[17] and near the centre of Liverpool a similar
figure could be expected. These high prices reflect not only the
attraction of the cities, but also the scarcity of land. Lack of room for
industry has been a major restriction on industrial development in
Manchester, helping to explain the relatively poor performance of the
city noted in the previous chapter. Liverpool, less hemmed in by
satellite towns, and with large industrial estates at Aintree, Kirkby
and Speke, has been better placed. But even here sites are now scarce,
and the recent establishment of an industrial estate of over 100 acres
by the Board of Trade at Knowsley on the East Lancashire Road was
welcomed as a timely addition to the local stock of industrial land.[18]
Land has been much more freely available on the southern side of the
Mersey estuary, where large undeveloped areas close to the Manchester
Ship Canal and dock facilities have been a major factor in the rapid
industrial growth around Bebbington and Ellesmere Port.

The ridge of high land values between Merseyside and Manchester
has two local peaks. These are Haydock, strategically placed at the
intersection of the East Lancashire Road and the M6, and Warrington
which showed up as a growth point in the previous chapter. Here
£10,000 an acre is a representative average figure, and the cost in
St Helens is reported to have risen from something like £5,000 to

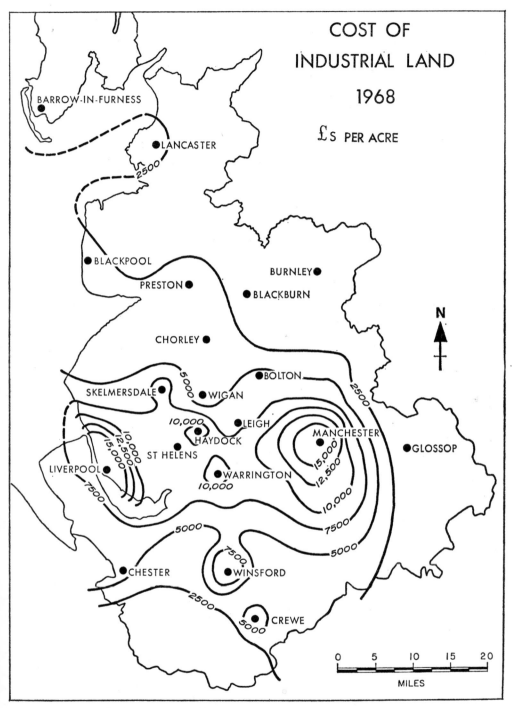

Fig 22. A generalised land-cost surface, based on the cost of representative industrial sites. (Source: LAMIDA.) In the case of rented land, purchase price is taken to be ten times the annual rental.

about £9,000 since the town was included in the Merseyside Development Area in 1966. Development-area grants also explain the relatively high cost of land in Winsford and Skelmersdale New Town, while in nearby places such as Wigan and Northwich, lacking the advantage of government assistance, industrial land may be very much cheaper.

The cheapest sites are in Furness where land is plentiful, northern Lancashire where there is little demand, and the old mill towns. Here £2,000 to £3,000 an acre is a general average, and this also appears to apply to some of the central and south Cheshire towns. But even these figures are high compared with the North East and Scotland, where good sites can be obtained for £1,000 to £2,000. Land in Merseyside, Winsford and Skelmersdale is high in relation to development areas in other regions, and firms seeking government assistance who are very sensitive to the cost of land are likely to go to Furness or outside the North West.

In general, the effect of the cost and availability of land on industrial development in the North West may be summarised as follows. The relatively high cost in the Merseyside to Manchester belt seems to have exercised little restrictive effect on industrial growth, except within the two major cities. At the same time, cheap land has been unable to attract much new industry to the old coal and cotton towns. For many firms the quality and size of a site is very important, and twenty (or a hundred) acres free of existing buildings and easily serviced may be more readily obtained around Merseyside or south Manchester than in some Pennine valley. Firms who can find the right piece of land seem generally prepared to pay what they have to for it; if it is a little more than they hoped to pay, this is likely to be more than offset by development-area grants or other local cost advantages.

The Availability of Premises

If government policy has tended to restrict new industrial development in many of the coal and cotton towns, and if their cheap land has not tempted new firms in, how it is that they have been able to achieve some diversification? How is it that some of them have performed better in recent years than their poor industrial structure suggested that they should have done? The answer is to be found partly in the availability of labour, but of greater importance appears to have been the presence of empty mills and other premises to provide cheap accommodation for new industry.

The Ferranti Transformer Division at Hollinwood, Oldham. This firm has been one of the most successful in the old textile districts in recent years. A wide range of electronic equipment is manufactured, with converted mills providing much of the production space.

Page 125: GROWTH INDUSTRIES IN THE COTTON TOWNS

The Mullard factory in Blackburn. This large plant producing radio apparatus is representative of the modern industries which have brought diversifications to the textile towns of north-east Lancashire.

The Senior Service factory at Hyde. A typical Victorian red-brick cotton mill, converted for cigarette making. Such premises can still be obtained cheaply in many of the old cotton towns, and have been a major factor in the growth of replacement industries.

Page 126: NEW INDUSTRIES IN CONVERTED COTTON MILLS

The British Vita foam-rubber factories at Middleton. The growth of the Vita foam concern has been one of the success stories of the recent diversification of the textile districts. The conversion of cotton mills has been a major factor in the firm's expansion.

The conversion of old mills is certainly not a new phenomenon in the North West. The Rossendale slipper industry grew up in defunct textile mills in the latter part of the nineteenth century, some leading firms, notably Ferranti, took advantage of empty mills before the Second World War, and the wartime concentration of the cotton industry freed premises for more essential activities, some of which remained in their new homes. But it is since the collapse of the Lancashire cotton industry at the beginning of the 1950s that the reoccupation of mills has assumed particular importance. Accommodation has been provided for new activities ranging from electrical engineering to mail order businesses, from foam-rubber manufacturing to poultry breeding, in what must be one of the most rapid and extensive industrial recolonisations in history.

The occupation of an empty textile mill has two major advantages. The first is that the accommodation is cheap; the purchase price can be lower that 2s per sq ft compared with up to £4 for a modern purpose-built factory; an average mill of 500,000 sq ft might be obtained for from £50,000 to £60,000. For rented factory space current annual figures for new premises are in the region of 6s 6d to 7s 6d a sq ft, while mill space may be had at as low as 6d a sq ft for upper floor accommodation with somewhat higher rentals for the ground floor.[19] A specific example of reoccupation is an 800,000 sq ft mill in Oldham which is reported to have cost Ferranti 3s 4d a sq ft. Another is provided by six mills occupied by Ward & Goldstone, the Salford electrical engineering firm, which cost less than 4s a sq ft to buy and the same to rehabilitate, but still came out at only a fifth of the cost of a new factory.[20] Such savings are particularly important to projects where the initial cost of a building is a large element in total costs.

The second advantage is that reoccupation of existing premises does not require an IDC. The purchase of an empty mill thus enables firms to set up or expand in locations where the Board of Trade approval for a new factory would be difficult or impossible to obtain.

Two maps in Fig 23 give some idea of the geographical distribution of mills reoccupied. The first, based on field investigations by R. L. Holt for 1951–62, shows the concentration in the Blackburn and Burnley areas and in Oldham and other cotton towns near Manchester. But there are interesting differences in the proportion of closed mills which were reoccupied. Single-storey weaving sheds are more easily adapted to modern industry than the multi-storey spinning mills, and Holt found that 83 per cent of the closed weaving sheds had been reoccupied compared with 69 per cent of spinning mills, and only

H

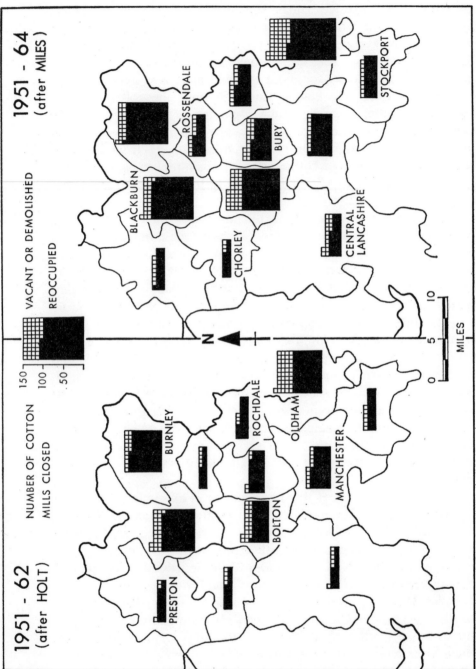

Fig 23. Two views of the distribution of cotton-mill reoccupation. (Source: Holt, R. A. *The Changing Industrial Geography*

39 per cent of the much less easily adapted finishing works.[21] This meant that a greater proportion of mills in north-east Lancashire were reoccupied than in the spinning area centred on Manchester; in the Blackburn–Burnley areas the conversion rate was about 80 per cent compared with only 65 per cent in the two leading spinning areas of Bolton and Oldham. In Manchester itself, with a high level of demand for premises, the rate was about 90 per cent.

Caroline Miles' analysis of the LAMIDA files on mill conversions over 1951–64 (Fig 23) confirms Holt's findings. Again, local differences in the percentage of mills reoccupied can be related to the type of textile specialisation and to demand for premises. The conversion rate in the Blackburn and Burnley weaving areas is 80 per cent; it drops to little over 70 per cent in Rossendale, Bolton, Bury and Oldham, and to about 60 per cent in south Lancashire.

Holt's survey provides a useful indication of the type of activity which has moved into the mills. Of 414 mills fully reoccupied between 1951 and 1962, about a quarter were taken over by other textile and clothing firms (Table 11), followed closely by engineering. The third use, flatted factories, involves the subdivision of a mill between a number of different occupants, a familiar development in other textile

Table 11

CONVERSION OF COTTON MILLS 1951–62

Use of mills closed since 1951 at September 1962	Number of mills	
Mills fully converted to other uses		
Other textiles and clothing	101	
Engineering	89	
Flatted factories	55	
Storage and warehouses	36	
Food, drink and tobacco (including broiler houses)	26	
Furniture and joinery	17	
Plastics	17	
Mail order businesses	11	
Miscellaneous industrial and commercial activity	62	
Total		414
Mills partially converted		
Partly empty, partly new industry	38	
Partly cotton, partly new industry	25	
Total		63
Mills not reoccupied		
Vacant and for sale	111	
Demolished	34	
Total		145

Source: Holt, R. A. *The Changing Industrial Geography of the Lancashire Cotton Area.* Unpublished MA Thesis, University of Manchester, 1964.

regions such as the Nottingham lace-making district and the New England cotton towns in the USA. Despite the antiquity of many of the mills, only about one in twelve had been demolished. Another survey, by LAMIDA,[22] indicated the fate of 103 mills closed between December 1964 and November 1967. Of the 41 already reoccupied by the end of this period, 11 housed engineering and electrical goods firms, 8 others had textile and clothing manufacturing, five paper and printing, 11 contained other manufacturing industries, and the remaining 6 were used for storage. One, at Helmshore, may be converted into a museum!

Much of the credit for achieving so many reoccupations must go to LAMIDA which, for the past ten years, has been promoting the resale of mills in a systematic way, and offers manufacturers looking for premises full information on the choice available, along with its other advisory services. Without this organisation, of which there is no equivalent in any other region, the diversification of many of the cotton towns would have proceeded much less effectively.

The number of jobs created by the reoccupation of mills is very difficult to estimate. A figure of 120,000 has been suggested for 1951–61, representing about two-thirds of the loss of employment in textiles over the same period; in 1963 LAMIDA's Director put it at 125,000 since 1951.[23] What is clear is that conversions seldom provide as many jobs as the mills originally offered: Holt cites eighteen mills in Nelson employing 4,625 people in cotton manufacturing in 1951 but only about 2,000 in other uses in 1962, and eleven in Royton employing 2,400 in 1951 but only 550 in the two which had been reoccupied by 1962.[24] The area of premises reoccupied is more easily estimated than employment, and has recently been 3 to 5 million sq ft a year.

Whatever the exact number of jobs created, mill reoccupation has brought valuable new industry, often with considerable growth potential, into the textile towns. It explains why some of the employment trends observed in the previous chapter were not considerably worse. Many of the region's best-known firms occupy former mills; Dunlop Rubber, Antler (luggage), ICI, Joseph Lucas, Lintafoam, Vitafoam, Senior Service and BICC are a few selected at random. But others of less prominence form the bulk of the new occupants. The cheap accommodation is an attraction to young firms who would find it difficult or impossible to build their own premises, so the old mills act as a kind of industrial nursery,[25] and many of the firms they have helped to get started have subsequently expanded to make an important contribution to local employment opportunity.

So far this section has concentrated on the advantages of mill conversion to the regional economy. But there are also some serious problems. Many very successful conversions have taken place, but abandoned mills often provide a poor alternative to a new purpose-built factory. They may be difficult to adapt successfully for modern industry, and thus may hamper efficiency. It is clear that LAMIDA is becoming increasingly concerned about so much industry going into old premises, describing it as a root cause of the relatively poor rise in the region's prosperity, and a contributor to the out-dated image and poor quality of environment perpetuated in many of the region's towns.[26] Caroline Miles has gone so far as to suggest that the very success of LAMIDA and individual local authorities in selling mills to new users may have limited the general progress of the area, given the way in which regional development legislation has operated.[27] Certainly, if mills had not been reoccupied to the extent that they have the level of unemployment would have brought development-area assistance to the whole of the textile districts long ago, with new industry in new premises. Even the cheapness of old mills may be partly an illusion. A mill of 100,000 sq ft might be bought and rehabilitated for, say 7s a sq ft, giving a total cost of £35,000 compared with £200,000 for a new factory at £2 a sq ft. But a development-area grant could provide a reduction of up to 35 per cent in the cost of the new building, which would have a longer and more efficient life, and no doubt a better situation than many back-street mills with poor vehicular access, loading facilities and inadequate parking space. And on top of this would be other capital grants and the employment subsidy which development-area status would bring.

Mill conversion has certainly provided a partial short-run solution to local employment problems. But in the long run cheap premises may not be such a cost-reducing factor as they now appear. The time may come when the amount of new industry in inadequate buildings and cramped locations will prove to be a major liability to many Lancashire towns.

The reoccupation of premises vacated by other firms has not been confined to the textile towns and their mills. Closures in other industries, including textile machinery, railway engineering and even aircraft, have placed very substantial buildings on the market at relatively low cost. The largest vacant premises in the region until recently was the former Squires Gate aircraft works south of Black-pool; this now houses engineering, furnishing, dental equipment, chemicals and food firms, bringing useful diversity to the Fylde. A large Preston works with 500,000 sq ft now houses engineering and printing firms and a number of storage depots, and the former locomotive works at Earlstown is being used as an industrial estate. Many examples of the reoccupation of smaller premises could be cited. At the end of 1967 over 26 million sq ft of existing industrial floor space was available for reoccupation in the North West, including over 15 million in cotton mills. The sub-regional distribution (Table 12) shows

Table 12

VACANT INDUSTRIAL PREMISES AT 31 DECEMBER 1967

Subdivision	Textile mills		Other premises	
	number of mills or sections	area (1,000 sq ft)	number of buildings or sections	area (1,000 sq ft)
North-East Lancashire	53	3,298	37	1,160
South Lancashire	6	910	27	968
East Lancashire	72	7,965	36	1,160
Preston and the coast	6	542	21	1,227
Furness	0	0	5	92
Greater Manchester	24	2,172	99	3,308
South Cheshire and Peak.	8	455	8	224
Merseyside	0	0	71	2,735
Total	169	15,342	304	10,874

Source: LAMIDA. *Twenty Second Annual Report*, 1968, pp 35-6.

that the largest area available is still in the cotton towns of eastern and north-east Lancashire and the Manchester area. The greatest stock of buildings other than mills is in the two major conurbations, but significant areas exist in other parts of the region. Like the cotton mills, the other reoccupied premises often attract less than a full replacement of employment lost in the original closure, and the new jobs are not necessarily of the same character, skill or sex structure as previously.

There are some cases where non-industrial premises suitable for manufacturing come onto the market. A major current example is the former RAF depot at Broadfield, Heywood, with about 1 million sq ft on a 167 acre site with rail sidings, and only two miles from an access point on the new Lancashire–Yorkshire motorway (M62). With a sympathetic Board of Trade IDC policy, such a site could become an important growth point in an area where new employment is still needed. But the availability of these and other vacant premises is too much a matter of chance for great reliance to be placed on them as an aid to local industrial diversification.

One final aspect of the availability of premises is the Board of Trade advance factories, which are built to attract industry to specific towns. But of 124 advance factories announced since 1964 only 8 have been in the North West, which LAMIDA sees as a further indication of government failure to give fair treatment to the region.[28] Certainly 7 per cent of the total advance factory floor space seems small in relation to the region's development-area population, not to mention the unscheduled coal and cotton towns. Although important to the firms which have occupied them, and providing small local increases in employment around Merseyside and in Barrow, the advance factories have had very little impact on the region as a whole, and none on the badly-hit cotton towns.

Labour Supply

Obtaining labour for a new factory or extension has been difficult for many firms during the post-war years of virtually full employment. But in the North West, with pockets of relatively high unemployment and one major declining industry, there should have been substantial and easily identified local reserves of surplus labour to attract new industry. In practice, however, the situation has not been so simple, as the experiences of various parts of the region have shown.

It is Merseyside which has had the region's largest unemployment problem,[29] and the experiences of Ford and Vauxhall in connection with the local labour situation are revealing. With a combined employment of about 25,000 by 1968, these two motor factories represent the largest additions to the area's manufacturing sector since the war (see next chapter). In a survey of their labour recruitment up to 1965,[30] it was found that only about 1,100 of the 13,000 then working in the plants had been unemployed immediately prior to joining Ford or Vauxhall, and the majority of these had not been long-term unemployed—three-quarters had been out of work for less than six months. Avoiding those with a history of unemployment or irregular working habits was company policy in both cases, as was the preference for men under fifty and over twenty-one. Both took on large numbers of men who were potentially unemployed, ie redundant or about to be declared so, but the majority appear to have come from steady jobs with other firms, who thus lost many experienced and skilled workers. It appears that Ford and Vauxhall were able to build up satisfactory labour forces largely by competing with existing firms in the sphere of wages and conditions of service, leaving little impact on the hardcore unemployed, and the same may well be true of other major post-war newcomers to the area. The fact that one of the motor firms is now bringing workers in by bus from well outside Merseyside indicates that the local supply of suitable labour is becoming tight, whatever the above-average unemployment figures might suggest.

Substantial recent growth of new industry has also taken place in Furness, the other development area. A recent investigation of labour reserves there[31] has shown that most firms have got the labour they needed with little trouble, and generally without having to advertise. Furness, with an employment structure dominated by the Vickers ship-yard, has a very high proportion of male workers, and much of the new industry has attempted to tap the female-labour reserves. Females not registered as unemployed have apparently provided the bulk of new recruits for the factories, so, as on Merseyside, the ability of new firms to obtain labour has not been closely related to high official unemployment statistics.

The largest labour surpluses since the war have been in the cotton towns, where unemployment figures have not generally been very high. Labour freed by the contraction of the textile trade and some related activities such as textile engineering has been a major factor in the diversification of eastern Lancashire, though generally only in combination with the availability of premises. But the amount of labour available has been considerably less than the loss of something like 200,000 jobs in cotton might suggest. Migration, retirement, the reluctance of some women to consider jobs outside the familiar mills, and the growth of the service sector, have all reduced the number of potential recruits for new manufacturing concerns.

In many firms the quality of labour is more important as a location factor than the apparent quantity of surplus workers. The cotton towns have an obvious advantage for expanding sectors of the textile trade and for clothing firms, but the best engineering labour is in Greater Manchester, and firms in this industry would generally prefer a location here to one in eastern Lancashire or Merseyside. Ford and Vauxhall have been able to build up stable and efficient labour forces in an area without a strong engineering tradition, but some other Merseyside firms have had problems dealing with local militancy and a casual attitude to employment which has its roots in the old organisa-tion of labour in the docks. One firm in Winsford, which is taking overspill from Liverpool, prefers local labour as it is thought to be less troublesome than the newcomers from Merseyside.[32]

How these various factors balance out in terms of labour costs and efficiency in different parts of the region is very difficult to say. Labour may be somewhat more expensive in and around Manchester than in other areas, but for firms in the growth industries like engineering this may be offset by higher productivity. If cheap unskilled labour in relatively large quantities is needed a cotton town is a better bet than either of the major conurbations.

It is possible to be more precise about cost differentials at a regional level. The cost of living in the North West is less than in the Midlands and South East, and wages are generally lower. In vehicles the regional average weekly wage for men is about 20s below the national average, while in engineering the difference is 9s. But in paper, printing and publishing the saving in the North West is only 4s, and in chemicals the regional figure is 22s above the national average.[33] Thus manufacturers in certain industries may be attracted to the North West by the possibility of savings in labour costs as well as a generally easier supply than around Birmingham or London. But for many firms other factors such as development-area assistance and empty premises may be more important. In the major growth industries of engineering and vehicle manufacture, where capital intensity is increasing, the tendency may well be to choose the location largely on other grounds, relying on relatively high wages to compete for labour. There are always some firms, however, where labour costs are such an important item in their total costs that local reserves of suitable labour, hidden or suggested by the level of unemployment, provide the dominant influence on locational choice, and this appears to have applied to many firms who have developed in the North West since the war.

Access to Materials and Markets

Access to sources of materials and suppliers of components have been of less general importance to the location of post-war industrial development in the North West than the other factors so far considered. But there are important exceptions. Some industries are becoming increasingly dependent on large supplies of bulky materials from overseas, and in these cases proximity to the coast and to facilities for handling imports is an important location factor. This explains much of the development of petro-chemical industries along the Manchester Ship Canal and the location of some recent expansion in paper manufacturing (both considered further in the next chapter). The continued growth of food and related processing industries on Merseyside and near Manchester Docks is also clearly related to ease of access to bulky imported materials. Good transportation facilities, particularly by water and rail, are a major attraction of the Mersey growth zone.

The influence of the market on industrial location is also related to transportation. Although the North West is certainly not the best location from which to serve the national market, the M6 now provides rapid road access to the west Midlands, and the completion of the links with the M1 and M5 will help to make southern England and the metropolitan market closer. The success of mail order business in the region shows that the national market can be served effectively from well off centre, especially if cheap mill space is available for warehousing. The North West has, in fact, become the nation's leading growth centre for the mail order business, which is now worth over £400,000,000 a year in the country as a whole. Although this book is concerned with the industrial economy, the importance of the growth of wholesale and retail distribution must not be overlooked, for the expansion of the mail order business has helped considerably to offset the loss of jobs in textiles in Preston, Burnley, and the Bolton and Bury areas. If the perusal of a glossy catalogue ever replaces a visit to the shops to anything like the extent it has in the United States, mail order businesses could become very important indeed as a source of new employment, perhaps attracting manufacturing capacity to the region.

For firms or branches serving the regional market there are obvious locational preferences. A site near the motorway is a big advantage, and the Haydock intersection of the M6 and East Lancashire Road has attracted a major concentration of distribution depots. A location in Liverpool or Manchester is clearly the best place from which to serve Merseyside or the south-east Lancashire conurbation, but there is probably no better position than Haydock from which to serve the regional market as a whole.

For some activities the market is another industry. This is the case for the many firms making motor-vehicle components in the North West. New firms have come to Merseyside following the arrival of Ford and Vauxhall in 1960, but how much of this is directly explained by a local market is open to question (see next chapter). In some industries the linkages between suppliers of materials and their customers have become increasingly complex in recent years. The chemical industry is an obvious example, with an oil refinery perhaps providing material for a nearby petro-chemical works which, in its turn, may send products like plastics to other plants for final manufacture. The growth of such linkages has influenced the location of both suppliers and customers. But the efficiency with which some commodities can be transported relatively long distances means that closely-linked factories need not be side by side; the Shell plants at Stanlow and Carrington, connected by oil pipeline, operate as an integrated concern despite the twenty-three miles separating them. The general tendency is for improvements in transportation to lessen the pull of material supplies and the market on industrial location.

Locational Preference in the North West

The effect on post-war industrial location of the various factors considered above may be summarised as follows. Government policy has greatly restricted freedom of locational choice, by preventing development in some areas and encouraging it in others by cost-reducing subsidies. Shortage of land has been a major constraint on industrial growth in and around the two big cities, but areal variations in the cost of land appear to have been more a reflection of local supply and demand than an important determinant of plant location. The presence of cheap premises has probably done more than anything else to attract new industry to the mill towns, but its effect has certainly not been confined to these places. The relatively free supply of labour has been very important in bringing industry into the region from elsewhere and in determining which parts of the region have been attractive to labour-intensive activities, with the influence of particular qualities of labour of special significance. In some industries access to sources of materials and the market seems to be less important than formerly, due to improvements in transportation, but in others, particularly those using bulky materials, this is still critical.

In an attempt to assess the relative importance of the various location factors in the most recent past, a survey of all firms completing a new industrial-building project in 1967 was conducted (see Appendix A note 10). Of fifty-two firms who ranked various factors in order of importance as influences on choice of location for their new project, almost one-third put labour supply first. A long way behind, and roughly equal, were access to the market, suitable premises, access to sources of materials and components, land at reasonable cost or rent, and government financial assistance. As the second most important factor, land was indicated by almost one-third of the respondents, with labour close behind. The overall importance of a supply of labour thus stands out clearly. Only one firm put good transport facilities as its most important location factor; perhaps this is now taken for granted.

The selection of purely personal considerations as the leading factor by two firms provides a reminder that all locational decisions are not made on economic grounds alone. For some activities economic factors allow considerable freedom of choice without unduly affecting profits, and the manufacturer may indulge his personal whims and fancies within broad limits. Most of the firms contacted described choice of location within the North West as 'very important or critical' (30 per cent) or 'important' (35 per cent) to the profitability of their new project. But just over 20 per cent said it was 'not very important' or 'unimportant'.

Twenty-six of the firms which provided information had set up within a development area. Most of them felt that government financial assistance was important or very important in influencing their choice of location, but five described it as 'unimportant' or 'not very important'. More than half said that even without development-area assistance, and with no IDC problems, they would not have preferred an alternative location. This tends to support the view that a significant amount of development in the assisted areas, particularly Merseyside, would have taken place even without government subsidy. Further evidence along these lines was provided by the response of all firms to the question asking in which of eight broad sub-regions they would prefer to locate a new factory. They were asked to assume that there were no official constraints or inducements, and that the site of any existing plant in the region did not affect the decision. Merseyside was the most popular sub-region, with Greater Manchester second.

The locational preference of firms moving into the region from elsewhere has been an important determinant of local rates of economic growth during the post-war period. A recent Board of Trade survey indicated that between 1945 and 1965 215 firms moved into the region, to provide almost 105,000 new jobs by 1966.[34] These firms have not generally had existing plants in the region to influence choice of location, and many are of the so-called 'footloose' variety, but they have of course been subject to the requirements of government location policy. An examination of 235 moves between 1945 and 1967[35] emphasises once again the pull of Merseyside, chosen by 40 per cent of the firms, with the Kirkby industrial estate, and more recently Skelmersdale New Town, as the most popular locations. Greater Manchester was chosen by less than 20 per cent: IDCs have been hard to get here, and it has become increasingly difficult for the area to compete with the advantages of development-area subsidies on Merseyside. Thirty-three firms located in north-east Lancashire, and twenty-five in south Lancashire (mainly Wigan and St Helens). Lancashire north of the Ribble attracted only about twenty firms, almost half of them in the Furness Development Area and nearly all the rest in the Fylde. Most of the moves into central and southern Cheshire were to Winsford, which again reveals the guiding hand of government policy.

The general conclusion is, then, that for most manufacturing industry a location in or around the two major conurbations has been preferable to one in other parts of the region. The strength of the natural economic advantages of Merseyside compared with the Manchester area are difficult to judge, but development-area status has certainly tipped the scales in favour of the former. There can be little doubt that Merseyside has attracted industry which would have gone to Greater Manchester had it not been for the action of the Board of Trade. The area between Manchester and Liverpool also has a number of economic advantages, not least of which are access to the M6 and the Ship Canal, and some places here may now be as attractive to industry as many parts of the two conurbations. But the old textile districts of the Pennine fringe have had to rely largely on the short-run advantages of cheap premises and relatively free labour supply, with the North-East Lancashire Development Area's brief existence as the government's only real concession to the post-war economic difficulties of the mill towns.

This brings the discussion back to the point made in the first section of this chapter, where the structural element in industrial change was examined. Here it was shown that the performance of the old cotton and coalmining areas cannot be attributed to poor structure alone, and the sections which followed have failed to provide evidence to refute this. Apart from their empty mills and redundant workers many of these towns have little to offer as locations for modern industry, and it is difficult to see anything short of full development-area subsidies being able to bring in new firms on the scale needed to stabilise population. And even then it is difficult to see them competing with Merseyside and places like Winsford and Skelmersdale.

The effect of the existing structure on local variations in industrial performance has clearly been of some importance. Much development has been initiated by firms already established in the region in cases where the location of new capacity is largely determined by the location of the existing factory. The manufacturing sector thus has much built-in locational stability, but local industry may be more potentially mobile than is generally thought. Many extensions built without question onto existing factories might be just as viable in a new location, particularly if this means leaving a congested site for one on a new industrial estate. Of more than 850 enquiries relating to locations for new development dealt with by LAMIDA during the last three years, two-thirds were from firms already in the region.[36] This amounts to an average of almost 200 possible developments each year by existing firms with enough locational flexibility to seek advice on the subject, compared with only about 60 enquiries annually from firms in the Midlands and South East. It is the big arrivals from outside the region which have had the most dramatic impact on the industrial development of the North West in recent years, but as competition between the regions for 'footloose' industry intensifies, the North West may have to rely more and more on the potential mobility of existing industry if persisting local structural weaknesses are to be corrected.

References to this chapter are on pages 241 to 243.

5

The Critical Industries

IT WILL BE clear by now that certain industries have been of critical importance in determining the changes which have overtaken the regional economy in recent years. The particular significance of these activities lies in the size of their contribution to regional employment, the extent of their expansion or contraction, and their degree of geographical concentration. This chapter looks at the performance of these critical industries, and tries to explain what has happened; some tentative predictions about their future role are also made.

The Declining Industries

Textiles

It is inevitable that the decline of the Lancashire cotton industry should occupy the most prominent place in this chapter. The loss of employment since the beginning of the 1950s has been enormous: both the Ministry of Labour's estimates of insured employees and the figures compiled by the Textile Council (formerly the Cotton Board) for the number of workers on the cotton-mill books agree on an average annual reduction of about 12,000 jobs. Added to this is a very considerable fall in regional and national production, arising from the greatly reduced output of yarn and cloth, and the industry's change from a major exporter to an insecure competitor for the home market. The reasons for the textile industry's decline have been analysed in detail elsewhere, notably by Robson[1] and more recently by Caroline Miles.[2] All that can be attempted here is a summary of the facts, together with some discussion of the geography of contraction.

The rapid expansion of cotton manufacturing through the nineteenth century reached a peak at the outbreak of the First World War. By this time 620,000 people were working in more than 2,000 mills, which had spread steadily outwards from the Pennine valleys and across the coalfield, well into the lowlands of central Lancashire. The key to the industry's phenomenal success had been its ability to capture and retain a large share of the world market. For much of the nineteenth century nine-tenths of the output of cotton cloth was exported, and there was a common saying that the Lancashire mills supplied the home market by breakfast time. But the maintenance of a virtual monopoly of the overseas market was by no means assured, for it rested on the unsteady foundations of growing competitive disadvantage.

The relative importance of the cotton industry to the national economy has in a sense been declining since about the middle of the last century. The industry's share of Britain's exports, which was almost half by value at the middle of the nineteenth century, had been reduced to about a quarter by 1914, and there had also been some contraction of the country's share of the world cotton trade. But the beginning of the transformation from a major national industry to what is now almost a minor regional specialisation dates from the period following the First World War. Between 1914 and the end of the 1930s the number of firms in business was reduced to less than 1,200 and employment to 250,000, while the number of spindles went down by a third and looms by almost half.

This first major contraction was due entirely to a reduction in export markets. This was partly the result of a deteriorating competitive position, as Lancashire's costs rose in comparison with those of its emerging Asian rivals. But it also reflected the increasing number of coutries outside the major industrial blocks of Europe and North America which were establishing their own textile industries, often protected by tariffs on imports. By 1930 only a little more than half the installed machinery in Lancashire was at work, and spare capacity had become a major embarrassment. The nation's share of the world cotton trade, which had been 82 per cent in 1882–4, was reduced to 39 per cent by 1926–8, and to little more than 25 per cent by the end of the 1930s.[3] With the slump in the cotton industry accentuated by the general recession, the 1930s were a period of great distress in the Lancashire textile towns, with high unemployment and heavy outward population movement.

The contraction of the 20s and 30s was followed by large-scale mill closures at the instigation of the government during the Second World War. Cotton manufacturing, like other less essential industries, was subjected to a compulsory concentration scheme, to release labour and premises for the production of other goods. Almost 900 plants were closed, including finishing works, and by the end of

Part of the Vickers shipyards at Barrow-in-Furness. For a long time Barrow has been heavily dependent on shipbuilding: Vickers employ 14,000 out of about 30,000 workers in the town. Present production includes nuclear submarines.

Page 143: TWO SIDES OF INDUSTRY IN THE FURNESS AREA

The Ferranti microelectronics laboratories at Ormsgill, Barrow-in-Furness. This Board of Trade advance factory was completed in November 1965, to attract new industy, and was subsequently occupied by Ferranti. Production of microcircuits began in mid-1967 and employment will eventually rise to 1,000.

Docks on the Manchester Ship Canal at Ellesmere Port. The cars awaiting despatch to overseas markets are from the nearby Vauxhall factory, one of the region's major exporters.

Page 144: THE REGION'S TRADING OUTLETS

The northern part of the Liverpool Docks at Bootle. At the far end of the docks is the site of the Seaforth extension, now under construction, which will provide new deep-water berths and container handling facilities.

the war the industry's labour force and output had been reduced to about half the pre-war level.

When the war ended the need for a major reorganisation and re-equipment of the industry—the major lesson of the pre-war years—was overlooked for the sake of short-run profits. From 1946 to 1951 the industry experienced boom conditions, and although more than 250 of the mills which closed during the war failed to reopen, production of yarn and woven cloth rose by about 50 per cent between 1946 and 1951; employment increased by a similar proportion, to reach almost 300,000. But the trade collapsed in 1951-2 and entered two decades of headlong decline which has left it almost unrecognisable in both size and structure.

Before looking at the 1950s and 1960s, some attempt can be made to assess the geographical impact of the earlier phase of decline. The enormous loss of jobs was concentrated in only part of the North West, the area bounded roughly by Colne, Preston, Wigan and Stockport, and some parts of the textile district were affected more seriously than others. Some branches of the trade were hit particularly hard, and the tradition of local specialisation within Lancashire meant that decline was thus geographically selective. Specialisation included not only the well-known distinction between the spinning area centred on Manchester and the weaving area centred on the Blackburn–Burnley area, but also a high degree of more local concentration on particular types and qualities of goods.

The local geography of decline was clearly illustrated in a study of the 1931-51 period by Rodgers.[4] He showed that losses of employment were greater in weaving than spinning and least in the finishing sector, which meant that the northern belt of cotton towns fared worse than those of the Manchester lowland and its fringes. Within the weaving towns, those producing coarse cloth for tropical markets lost an average of two-thirds of their employment in textiles, roughly twice the rate in towns specialising in fine and coloured cloths for home and other markets less open to Asian competition. Thus the Blackburn area, the worst hit of all parts of the region, suffered to a greater extent than did the towns at the Burnley end of the lowland, and in the south the coarse-spinning towns grouped around Oldham felt the loss of exports more keenly than the fine-spinning district centred on Bolton. Rodgers also detected a tendency for many of the more remote towns on the edge of the region to suffer particularly badly, as their distance from the commercial centre of the trade in Manchester became a critical disadvantage. The area which lost least employment was the coalfield of central Lancashire, where the late arrival of the

I

industry meant that the mills were large and comparatively modern.

The slump following the post-war production peak of 1951 was the result of very specific economic conditions. Put briefly, the post-war rise in demand for clothing was becoming satisfied, the price of textiles was rising sharply, and expenditure was shifting to more durable consumer goods.[5] But there are more fundamental reasons why the Lancashire industry was so badly hit. Britain's relatively high prices had not been a real disadvantage in the seller's market of the 1946–51 boom, but the reduction in demand which followed revealed once again the seriousness of the country's competitive position. High wages compared with those of Asian producers was one reason for Britain's cost disadvantage, but another contributory factor of long standing was the antiquity of much of Lancashire's machinery and trading practices. Caroline Miles has recently described lack of interest in technological development and in the use of new production methods and equipment as a characteristic feature of the British cotton industry over the last fifty or more years, and has accused most of the domestic textile-machinery industry of lagging behind world development.[6] The inventive genius of the eighteenth-century industrial pioneers, and the enterprise with which it was exploited, had been replaced by a complacent belief in the indestructability of the Lancashire cotton trade. The impact of the 1951–2 slump in terms of reduced employment, output and capacity is indicated in Fig 24.

During the 1950s a new threat to the cotton industry emerged— competition in the home market. Imports of cloth amounted to one-sixth of domestic consumption in 1951 and in the latter part of the 1950s the figure began to rise sharply. In 1958, for the first time in history, Britain imported more cotton cloth than was exported, and the illusion that however difficult competition overseas might be the home market would be safe from impertinent foreign intrusion was finally dispelled.

The events of the 1950s emphasised what had been apparent to some observers for many years, that drastic action was required if any of the Lancashire cotton industry was to survive. This action came in the form of the 1959 Cotton Industry Act. The object of the Act, under which government and private industry co-operated on an unprecedented scale, was to make the industry more competitive by reorganisation and re-equipment. It aimed at reducing the physical plant by at least 50 per cent in spinning and about 40 per cent in weaving and finishing, thus eliminating the spare capacity which was holding back the progress of the more viable parts of the industry.

The remaining firms were to be encouraged to re-equip with modern machinery, and this, like the scrapping of obsolete equipment, was to be assisted by financial subsidy.[7]

As a result of the operation of the Act, 203 of the 986 firms in the Lancashire textile industry closed down altogether. Almost all were small single-process firms: only 10 employed over 500 workers, and only 7 were engaged in more than one major branch of the trade. This brought about a shift in emphasis towards the large integrated concern, with a smaller share of the industry's labour force in firms employing less than 500, and more in firms with over 1,000.[8] Altogether almost half the installed spinning spindles were scrapped, almost 40 per cent of the looms, and more than a quarter of the doubling spindles.

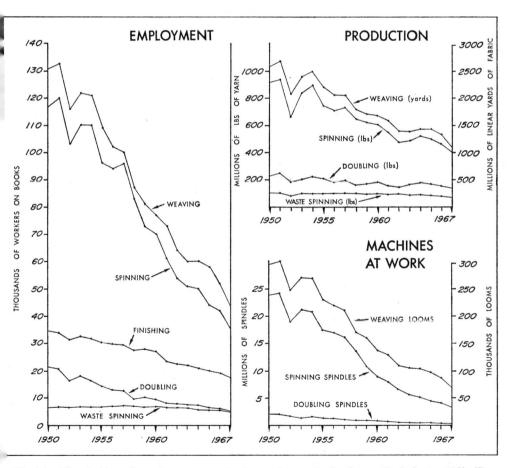

Fig 24.   The decline of employment, production and capacity in the textile industry 1950–67. (Source: Textile Council.) The number of waste-spinning machines at work is very small, and has been omitted.

The geographical impact of the contraction precipitated by the 1959 Act differed in some respects from the previously observed trends.[9] Local concentration on a high quality of output was no longer an advantage, and there was a rapid decline in Bolton's fine-spinning industry and in Nelson, the largest of the fine-weaving towns, while Bury, Rochdale and the Rossendale valley towns, with a tradition of coarse work, escaped serious loss. Again, the coalfield cotton towns of central Lancashire fared reasonably well, as did Preston, but there was a rapid rate of mill closure in Manchester and Stockport. The traditional division between the spinning and weaving areas became obscured, as the spinning towns generally lost more spindles than looms and *vice versa* in the weaving towns so that in place of the former two-fold division of the textile region a more complex pattern was emerging. The northern weaving zone remained highly specialised, but in Rossendale looms and spindles existed in roughly equal numbers by 1960. The old spinning area to the south was also taking on more of a mixed character, while west-central Lancashire, like Rossendale, was characterised by lack of specialisation and a better mill-survival rate.

How successful was the reorganisation of the 1959 Act as a solution to the problems of Lancashire's textile industry? It certainly removed some of the dead-wood, in terms of the scrapping of obsolete and largely unused machinery, and it achieved a considerable pruning of the number of firms in business. But many small firms resisted the temptation to liquidate; only a quarter of the weaving firms employing less than 500 left the industry, though the small-scale weaver was a particular target of the Act. And expenditure on re-equipment turned out to be considerably less than had been originally anticipated by the industry itself—£53,500,000 against £80,000,000 to £95,000,000. The main criticism of the Act, however, is that it failed to bring about the fundamental change in the structure of the industry needed to ensure its ultimate survival. This was, in fact, never an objective of the Act, and it has been left to the initiative of private industry to begin the process of rationalisation.[10]

Fig 24 shows that the downward trends of employment, production and machinery at work continued virtually unaffected by the scrapping and re-equipment of 1959. Despite some import restrictions, foreign manufacturers have continued to exploit the home market, and the UK trade deficit in cotton cloth (ie net imports) rose from 190 million sq yds in 1959 to 420 million sq yds in 1966. The relative stability of employment in the finishing sector is explained by the fact that about three-quarters of the imports are of 'grey' (unfinished) cloth which comes to Lancashire to be bleached, dyed, printed and so on. Overall, the Lancashire textile industry reduced the number of workers on its books from 314,000 in 1951 to a mere 105,000 at the end of 1967, a loss of more than 200,000 jobs in sixteen years. The loss in the past fifty years has been more than 500,000.

One encouraging trend indicated by the more rapid contraction of employment compared with output is a marked increase in productivity. This is a result of re-equipment, the spread of multi-shift working, and the structural reorganisation of the industry. Since 1951 output per man hour has risen by over 40 per cent in spinning and by at least 30 per cent in weaving, and there have also been increases in output per machine hour, particularly since 1959.[11]

The geographical pattern of contraction since 1950 is illustrated in Fig 25. The top two maps show the decline in the labour force of the four main branches of the industry, and indicate changes in the degree of local specialisation. The northern weaving belt has remained highly specialised, while only in the Oldham district does any strong emphasis on spinning survive. The decline in employment has been fairly evenly shared between the areas,[12] but there are some important exceptions to the general loss of 65 to 75 per cent of the 1950 labour force. The Haslingden district (ie the Rossendale valley towns) has suffered less seriously than any other district except Lancaster, a partial result of its local specialisation in heavy industrial textiles, waste spinning and finishing. Rochdale, the main district for the relatively stable waste-spinning section, also has a low loss, and to the south a concentration on finishing has been of some advantage to the Glossop district. The largest percentage losses have been on the south-western fringes of the textile region and in the Burnley area. Between 1957 and 1967 the number of mills fell from 1,329 to 621, and the map of mill closures generally confirms the pattern of decline indicated by employment trends. The figure for the Manchester district is somehow symbolic of the industry's decimation; the capital city of King Cotton's once great empire now has only about fifteen active mills, with a labour force of barely 4,000.[13]

It is hardly necessary to stress further the impact of the decline in the textile industry on the regional economy. The loss of jobs indicated in Fig 25 speaks for itself, particularly when it is realised that in many places the textile mills were still the major source of employment at the beginning of the 1950s, often occupying a majority of the town's industrial workers. The regional concentration of the industry and the distress caused by its contraction have often been put forward as matters of major public concern, yet the 1959 Act made no attempt

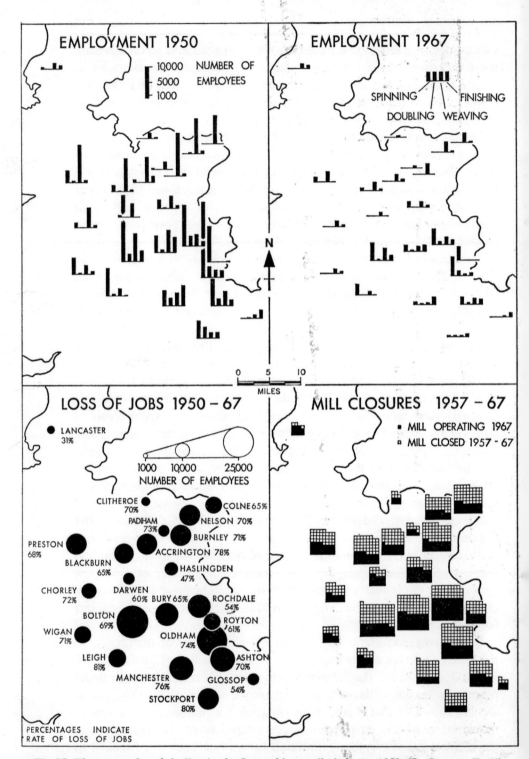

Fig 25. The geography of decline in the Lancashire textile industry 1950–67. (Source: Textile Council.) The figures are based on Textile Council districts, the boundaries of which have been omitted.

to restrict the impact of closures in areas with little alternative employment,[14] and there have been no development-area incentives to attract new industry. For obvious political reasons successive governments have been reluctant to alleviate the problem by providing full protection from imports from the Commonwealth, developing countries, and Britain's EFTA partners, and there seems little prospect of a much harsher tariff policy despite pressure from the industry.[15]

Against these difficulties must be set certain benefits which the region has derived from contraction at this particular time. Textile manufacturing has a relatively low value of output per employee and almost the lowest wages in any industry, and large numbers of workers have been released for more productive and remunerative activities. If Lancashire had to loose its hold on the world cotton trade this century, the final eclipse during the post-war years could have happened at a far worse time. The generally high level of employment and the national growth of other industries has meant that most redundant cotton operatives who wanted new jobs have had little trouble getting them, even if this has meant leaving Lancashire. A repetition of the tragedy of the 1930s has been avoided, though the impact of outward population migration from the cotton towns must not be overlooked.

In attempting to assess the future role of the textile industry in the regional economy, the most important consideration is probably the major structural changes which were initiated in the mid-1960s. Leading in the formation of large vertically-integrated groups (as opposed to the traditional horizontal integration of the Lancashire industry) have been Courtaulds and Viyella International, the latter originally backed by ICI. Other major groups which have emerged are English Calico (English Sewing Cotton and the Calico Printers Association), Carrington & Dewhurst who are prominent in the weaving sector, and the Coates Patons combine with its big yarn interests. The largest concern, Courtaulds is the major producer of man-made fibres in Britain, and has a third of the prosperous warp-knitting industry and a similar proportion of Lancashire's spinning. These large integrated concerns should be in a much better competitive position than the small one-process firms they are replacing. They have enormous capital resources to finance re-equipment and research, and control of the production process from beginning to end has obvious advantages over the old organisation.

An important change is also taking place in the type of goods produced. The gradual shift from cotton to artificial fibres since the war is well-known, but more recently the severity of foreign competition in the market for the traditional cotton cloths, including shirtings, dress goods, sheetings and towellings, has accelerated this trend. This is particularly true of the knitting section. Knitted goods have proved ready substitutes for those of woven cloth in recent years, and warp knitting is one of the major growth sections of the textile trade. At present the production of textured-filament yarns is also expanding rapidly. Other interesting recent developments include innovations in carpet manufacturing, and new methods of bonding fabric with other fabric and with foam rubber. The tendency is, then, for Lancashire to move towards synthetic yarns, knitted fabrics and various specialities and novelty items, leaving the traditional cloths to be mass-produced abroad.

Even with this increasing specialisation it is essential for Lancashire manufacturers to keep their prices down. The relatively high labour costs must be compensated for by reductions elsewhere. The external economies arising from a location within a major textile-manufacturing agglomeration are unlikely to be of much help to the major integrated concerns, but reductions in capital costs may be possible by the more intensive use of machinery.

Unfortunately for the old textile towns, there are signs that under present conditions the traditional areas may not be the best locations for the new industry which is in the making. One of the largest warp-knitting plants in Europe has been built on the outskirts of Liverpool, and the Courtaulds decision to build new capacity at Skelmersdale, Carlisle, Lillyhall in Cumberland, and Spennymoor in County Durham further underlines the importance of government subsidies in the development areas as a major cost-reducing factor in an increasingly capital-intensive industry. The prospect of a great London-based combine putting up weaving sheds in development areas while closing mills in Bolton, Nelson and Padiham is greeted with understandable alarm in some quarters, despite the money spent by Courtaulds and others in modernising older units in the eastern part of the region; but it does serve to emphasise that the advantages which originally attracted the cotton industry to Lancashire were not bestowed indefinitely. The Viyella project for a £14,000,000 warp-knitting plant at Chorley, on the western edge of the old textile district and in the area of the proposed central Lancashire city, may be a pointer to future locational trends within the region.

Mr Shinzo Ohya, the president of the Japanese Teijin concern, was recently quoted as saying that Lancashire should have got out of cotton generations ago, and left it for the poor under-developed countries.[16] He may well have been right. But the North West seems certain to retain its major integrated groups, highly capitalised and in the forefront of technical and organisational innovation, together with some smaller, specialised producers. Further contraction will undoubtedly take place, and Viyella has recently predicted that employment in the spinning and weaving sectors will fall to 55,000 by 1975. Thus the textile industry's future in the North West seems to be as one of a number of secondary regional specialisations; as a source of new employment at other than a local level it can now be forgotten.

Coal Mining

Compared with the contraction in textiles, the regional impact of the decline in coal mining has been relatively small. The loss of jobs during the post-war period has been only about one-seventh of the loss from mill closures. But the very high degree of geographical concentration of the mining industry has made the impact on certain localities very considerable indeed.

In 1950 there were seventy pits operating in the Lancashire coalfield, but by the end of 1968 this number had been reduced to thirteen. Between 1950 and 1958 twelve were closed, and after this the rate went up, with twenty-two in the four years up to 1962, and a further twelve in the next three years. Then in November 1965 the Coal Board announced an accelerated national programme for the closure of uneconomic pits, involving thirteen in Lancashire employing 8,000 men. This phase of the industry's contraction has now been virtually completed, with six closures in 1968. Among the most recent casualties of the coal industry's desperate fight for efficiency have been Bradford Colliery in Manchester and Mosley Common Colliery at Worsley, where even extensive modernisation has failed to make the pits profitable.[17]

As a result of all these closures, employment in Lancashire has gone down from almost 50,000 in 1950 to about 20,000 in 1968; most of the reduction has been in the last ten years since in 1958 there were still 48,000 at work. Because of retirements, and vacancies in surviving pits, the closures have been implemented virtually without redundancies, but the reduction in employment nevertheless represents a substantial loss of jobs for men in the coalmining areas. And losses of employment opportunities have led to outward population movement, just as in the textile districts.

Although production of coal in Lancashire has fallen from 12·5 million tons in 1950 (compared with a peak of 20·5 million in 1907) to less than 9 million, the rate of decrease has been much less than in employment. This is a reflection of increased productivity. The closure of the least efficient pits, the modernisation of others, and the sinking of two new shafts has led to a substantial rise in output per man shift, and the Lancashire industry as a whole is moving nearer to profitability. The first of the new pits was Agecroft at Pendlebury, opened in 1960 and top producer in the region with 817,000 tons in 1967–8. Then came Parkside Colliery at Newton-le-Willows in 1964. Between them they employ 3,500 miners, and will ultimately produce 1·75 million tons of coal a year.

The largest user of Lancashire coal is electricity generation, which takes almost half the output. The market is close at hand; half Agecroft's production goes to an adjoining Central Electricity Generating Board unit, and Bold Colliery near St Helens feeds into another power station. The second market is industry, taking a little more than a quarter of Lancashire's coal, followed by domestic consumption with 16 per cent. But with its reduced output the region now produces only about half the coal it needs.

The decline of coal mining is easily explained. The demands of industry, particularly cotton, led to vigorous and often careless exploitation during the nineteenth century, when Lancashire was one of the most productive coalfields in Britain. The best seams were thus worked out early, and during the present century the field has become increasingly uncompetitive compared with the low-cost pits of Yorkshire and the East Midlands. Large reserves exist, but difficult geological conditions make their exploitation expensive. A Coal Board official was recently quoted as saying that if every machine was run for an extra seventeen minutes a shift the North West coalfield's loss could be wiped out.[18] But this loss amounts to almost £250,000 each week, 17s 6d per ton of output, or 23s a day for every miner in the region. With a contracting national market for coal, Lancashire's competitive position is weak.

Something of the geography of the mining industry's recent decline is shown in Fig 26. There are two main producing areas, south Lancashire and the Burnley district in the north east, with the former of much greater importance. They are separated by the Rossendale uplands. The area containing the majority of pit closures since 1950 extends from Leigh westwards, then up through Wigan almost as far as Chorley; most of the others have been around Burnley, including the small group of mines north of Bacup all of which have now ceased operation. Mining is today virtually confined to a narrow belt along the southern margin of the exposed coalfield, and the small adjoining band of concealed coal measures. The maps show that the

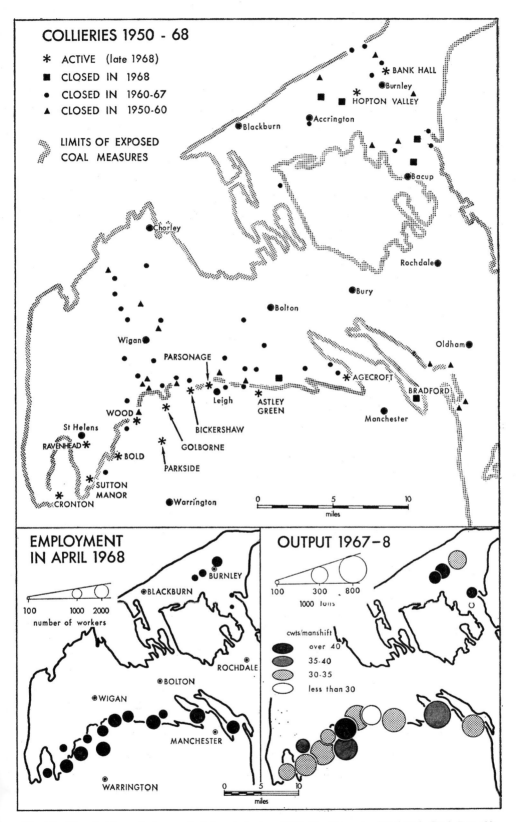

Fig 26. The decline of the coalmining industry 1950–68. (Source: National Coal Board.)

surviving pits are relatively large; almost all employ over 500 miners, six have at least 1,500, and most produce 0·3 million tons or more a year. Productivity varies considerably; Golborne had the highest output per man shift in the year ending March 1968, with the two new units, Agecroft and Parkside, also doing well. But two of the pits closed in the north east in 1968, Thorney Bank and Deerplay, also had very high output per man shift by Lancashire standards— no guarantee of survival if total output is relatively small.

Most of the loss of employment has been in the south-western section of the coalfield. The Ministry of Labour's estimates of insured employees show a reduction of 27,000 here between 1953 and 1965, with over 10,000 of these in the Ashton-in-Makerfield and Atherton exchange areas. This compares with a loss of about 1,500 at the eastern end of the field in Oldham and Ashton-under-Lyne, and 1,100 in the Burnley area. The latest closures have added to these figures. The absorption of displaced miners at other pits has helped to keep local unemployment down, but at the expense of lengthening journeys to work; substantial numbers of miners must now travel ten miles or more.[19] The modern miner, like his counterpart in other activities, is becoming more of a commuter, for the days of the short walk from cottages huddled around the pit head have virtually gone.

The future of any area dependent on coal mining for its employment must remain uncertain. The increasing use of oil, nuclear power, and cheap North Sea gas will continue to place pressure on the market for coal. Early in 1967 a national production of 180 million tons seemed a reasonable future expectation, with 5 per cent coming from Lancashire. But a more recent White Paper talked in terms of a reduction to 120 million by 1975.[20] This could reduce Lancashire's output to 5 million tons, and more closures would be inevitable. Looking further ahead, Lord Robens has stated that only one pit will be in operation in Lancashire by 1981, and as the colliery he referred to, Bradford, closed in 1968 it can be inferred that the NCB see the coalmining industry ceasing altogether in this region during the late 1970s. Like cotton manufacturing, coal mining is now so reduced in its scale that its complete disappearance as a source of employment would not be catastrophic to the region, though further contraction could still bring serious local problems.

The Clothing Industries

The various clothing industries have together suffered a net reduction of over 25,000 jobs since the early 1950s. This is comparable with the loss in coal mining, but the clothing industries have reacted in a very different manner in different areas, with big local contractions partially offset by growth elsewhere. And by far the largest reduction in employment, in the city of Manchester, has taken place in an area where other work is seldom hard to find.

The Manchester and Salford garment industry specialises in rainwear, shirts, dresses and similar goods, made from fabrics of local manufacture or finish. Much of the industry occupies converted houses and other old property. It is in general a trade of small-scale operators with little capital, and is highly labour intensive. Any amalgamations or reorganisation of production techniques are bound to reduce the number of workers, and the industry's concentration in blighted areas of the cities has meant the displacement of many firms as urban renewal proceeds. Manchester and Salford have thus lost over 20,000 jobs in clothing during the past two decades. The loss in Liverpool, which has a much smaller industry operating under similar conditions, has approached 2,000. Against this has been the limited expansion of garment manufacturing in some of the mill towns, using vacant premises and surplus female labour.[21] The leading growth centre, Oldham, has increased employment by almost 1,500 since 1953.

Footwear manufacturing has been a more stable employer in the region as a whole, with the loss of only about 2,000 jobs between 1953 and 1967. But local expansion, notably in the Furness area, obscures a more serious contraction in the Rossendale valley. The Rossendale industry grew up towards the end of the nineteenth century to specialise in slippers made from locally-produced felt, and later in women's and children's shoes. After a fairly prosperous period following the Second World War demand fell, and what expansion there has been has tended to be outside the valley in places like Preston and Burnley.[22] Employment in footwear in Rawtenstall and Bacup alone has gone down by about 2,000 since the early 1950s, and there seems little hope of a reversal of this trend.

Contraction in the hatting industry has reduced employment in clothing in Denton and Stockport by about 1,500 since 1953; the hatters have gained little from the increasing interest in men's clothing and today's fashion-conscious young man prefers not to hide his hair. Unless the world of pop culture sees fit to resurrect the hatted hero of the immediate post-war cinema, there seems little prospect of renewed growth in this locally-important section of the clothing industry.

The Growth Industries

Engineering, Electrical and Metal Goods

It is an interesting and perhaps rather significant feature of the literature on the region's economic development that declining industries seem to attract more attention than those which are expanding. Many studies of the cotton industry and its problems can be found, and the plight of the coal industry has also prompted much concern, but the student of regional affairs looks in vain for similar treatments of the growth industries. The engineering, electrical and metal goods industries (not including vehicles) have been providing the North West with about 5,000 additional jobs each year during the post-war period, but remarkably little systematic information exists to indicate why certain localities have been preferred to others.

It is this problem of information alone which justifies the treatment of a very varied group of activities under one broad heading. Some-

Table 13

EMPLOYMENT IN ENGINEERING, ELECTRICAL
AND METAL INDUSTRIES 1959-67

Industry	*Number of insured employees 1967*	*Increase or decrease (—) 1959–67*	
		number	*per cent*
Mechanical engineering			
Machine tools	12,100	— 100	— 1
Textile machinery	20,600	— 1,100	— 5
Other machinery	75,100	16,700	28
Industrial plant and steelwork	25,800	6,200	32
Other mechanical engineering	24,400	3,500	17
Electrical goods			
Electrical machinery	58,600	2,800	5
Insulated wires and cables	24,000	5,200	28
Telegraph and telephone apparatus	17,630	7,000	65
Radio etc and domestic appliances	31,100	9,000	41
Other electrical goods	17,700	4,000	29
Miscellaneous engineering and metal goods			
Small arms, instruments, watches, jewellery etc	11,700	— 3,900	—20
Tools, cutlery, nuts and bolts, wire, metal containers etc	19,700	900	5
Other metal industries	41,600	7,900	24
Total	380,000	59,000	22

Source: Ministry of Labour. The industries specified comprise Minimum List Headings of the SIC, in some cases amalgamated.

thing of the composition of the engineering group is shown in Table 13, which helps to identify the more important growth sections. The most spectacular expansion in relative terms has been in the telegraph and telephone apparatus category, with radio and domestic appliances second. Employment increases of at least 25 per cent in eight years are shown in more than half the industries listed, and the overall growth rate since 1959 has been almost 3 per cent a year.

Taken as a whole, the electrical goods section has grown most rapidly. The region is fortunate in having a number of Britain's major producers in this field, and their contribution to the build-up of new employment has been considerable. Ferranti employ about 10,000 in and around Manchester, with their three plants in Oldham making a variety of electrical equipment, a measuring instruments factory at Moston, the automation systems division at Wythenshawe, and the company's headquarters and largest manufacturing unit at Hollinwood. Four of these plants are in converted cotton mills. Of comparable importance in Liverpool are English Electric, with 13,000 employees and a wide range of products, and the Plessey telephone-equipment concern. The large increase in employment in the wires and cables branch can be mainly attributed to the activities of British Insulated Callender's Cables, with about 18,000 workers in the region. The company's main works is at Prescot, where it has four manufacturing divisions including a wire mill, telephone-cables plant, and copper refinery, and there are other BICC establishments in the Liverpool area and elsewhere in Lancashire. Another major employer is Associated Electrical Industries, now merged with GEC, with over 16,000 workers at its great Trafford Park complex.

The location of these and other major electronics firms in and around Merseyside and Greater Manchester goes a long way towards explaining the post-war expansion of employment in the Mersey growth zone. But the impact of the recent success of this industry has been felt in other parts of the region, including some with local employment problems. Mullards and Joseph Lucas have provided valuable jobs in north-east Lancashire, and in 1967 Ferranti set up microelectronic assembly laboratories in a government advance factory at Barrow-in-Furness, with a planned employment of 1,000. At Winsford a new English Electric computer factory already employs 1,250, and British Driver-Harris have moved their cable division here from Manchester.

The mechanical-engineering industries also have their very big concerns, though these occupy less of a dominant position than in electronics. The success of the large firms in obtaining export orders has been a major factor in the recent growth of this sector, and their location has been important in determining where the new jobs have been created. In Stockport, for example, factories of the Simon engineering group employ 3,500 workers, meeting foreign orders for various kinds of industrial plant, and Mirlees National, with a big export trade in diesel engines, have 2,500 employed. The success of firms like these helps to explain the growth of employment in the Stockport district, despite the contraction of the textile trade. Another example is provided by Walmsleys, the leading manufacturers of papermaking machinery, with big contracts to install machines in foreign pulp and paper mills. Their employment of 3,000 in Bury and Wigan constitutes an important element of stability in towns hit by colliery and cotton-mill closures.

One of the oldest engineering industries in the region is, of course, textile machinery. This has been severely affected by the contraction of the local market, but there are signs that its decline is slowing, and some important new developments are taking place. Between 1953 and 1959 about 12,000 jobs were lost in textile engineering but recent losses have been less substantial (Table 13). Demand for machinery from producers of man-made fibres is keeping some firms busy, and the likelihood of frequent re-equipment as the reorganised Lancashire textile industry fights for its markets clearly offers scope for the enterprising and innovating machinery manufacturers. One recent development of some interest is in tufted-carpet machinery, with a number of firms in this business in Blackburn.

Many of the textile-machine makers have survived by diversification; for example, the Mather & Platt group, with 6,000 workers in the Manchester area, makes such products as sprinkler systems and food-processing machinery, and the Stone-Platt group's spinning-machinery production has been concentrated at Accrington, to leave its Oldham factory to do general engineering.[23] This kind of move out of textile machinery, with the transfer of capital and labour to other forms of engineering, is a common feature of Britain's textile regions, and has been going on in Lancashire since the last century. Metal-working skills can easily be turned to new and profitable endeavours, whereas skill with the spindle and the loom has proved to be of more transitory value.

In addition to electrical and mechanical engineering, a group of miscellaneous metal industries have been important providers of additional employment in recent years. These include the manufacture of metal containers, office furniture, and a variety of other metal goods.

Two views of the distribution of recent growth in the engineering

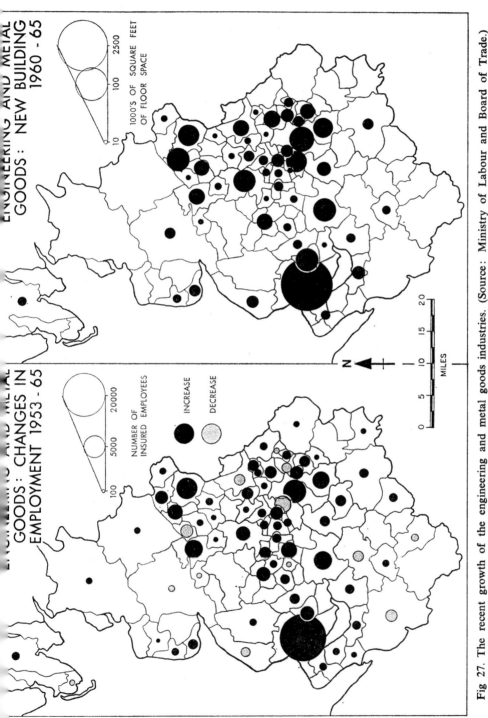

Fig 27. The recent growth of the engineering and metal goods industries. (Source: Ministry of Labour and Board of Trade.) In the left-hand map the absence of a symbol in an area indicates a negligible change, in the right-hand map it indicates no building recorded.

and metal industries are given in Fig 27. Changes in employment between 1953 and 1965 show Liverpool (20,000 additional jobs), Greater Manchester (over 10,000) and the intervening towns, as the major area of development. North-east Lancashire stands out well, with about 10,000 new jobs, mainly in electronics. Very small increases, with some decreases, are the rule in most other parts of the region. The Board of Trade statistics for factory building completed show a similar pattern; of 9·5 million sq ft constructed in 1960–5, about three-quarters was in the Merseyside to Manchester belt, while northern Lancashire, most of southern Cheshire, Rossendale and much of the Pennine fringe is conspicuously bare.

It is clear, then, that recent development has shown a strong locational preference. Much of the growth has been on the industrial estates of Manchester and Liverpool, or other extensive sites around the fringe of the two conurbations. Relatively little has taken place in the smaller cotton towns, where to add to their misfortune much of the existing engineering has been in textile machinery. The obvious success of firms like Ferranti in converted cotton mills, and those enticed into north-east Lancashire, shows that the region's main growth zone need not monopolise the expansion of the engineering industries. But the fact remains that Manchester and Merseyside have formidable advantages with respect to such things as good transport facilities, skilled labour available to those prepared to compete for it, and access to materials, component suppliers and the market. The hope for development in most other areas remains dependent on the less certain factors of cheap premises, surplus of not always highly skilled labour, and the enterprise of indigenous firms.

Motor Vehicles

The engineering industries have produced the most new jobs in recent years, but the most dramatic growth has been in motor vehicles. Almost all the 35,000 increase in employment in the vehicles and aircraft group between 1953 and 1967 was in the motor-vehicles section, and the majority of this has been the result of three major developments on Merseyside.

Until 1960 the production of motor vehicles was largely confined to two areas outside what has become the region's main growth zone. In the north was Leyland Motors, with factories at Leyland, Farrington and Chorley making trucks and buses. In the south was the Rolls-Royce car factory at Crewe, and two manufacturers of commercial vehicles, Fodens and ERF, in Sandbach. These firms were of local origin except for Rolls-Royce who established their motor-car division in Crewe in 1946.

The recent growth of motor manufacturing on Merseyside arose from the boom which built up in the industry during the 1950s, and from the Board of Trade's industrial-location policy. Faced with refusal of permission for major extensions to plants in the Midlands and southern England, the manufacturers had to look to the development areas. Although Rootes went to Scotland, three others, Ford, Vauxhall and Standard-Triumph, all decided on Merseyside, which was the closest area to the parent plants at Dagenham, Luton and Coventry acceptable to the government, with the exception of South Wales.

The largest of the three developments is that of Ford, with a site of almost 350 acres at Halewood on the eastern edge of Liverpool. The factory represents an investment of over £70,000,000, and employed 14,000 by 1969. This location was chosen after considering Scotland, the North East and South Wales, the main advantages of Halewood being the large site with adequate room for expansion, and the road, rail and docking facilities.[24] The communications position is particularly good; the main railway line running past the factory provides an excellent link with Ford's Dagenham plant, Garston and Liverpool docks can handle the very considerable export trade, and Speke Airport less than a mile away can be used for air-freight and visiting executives. Against these advantages had to be set distance from Dagenham, and the problem of attracting and retaining a satisfactory labour force. The Halewood plant, concerned with metal stamping, body and gearbox production, and the assembly of vehicles, has to rely on Dagenham and other suppliers for most components. Three trains a day bring engines, rear axles, forgings and castings from the parent factory, taking from Halewood in return, gearboxes, stampings and trim, and this is bound to add to production costs. Despite the unemployment which was the main reason for moving the motor industry to Merseyside, there was no pool of suitable labour, and no local experience in motor manufacturing with its flow-production techniques. Ford thus had to spend £2,000,000 on a labour-training programme before production could begin.

Vauxhall's development on a 400 acre site at Hooton Park near Ellesmere Port has been on a comparable scale with that of Ford, but investment (£66,000,000) and employment (almost 11,500 at mid-1968) are slightly lower. The main advantages of a Merseyside location were ample land and good communications. The original plan was to use the Ellesmere Port factory mainly for component production but it has subsequently become a fully-integrated manufacturing unit. It is much more independent of Vauxhall's Luton factory than Ford at Halewood is of Dagenham, producing engines as well as transmissions and bodies from the raw-steel stage. Vauxhall use road rather than rail for what movement of goods is necessary, and the Hooton Park site is very well-placed for connection with Luton and the other plant at Dunstable via the M6 and M1 motorways.

The third major project, that of Standard-Triumph International, is smaller than Ford and Vauxhall. It started with the acquisition of the Hall Engineering Company at Speke in 1960, and considerable expansion has taken place here and on another large site nearby. Production at Speke is confined to car bodies, which are shipped to Coventry for final assembly. Since 1960 Standard-Triumph has been owned by Leyland, and in 1968 the merger with the British Motor Holdings to form the British Leyland group raised some questions over the future of the Speke plants. But it is too early to say what impact the merger might have on Speke, and indeed on the other Leyland factories in the North West.

Although these three major firms have held the centre of the stage in the motor industry's recent development, there has also been growth elsewhere. In southern Cheshire employment at Rolls-Royce has risen to almost 5,000, the Sandbach vehicle industry has taken on about 1,000 additional workers since the early 1950s, and expansion of the Leyland factories has raised employment by 2,000.

Other important developments have taken place in the components industry. In 1961 Joseph Lucas bought the former Royal Ordnance Factory at Aintree, Liverpool, and now employ 3,000 in producing electrical equipment for the motor industry. They have also extended their Burnley plant. The Lucas subsidiary, Girling, has moved onto the Bromborough Port industrial estate. The Kirkby plant of the AC-Delco Division of General Motors, set up in 1958 to make fuel pumps, instruments, gauges, horns and other components, now employs almost 3,000 workers. Michelin have expanded their tyre plant at Burnley. The Leamington firm of Automotive Products have moved their filter production to a 250,000 sq ft cotton mill in Bolton, and Rist's Wires & Cables (another Lucas subsidiary) have taken an Accrington mill. Many other examples could be given; in 1965 LAMIDA noted twenty important recent developments in the component field, and listed almost sixty motor component and accessory manufacturers in the region.[25] Half the new projects were in or around Merseyside, and many of the rest in Greater Manchester. Merseyside's status as the major growth point for both the production and components sections of the motor industry is emphasised by more recent developments, including a large factory for Champion Plugs at Birkenhead. It has been estimated that expansion in motor accessories in the last few years represents an investment of about £15,000,000, giving the Merseyside district 10,000 new jobs.[26]

How much of this growth can be attributed directly to the arrival of Ford and Vauxhall? This is very difficult to answer, but the evidence suggests that the direct impact of the major manufacturers in stimulating ancillary development has been less extensive, and certainly less rapid, than was originally anticipated. One recent study estimated that by late 1965 no more than 500 new jobs for men and 150 for women could be attributed to the coming of Ford, Vauxhall and Standard-Triumph, and this included employment in the distribution of finished vehicles. The conclusion was that most vehicle-accessory firms had been in Merseyside before the major manufacturers arrived, and that their expansion had been tied more to the growth of the motor industry nationally than to the local expansion.[27] Some firms certainly have come in to supply the local market, for example, an Essex firm employs 250 workers in Widnes making door panels, glove boxes and so on specifically for Ford at Halewood five miles away. But others supply a much wider market; AC-Delco's fuel pumps go into about three-quarters of all British vehicles. Whether directly connected with Ford and Vauxhall or not, much development has taken place since 1960, and each new project contributes to a growing sub-regional motor-vehicle complex with strong inter-industry linkages, of the kind on which much of the post-war prosperity of the West Midlands has been based.

As a location for the motor industry, Merseyside now looks very good. The initial problem of labour supply has been solved to the satisfaction of both the major newcomers; by careful selection they have built up efficient and reasonably stable workforces, avoiding the long-term unemployed and Merseyside's more irregular and reluctant workers.[28] The wages paid have been high enough to attract loyal and skilled operatives from other industries, particularly engineering; in October 1967 the vehicle industry was paying an average of 10s 3½d an hour in the North West, compared with 9s 2½d paid in engineering.[29] To offset the increase in costs arising from distance from parent plants and from some sources of components are the very considerable grants paid in the Merseyside Development Area. The regional employment premium is a particularly important labour-cost subsidy for a big motor firm, who can thus save about £1,000,000 a year. Far from being a poor second-best to the Midlands and southern England,

Merseyside may now have become a low-cost location for motor manufacturing. It has recently been suggested that Vauxhall produce their 'Viva' at Ellesmere Port and Ford their 'Escort' at Halewood more cheaply than any other firms in Britain could turn out comparable cars.[30] If this is so, it is probably less the result of economic conditions on Merseyside than a function of the large-scale manufacture of successful products, with the degree of technical efficiency which massive capital expenditure can create. In other words, a high volume of output on the latest assembly lines may well be a more important determinant of profits in the modern motor industry than the exact location within spatial limits which certainly include the North West's growth zone.

Paper, Printing and Publishing

Third of the region's growth industries in terms of employment increase is the paper group. The 20,000 or so new jobs created since the early 1950s are particularly important because this is on average the best-paid manufacturing industry in the region.[31] Paper manufacturing is a very old activity, and there have been mills on Lancashire streams since the eighteenth century. During the Industrial Revolution it became concentrated in a zone extending from Preston to Blackburn south-east to include Bolton and Bury, and then to the flanks of the Pennines east of Manchester.[32] Printing and publishing is largely concentrated in Liverpool and Manchester, where employment has increased steadily in recent years.

The location of paper making in a number of the Lancashire textile towns has proved fortunate, for the increases in employment have often been considerable. Among those which can be detected from the Ministry of Labour figures for 1953–65 are a rise of almost 1,000 in Oldham, 850 in Blackburn, 700 in Nelson, 650 in Darwen, and 500 in Stockport. Against these, the losses of 300–400 in Bury, Glossop and Rochdale are small, though locally unfortunate.

But much of the more recent growth has been in the western part of the region, away from the traditional area. In Warrington, with its large firms making cardboard and cases, employment has risen by almost 2,000 since the early 1950s. Major development has taken place near Ellesmere Port, where the Bowater group has a groundwood pulp mill and large factories producing such things as newsprint and paper sacks. There has also been an increase of almost 1,000 in Wigan, where Reed Corrugated Cases have a factory. Of special importance has been the development of paper manufacturing in the Furness area;

to an existing paper industry in Barrow has been added a £3,000,000 factory built in 1959 by British Cellophane, and a large paper-tissue plant for Bowater-Scott opened in May 1968. Barrow was chosen by Bowater from thirty-five alternative locations in the development areas of northern England, largely on the basis of adequate supplies of water of the desired quality, a suitable site, and existing wood-pulp handling facilities at the docks. About 300 workers are now employed, a £2,000,000 expansion should be completed in 1969, and further development is expected.

The North West is fortunate in having a good stake in the paper industry. It was recently forecast that the world demand for paper will at least double every fifteen years, and exports from Britain rose significantly in 1968. New uses for paper in clothing, furnishings and disposal products such as tableware could create important new markets. Coastal locations like Ellesmere Port and Barrow, with the necessary facilities to handle large volumes of imported timber or pulp, are ideally placed under present economic conditions, and further growth can also be expected in some of the older centres inland.

Chemicals

The varied activities which make up the chemicals industry are generally highly capital intensive. Their growth is not effectively measured by employment; in fact there has tended to be a reduction in the number of workers during the 1960s, after a rise during the previous decade. But as the third industrial group in the region in terms of floor space constructed during the first half of the 1960s, chemicals should be considered an important growth industry. In recent years the British chemicals industry has been increasing its output at about double the rate in manufacturing as a whole, and in 1968 it was reported that investment in chemicals and petroleum plant in the North West during the previous year exceeded £200,000,000.[33]

The manufacture of chemicals began with the production of alkalis for the region's soap and textile industries. The salt deposits of mid-Cheshire and the limestone of the Peak District and North Wales provided two important raw materials, while a third, sulphuric acid, was made from minerals imported through Liverpool. The need for fuel brought the industry into the Lancashire coalfield, so that a north–south belt developed from St Helens through Widnes and Runcorn into the Cheshire saltfield, with the Weaver-Sankey Navigation as its central transport artery.

Since the Second World War the nature of the chemical industries has changed in a fundamental way, and this has brought important locational changes. Much of the industry is now based on oil, which is the raw material for about three-quarters of Britain's production of organic chemicals, in addition to its role in the manufacture of plastics and fibres. During the past thirty years national consumption of oil has risen from less than 10 million tons to about 75 million. The petro-chemical industry has rather stringent locational requirements; dependent on one major bulky material which has to be imported, it prefers waterside sites where the giant oil tankers can pour their contents directly into the works. The Mersey estuary and the Ship Canal have proved ideal in this respect, and a string of refineries and chemical plants extends from Ellesmere Port to Manchester Docks. The north–south chemical manufacturing belt of the nineteenth century is thus being replaced by an east–west axis, based on a different waterway.[34]

By far the most extensive petro-chemical complex is Shell's refinery and chemical works at Stanlow near Ellesmere Port. This refinery has become one of the largest and most comprehensive in Europe, with an annual capacity of over 10 million tons and a wide range of petroleum products. It occupies almost 2,000 acres adjoining the Ship Canal, and the total investment of over £70,000,000 is on a similar scale to that of Ford at Halewood. Stanlow is the centre of a complicated system of oil intake and distribution. The largest tankers dock at the Tranmere Oil Terminal south of Birkenhead, constructed jointly by the Mersey Docks & Harbour Board and the Shell Refinery Company, and a pipeline carries oil the eleven miles to Stanlow. Other tankers use the Queen Elizabeth II Dock at Eastham, built by the Manchester Ship Canal Company, and berths also exist on the Canal alongside the refinery itself. About one-third of Stanlow's output goes by pipeline to power stations and other industrial markets. The refinery has pipeline connections with the large Shell chemicals plant at Carrington ten miles west of Manchester, where a major expansion scheme is underway. A similar link has been completed to Shell's smaller refinery at Heysham on Morecambe Bay almost seventy miles away. Among recent developments at the Ellesmere Port complex is an £18,000,000 fertiliser plant on the Ince marshes to be run by Shellstar—a joint venture with an American company.

Firms other than Shell have made big contributions to the spectacular growth of petrochemicals on the southern side of the Mersey estuary; there are three other important refineries, and most of the major oil companies have installations there.

The other great corporation heavily involved in the chemical industry's recent growth is ICI. The interests of ICI are different from those of Shell; the company has deep roots in the region's alkali industry, and is not concerned with oil at the initial-processing stage. ICI's alkali and general chemicals divisions were amalgamated in 1964 to form the Mond Division, which has its headquarters at Runcorn, and a total labour force of over 20,000. A new research complex has been built at Runcorn Heath, overlooking the huge chemical works at Weston Point. The importance of this location goes back to when the junction of the Weaver Navigation and the Mersey Estuary was a particularly strategic spot for the chemical industry; now Western Point has a brine pipeline to the saltfield, and the works are served by the Ship Canal. The Mond Division has other plants in Cheshire including the big Winnington soda-ash and chlorine works, and at Widnes and Fleetwood.

ICI has many other interests in the North West. The pharmaceutical division has its headquarters in Wilmslow, new laboratories employing over 500 people nearby at Alderley Park, and other production capacity in Macclesfield and Manchester. There are paint works at Oldham, Rochdale and Radcliffe, as well as at Hyde where much employment growth has taken place. Plastics are made in Darwen and the Fleetwood works, dyestuffs in Manchester and Fleetwood, and agricultural-chemical products at Clitheroe.

The developments in pharmaceutical goods are important replacements for declining industries, as they are more labour intensive than most chemical manufacturing. In addition to ICI, Geigy have expanded their capacity, including a new £3,000,000 extension at Trafford Park, and the Glaxo antibiotics factory in Barrow has brought valuable new jobs to Furness. Among other significant developments is that of Ashe Laboratories, who have occupied a former textile mill in Littleborough, and are a useful acquisition for one of the more isolated Pennine-fringe mill towns.

In general, the recent expansion of the chemicals industry has been concentrated at the two ends of the Mersey growth zone. New developments completed in the first half of the 1960s amounted to 1·75 million sq ft in Manchester, mainly around the docks and eastern end of the Ship Canal, and almost 1·1 million sq ft on Merseyside including Widnes and Runcorn. These two areas accounted for three-quarters of all development in the region. Growth has thus been away from the traditional chemical centres, with little development taking place in mid-Cheshire and in the dyestuffs industry of the textile districts. The shift of emphasis towards locations well-placed for the importation of bulky materials is similar to that which is taking place in the paper industry.

With its excellent location for oil refining and chemicals manufacture, the North West should share to the full in the continued expansion of these important national growth industries. The modern chemicals industry may well prove to be one of the region's most important assets during the remainder of this century as its range of products continues to increase and as its linkages with other industries are extended. The growing concentration of the chemicals industries in the Merseyside–Manchester belt, with its wide range of engineering and electronics industries and its emerging motor-vehicle complex, serves to further emphasise the considerable economic attractions and growth potential which this part of the region possesses.

References to this chapter are on pages 243 and 244.

6

The Regional Geography of Economic Health

PREVIOUS CHAPTERS HAVE identified important differences within the North West in the social character and material prosperity of the population, in the structure of the economy, in the rate of industrial growth or decline, and in the attraction of different areas as a location for new development. As each pattern has been presented the overall impression has become steadily more complex, though some fairly obvious distinctions between one part of the region and another have begun to emerge. It is now time to clarify these patterns, through a study of the region's internal makeup in terms of some broad conception of economic well-being.[1]

Subdividing the region on the basis of economic health requires the choice of suitable criteria. Until the Hunt Committee investigation of the 'grey' areas in 1968,[2] the measurement of economic well-being for official purposes in Britain had been based almost entirely on the level of unemployment. But local problems of industrial decline, factory closures, redundancies, and shortage of new employment opportunity are not necessarily reflected in a high unemployment figure, for reasons indicated at the end of Chapter 2. In fact, the statistical correlation between the percentage out of work and other possible measures of industrial health is often relatively low in the North West, and in some cases in the opposite direction to that which might have been expected.[3]

If unemployment is inadequate on its own as an indicator of areal variations in economic health, what are the alternatives? Ideally, this should be measured in as many ways as are practicable and relevant, with some general consensus extracted from the conflicting patterns of individual criteria. How this can be done must be considered briefly before subdivisions of the North West are proposed.

171

The Measurement of Economic Health

The choice of criteria involves deciding just what is meant by economic health. Should it be thought of entirely in terms of industrial matters such as structure, performance and employment opportunity, or should social structure, living standards and the quality of the environment also be included? Clearly, the definition must be related to the purpose of the enquiry. In the present case, this is to summarise general levels of industrial development and local economic well-being, and to provide a spatial framework within which sub-regional economic problems can be reviewed. For this reason a rather broad view of economic health is adopted here.

Unfortunately, shortcomings in official statistics make it impossible to obtain local information on some important matters, such as *per capita* income and value of industrial production. And there are other less tangible things which could usefully be considered, like local attitudes and the air of decay which pervades some old industrial communities, for which there is no information in numerical form. Another difficulty arises from the fact that some official figures are compiled by local-authority areas while others relate to employment-exchange areas, which means that this analysis has to be split into two parallel investigations. So two major dimensions of economic health are recognised, an industrial dimension and a socio-economic dimension. The former uses information by exchange areas and the latter by local-authority areas.

Economic health in the industrial dimension is defined as a function of three characteristics represented by fourteen criteria, or variables. These are listed in Table 14 on page 174. The first characteristic is the rate and nature of economic change, with the emphasis on the industrial sector. There are four measures of employment change (Nos 1–4 in Table 14), one relating to the amount of recent industrial building (No 5), and the local index of structural change (No 6). All appeared in Chapter 3, where most of them are mapped. The second characteristic is the level of employment, involving two measures of unemployment and one of female-employment opportunity (Nos 7–9). Finally, there are five variables (Nos 10–14) relating to structure, indicating the contribution of the industrial sector, the importance of the main growth and declining industrial groups, the degree of specialisation, and the structural predisposition in terms of expansion or contraction of employment (explained in Chapter 4). The emphasis on employment in nearly all these variables is due as much to lack of other ways of measuring industrial structure and performance as to its importance as a contributor to economic health.

The socio-economic dimension is defined in terms of the demographic character, physical health, socio-economic structure, and material well-being of the population (see Table 15, p 182). Four measures of population change are used (Nos 1–4), with a fifth to show the proportion of aged people the community has to support. The health of the people is measured by a death-rate index, adjusted to take into account local differences in age and sex structure, and by infant mortality. Then come measures of the educational level of the population and occupational or socio-economic structure. Material well-being is measured by quality of housing and car ownership (Nos 11–14). The inevitable absence of information on local income levels is a major omission, but this is largely compensated for by other variables which should correlate fairly well with income.

The problem now is to classify areas with respect to each of these two major dimensions of economic health. What is needed is an objective numerical method of allocating areas into groups, each representing a specific level of economic health, with its members being broadly similar in character. The method adopted here is based on a technique which has been used successfully to tackle similar problems in North America.[4] Because many of the criteria selected above tell basically similar stories about spatial variations in economic health, it is possible by the use of statistical analysis to identify a small number of underlying *factors* which take into account a relatively large share of the total information available. These factors in effect provide formulae from which can be calculated factor scores for each area, which represent indexes of economic health. Areas can then be grouped on the basis of these scores. (This is a greatly simplified account of the procedure involved; a more technical explanation with references is to be found in Appendix A note 11. Readers for whom this method is difficult to grasp should find that the general principle becomes clear if the illustrations and tables are examined carefully in conjunction with the text in the sections which follow.)

The Industrial Analysis

A factor analysis of data relating to the industrial criteria for the ninety-five employment-exchange areas produced two leading components, which together accounted for almost half the areal variations (variance) in the fourteen original criteria.[5] The nature of these components is indicated by the factor loadings (Table 14), which measure the degree of correlation between the original variables and the two composite measures. Factor 1 is identified as the industrial-change factor: it has very high loadings on variables 1, 2, 4 and 5, three of which measure the rate of industrial change. Factor 2 is designated the industrial-structure factor, loading high positively on employment in textiles and clothing (No 12), and high negatively on employment in engineering and metals (No 11) and structural change (No 14).

For each factor, indexes of economic health can be calculated for the exchange area by combining an area's values for the original fourteen criteria in proportions represented by the factor loadings (see Appendix A note 11). Thus areas with big positive increases in employment (Nos 1, 2 and 4) will tend to have high indexes, or scores,

Table 14

FOURTEEN SELECTED INDUSTRIAL CRITERIA USED TO MEASURE ECONOMIC HEALTH: LOADINGS ON THE FIRST TWO FACTORS

Criteria	Factor 1 Industrial change	Factor 2 Industrial structure
1 Change in industrial employment 1959–65 (‰ per year)	0·773	−0·053
2 Change in industrial employment 1953–65 (‰ per year)	0·878	0·001
3 Change in service employment 1953–65 (‰ per year)	0·297	−0·248
4 Change in total employment 1953–65 (‰ per year)	0·805	−0·237
5 Industrial floor space built 1960–65 (sq ft per industrial worker in 1959)	0·725	0·171
6 Index of structural change 1953–65	0·546	0·117
7 Average monthly unemployment 1966 (‰ insured employees)	0·556	−0·212
8 Index of unemployment variability 1966 (highest month ÷ lowest month)	−0·060	0·458
9 Females employed in industry 1965 (% of all employees)	0·055	0·530
10 Industrial employees 1965 (‰ of all employees)	−0·417	0·364
11 Employment in engineering and metal industries 1965 (‰ of all industrial employees)	−0·040	−0·602
12 Employment in textile and clothing industries 1965 (‰ of all industrial employees)	−0·329	0·757
13 Coefficient of industrial specialisation 1965	0·096	0·378
14 Structural change in industrial employment 1953–65 (‰ industrial employees in 1953)	0·336	0·774
Proportion of total variance accounted for	26·1	17·8

Sources of statistics: Ministry of Labour, except No. 5 which is Board of Trade.

on Factor 1, while areas with decreases will have low (or negative) scores. The higher an area's score on Factor 1, the better its economic health. For reasons which need not be considered here, scores on Factor 2 give an inverse measure of economic health; high positive scores mean poor health and high negative scores good health.

Mapping the scores on each of the factors provides one means of classifying areas on the basis of economic health. This has been done in Fig 28. The industrial-change factor reveals a clear geographical pattern, with a fairly regular improvement from east to west. The lowest category is concentrated along the Pennine fringe and in central Lancashire. The healthiest areas are mostly on the western side of the region, but also include parts of the southern edge of the Manchester conurbation. Most of industrial Lancashire not in the lowest category is in the next lowest, while almost all Cheshire and northern Lancashire fall into the higher of the two intermediate categories. Among the exceptions to the general east-west trend, the relatively poor position of Barrow and Birkenhead in the generally healthy Furness and Merseyside Development Areas is worth noting. Also of interest is the presence of some healthy areas in the east, notably Heywood and Middleton to the north of Manchester, and Padiham in north-east Lancashire. This highlights some of the places where successful diversification has enabled a reasonable rate of industrial expansion to be achieved in part of the region which otherwise looks unhealthy on the industrial-change factor.

The structure factor reveals a similar basic pattern, but with some important local differences. Members of the lowest category are more scattered, but still concentrated along the eastern edge of the region, while the main block of healthiest areas now stretches inland continuously to Stockport and Denton. Many of the intermediate areas of industrial Lancashire look better on the structure factor than on change, which is probably indicative of the diversification which has taken place with the rapid decline in textiles. But some areas, like southern Cheshire, score better on change than structure.

These two maps provide an effective summary of many of the patterns of industrial change and structural character presented in earlier chapters. The next step is to produce an areal classification based on both these factors together. The grouping procedure used is explained in Appendix A note 11, and all that need be said here is that it creates a number of groups of areas the members of which have a similar level of economic health, while each group is markedly different from other groups. The results are set out graphically in Fig 29, and the classification is mapped in Fig 30.

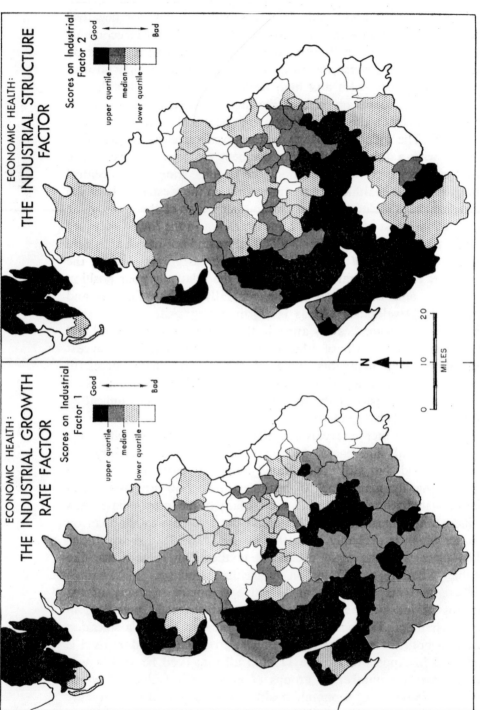

Fig 28. Levels of economic health, based on scores on the two principle factors extracted from fourteen industrial criteria. (Based on a map published in *Regional Studies*, Vol 2, 1968.)

In Fig 29 every exchange area in the North West is plotted according to its scores on the two factors. As high positive scores indicate good economic health on Factor 1 while high negative scores are good on Factor 2, the general level of economic health improves from bottom right to top left of the graph. The distance between any two places on the graph indicates their similarity—the nearer they are the more similar their level of economic health. The effect of using both factors at once will be clear from a careful examination of the graph. For example, Altrincham and Padiham are closely similar in the industrial-change direction, both having achieved reasonable growth, but they have vastly different scores on industrial structure, for Altrincham has a lot of growth industries while Padiham is still partially dependent on textiles. Examples of places with a similar position in respect of both factors are Runcorn and Blackpool, and New Mills and Horwich.

Much could be said about the position of individual areas, but the aim here is to generalise by producing relatively simple classification. The procedure adopted led to the formation of six major groups, lettered A to F in Fig 29. The position of each group of areas on the graph indicates its general economic-health status. Group A clearly represents the most favoured areas, scoring high on both the change and the structure factors. Towards the top of the graph, and amalgamated with group A, are the areas with the best growth performance, though some (ie Thornton, Wallasey and Winsford) look less healthy in terms of structure. Groups B, C and D are intermediate areas. The boundary between them on the graph is a little indistinct in places, particularly between B and D, but each represents a different industrial situation with respect to the structure and change factors. Groups E and F, at bottom left, are the least fortunate areas, with poor scores on both factors. Apart from the position of Nelson, which fell into F only by a hair's breadth, these two groups are quite distinct, F representing the hard core of what, for want of a better expression, are termed the distressed areas.

The final areal classification according to industrial criteria is mapped in Fig 30. This reveals a clear tendency towards the geographical concentration of members of most of the six groups recognised on the graph. In this map will be found echoes of patterns of industrial development and structure illustrated in previous chapters. But, based as it is on fourteen separate industrial criteria, it gives a far more comprehensive view of the geography of industrial health than any single indicator can provide.

The distressed areas comprise the now familiar belt along the fringe

L

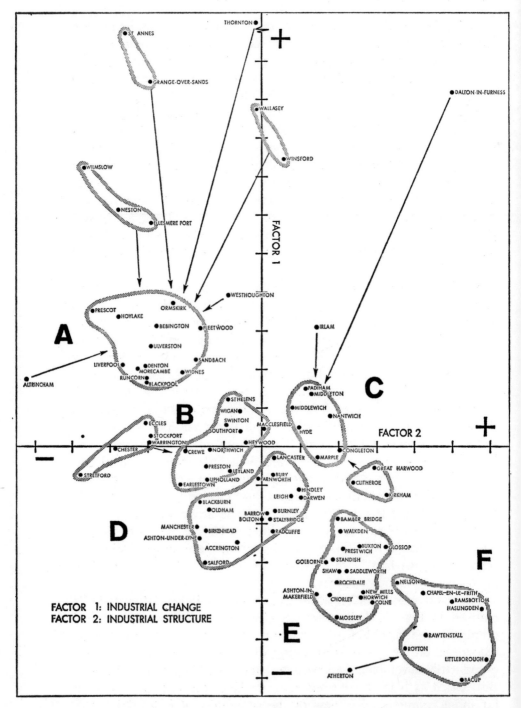

Fig 29. The grouping of exchange areas according to scores on the industrial-change and industrial-structure factors.

of the Pennines, together with parts of central Lancashire. In the east
the lowest levels are reached in the Rossendale valley towns, Ramsbottom, Royton and Littleborough. The relatively healthy position of
much of north-east Lancashire is worth noting, for recent industrial
readjustment has been such that only Nelson and Colne fall into the
distressed category. This is not, of course, to say that all is now well
in north-east Lancashire; the position of Burnley, Darwen and Great
Harwood on the graph (Fig 29) show that they are among the least
healthy members of the group to which they have been allocated. But
it does stress the very serious position of some of the other old textile-
manufacturing districts outside the Blackburn to Burnley area. The
distressed areas of central Lancashire largely reflect the problems
arising from dependence on cotton and coal. Only Atherton falls into
the hard-core distressed category, its very poor score on the change
factor arising mainly from loss of colliery employment.

The two main distressed districts are separated by areas which
almost exclusively belong to group D. This is, in general, the least
healthy of the three intermediate groups, mainly on the grounds of
poor performance on the industrial-change factor. Fig 29 shows that
it is in fact made up of two quite distinct sub-groups. The first (on
the left) has poor scores on Factor 1, but reasonably good scores on
structure. It includes most of the group D areas centred on Manchester,
with engineering industries well represented in their structures but
with performance adversely affected by declining employment in
textiles and clothing. The second sub-group looks a little better on
the change factor but all its members have negative scores on Factor
2. Included here are a number of places where the economy has clearly
performed better than in the other sub-group, despite a poorer
industrial structure.

The members of group C show less geographical concentration than
the other groups. These areas in general score poorly on the structural
factor but relatively well on change. They include textile towns where
diversification has been particularly successful—Padiham, Middleton
and Hyde—and towns heavily dependent on textiles which have kept
out of the distressed category on the basis of performance, eg Congleton, Great Harwood and Clitheroe.

Group B is the healthiest of the intermediate categories. Again, a
fairly clear geographical pattern emerges; there is an almost continuous
ring around the outer edge of Merseyside, and other groups around
Manchester and in north-central Lancashire. Of special interest is the
small sub-group (on the left-hand side of Fig 29) including Eccles,
Stockport and Stretford, with their engineering industries giving very

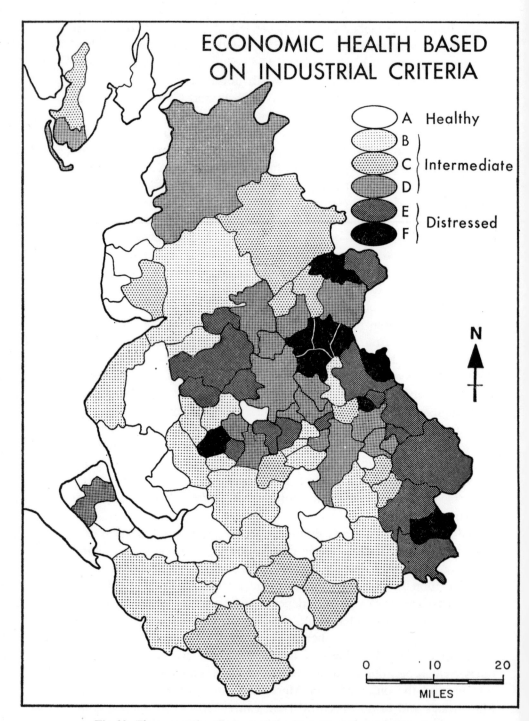

Fig 30. The geography of economic health in the industrial dimension.

high scores on the structure factor, but with only moderate scores on change. This follows the pattern found in group D, with a number of other parts of Greater Manchester scoring well on Factor 2 but poorly on Factor 1. Group A shows Altrincham displaying the same characteristic. The position of so many places in the Manchester area on the lower-left fringe of the scatter of places on the graph is very important. It stresses the fact that the problems of Manchester and many of its near neighbours are in performance rather than in structure, and it adds weight to the view that industrial structure alone cannot explain the poor (or negative) growth of manufacturing in Manchester and some neighbouring towns.

Finally, group A represents the healthiest parts of the region from an industrial point of view, with generally high scores on both factors. The graph shows that this group is fairly clearly defined, with an obvious zone of separation from group B. The whole of the Merseyside Development Area except Birkenhead looks remarkably healthy, as does the Fylde coast and much of Furness. Also in group A are Altrincham and Wilmslow, and the happy position of Denton east of Manchester and Westhoughton in central Lancashire helps to relieve a little of the economic gloom which pervades many of their neighbours.

The Socio-Economic Analysis

The fourteen socio-economic criteria can be expected to produce a different picture of the regional geography of economic health from that described above. They measure different aspects from those expressed by the industrial criteria, and the local-authority areas used to compile the socio-economic data permit a more detailed areal classification than is possible using employment-exchange areas.

The procedure is identical to that applied to the industrial data. Two leading factors were extracted, together accounting for just over 60 per cent of the variance. This is a higher proportion than the 44 per cent in the industrial analysis, which is explained by the generally higher inter-correlation between the socio-economic variables. The final classification is thus based on a rather higher share of the original information than in the industrial analysis.

Table 15 shows that the first socio-economic factor loads very high in a positive direction on professional employees, proportion educated beyond fifteen, and the two measures of car ownership. It has a high negative loading on proportion of semi-skilled and unskilled workers and fairly high loadings in the same direction on death rate and the two measures of housing quality. Factor 1 is thus identified as a broad social structure and affluence factor (the affluence factor for short). It accounts for as much as 41·4 per cent of the total variance. Factor 2, loading high on criteria 1, 2 and 3, is clearly the population-change factor.

Scores on each of the factors are mapped in Fig 31. The affluence factor clearly distinguishes between the region's major industrial districts, with relatively poor conditions, and the peripheral suburbs and rural areas, most of which fall into the healthiest category. The population-change factor shows up the Mersey growth zone as belong-

Table 15

FOURTEEN SELECTED SOCIO-ECONOMIC CRITERIA USED TO
MEASURE ECONOMIC HEALTH: LOADINGS ON THE FIRST TWO
FACTORS

Criteria	Factor 1 Social structure and affluence	Factor 2 Population change
1 Population change 1951–61 (‰ of 1951 population)	0·174	0·864
2 Natural increase 1951–61 (‰ of 1951 population)	−0·210	0·721
3 Migrational change 1951–61 (‰ of 1951 population	0·220	0·790
4 Population change 1961–65 (‰ of 1961 population)	0·447	0·248
5 Persons over 60 years of age 1966 (‰ of total)	0·165	−0·617
6 Death-rate index 1965 (national rate = 100)	−0·705	0·018
7 Infant mortality 1965 (‰ of live births)	−0·297	0·160
8 Persons over 25 having left school at age of 15 or later 1961 (‰ of total)	0·920	0·028
9 Professional workers etc 1966 (‰ of economically active and retired males aged 15 and over)	0·924	−0·099
10 Semi-skilled and unskilled manual workers 1966 (‰ of economically active and retired males aged 15 and over)	−0·843	0·153
11 Dwellings with rateable value less than £30 1966 (‰ of total)	−0·611	−0·444
12 Households without a fixed bath 1966 (‰ of total	−0·696	−0·375
13 Number of motor cars 1966 (per 1000 households)	0·911	0·048
14 Households with two or more cars 1966 (‰ of total)	0·878	−0·020
Proportion of total variance accounted for	41·4	19·5

Sources of statistics: Census of England and Wales, 1961 (Nos 1, 2, 3, 8); *Sample Census,* 1966 (Nos 4, 5, 9, 10, 12, 13, 14); *Registrar General's Statistical Review,* 1965 (Nos 6, 7); Ministry of Housing and Local Government (No 11).

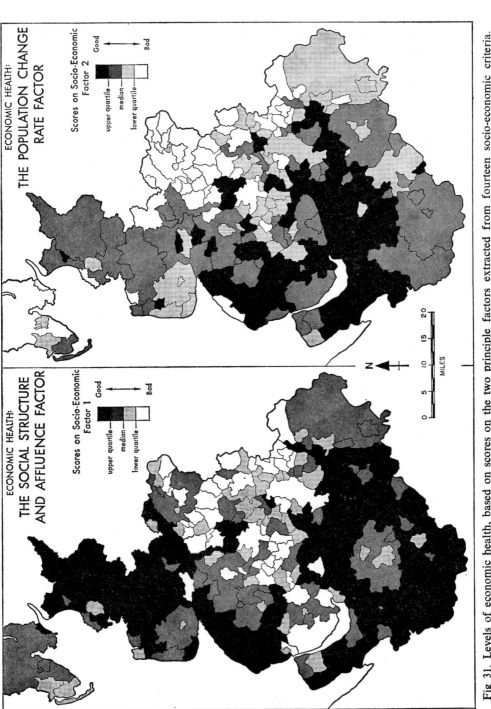

Fig 31. Levels of economic health, based on scores on the two principle factors extracted from fourteen socio-economic criteria. (Based on a map published in *Regional Studies*, Vol 2, 1968.)

ing to the upper quarter. Elsewhere this category is virtually confined
to a few residential areas and overspill reception towns for Manchester. The least healthy category highlights the poor position of the
whole of north-east Lancashire and Rossendale.

Scores on both socio-economic factors are plotted in Fig 32. A high
positive score for an area on either factor indicates a healthy situation,
while a high negative score represents the reverse, which means that
economic health improves from bottom left to top right of the graph,
and not from botton right to top left as in Fig 29. Six major groups
of areas are recognised, identified by the letters U to Z; a few minor
groups and outlying areas on the graph are connected with their
nearest group, as in the industrial analysis. Because it was felt that a
more detailed classification would be useful in the bottom half of the
graph, two sub-groups are recognised within each of the major groups
Y and Z.

Group Z is at the bottom of the socio-economic scale. It contains
42 of the region's 177 local-authority areas, which share the common
characteristic of poor scores on both factors. But these areas fall
clearly into two sub-groups, each with its own type of socio-economic
problem; sub-group Z1 has generally worse scores on population
change and better scores on the affluence factor than Z2. This division
takes on a special significance when membership of the two sub-groups
is mapped (Fig 33). The Z1 category clearly represents the old Pennine-
fringe mill town; it covers much of the north-east Lancashire industrial
area, the Rossendale towns, and a number of less extensive areas to
the south. The only place not originally a mill town is Dalton-in-
Furness. Sub-group Z2 is almost as clearly associated with the south-
western section of the Lancashire coalfield. Over half the places in
this category are in the mining area, and four of the places which are
not, Preston, Warrington, Salford and Oldham, all have a similar
status as highly industrialised cities on the level of the urban hierarchy
immediately below that of the major regional cities. There are thus
two distinct types of problem areas in the North West on the basis
of socio-economic criteria; on the one hand are the less fortunate of
the old mill towns, looking bad in terms of population change but
better on the social structure and affluence factor, while on the other
are places with very poor performance on affluence but not looking too
bad on population change. This helps to emphasise the fact that areas
vary in the nature as well as in the degree of their difficulties.

The next major group up the scale also divides into two sub-groups
—Y1 and Y2. The distinction here is largely in the population-change
factor, and again it has geographical significance. A large proportion

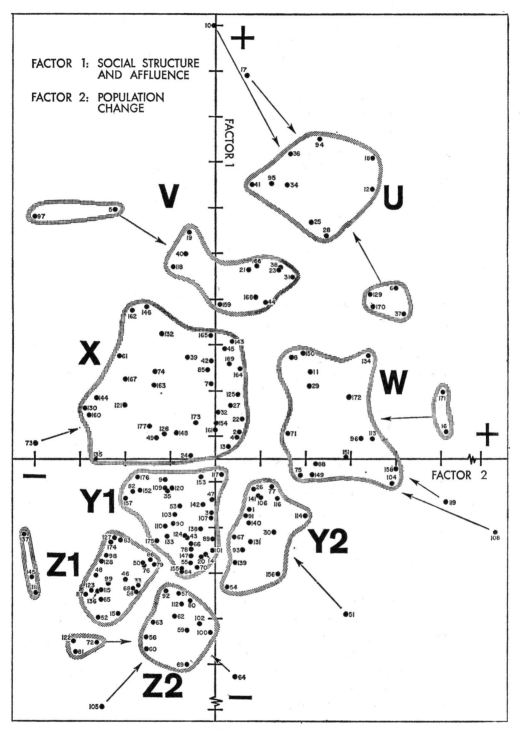

Fig 32. The grouping of local-authority areas according to scores on the social-structure and affluence factor and the population-change factor. (The local-authority areas, indicated here by numbers, are identified in Appendix C.)

of the area falling into the Y2 category is on Merseyside, including Liverpool, Bootle, Birkenhead, Widnes and Runcorn. These areas score rather poorly on the affluence factor, indeed some of them are no better than the mining and mill towns, but they look reasonably healthy in terms of population change. The areas in Y1 are generally similar to Y2 as far as affluence is concerned, but look less healthy on population change; they are strongly grouped in the industrial districts of Greater Manchester and the belt of former textile towns between the city and the Rossendale upland. Thus a broad qualitative distinction can be made between those parts of the two major conurbations falling into group Y.

But a warning is in order at this stage concerning the classification of Liverpool and Manchester, which are almost the least healthy members of their respective sub-groups. Liverpool, at the bottom extremity of Y2, keeps out of group Z only by virtue of population increases rather greater than would be expected in a city of this size, which in itself constitutes a major social and economic problem. A similar score to Manchester, Preston or Salford on the population-change factor would have taken Liverpool easily into group Z2. Manchester stands right at the bottom of Y1, and would have dropped into Z2 if its affluence score had been as low as that of Liverpool. Thus the two cities have problems closely similar to those found to be characteristic of the mining communities and certain of the second-order industrial cities. But both cities contain considerable socio-economic diversity, which is hidden by the fact that they cannot be subdivided for statistical purposes; in Manchester the separation of areas like the Wythenshawe estate from the slums of the inner-city residential areas would be very revealing, and would undoubtedly place large parts of the city into the lowest category. The exclusion of certain outer suburban areas would do the same for Liverpool. This is yet another of the difficulties imposed by the way official statistics are compiled.

Moving up Fig 32 again, group X comprises areas which generally score well or reasonably well on the affluence factor but often rather poorly on population change. As the map shows, this group includes many of the rural areas of northern Lancashire, southern Cheshire and the Peak District, where population tends to be fairly stable while high car ownership and recent residential development for middle-class commuters gives a healthy appearance on the affluence factor. Also included are a few largely residential towns where substantial growth is no longer taking place, eg Prestwich, Altrincham and Crosby, as well as the retirement and resort towns of Morecambe and Southport.

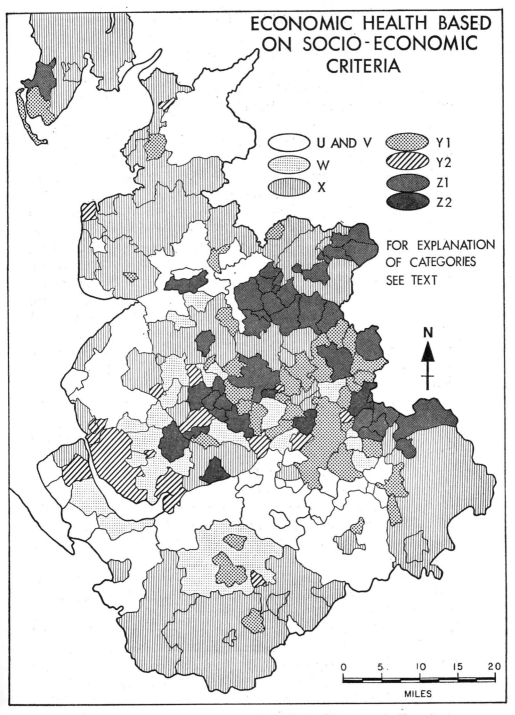

ECONOMIC HEALTH BASED
ON SOCIO-ECONOMIC
CRITERIA

U AND V   Y1
W   Y2
X   Z1
   Z2

FOR EXPLANATION
OF CATEGORIES
SEE TEXT

N

0   5   10   15   20
MILES

Fig 33. The geography of economic health in the socio-economic dimension.

The members of group W have in common relatively high scores on the population-change factor, but break into two distinct sub-groups on the affluence factor. The upper or more affluent group contains a few rapidly growing middle-class suburban areas, including Bredbury, Rainford and Bebbington. The lower group represents rapidly expanding areas of more working-class character, eg Leyland, Huyton, and some reception areas for Manchester overspill.

Also included in this group are some of the areas with the region's highest score on the population-change factor. At the extreme is Kirkby, with a unique socio-economic character befitting the 'Newtown' of Z Cars fame familiar to the nation's television viewers; it has recorded the fastest population increases of any local-authority area in the region since the war, as thousands of people have been transplanted from Liverpool's slums. But other things which have been taken as indicators of economic health reveal remarkable extremes. Kirkby is almost bottom of the car-ownership table, but top of the list in terms of houses with low rateable value and access to a fixed bath—more of its households have a bath than in Bowden or Hale! This small example serves to emphasise that single measures of economic well-being may, in extreme cases, produce widely conflicting results, which is why it is advisable to use a relatively large number of separate indicators.

The last two groups, U and V, represent affluent suburbia. The members of group V share roughly the same position on the affluence factor, clearly better than W and X but not quite as good as U, but differ considerably on the population change. At the one extreme are Grange-over-Sands, Alderley Edge, Hoylake, St Anne's and Disley, with poor scores on Factor 2 arising from low or negative population change and a disproportionate number of elderly residents. At the other are the more rapidly growing if slightly less affluent areas such as Lymm, Sale, Knutsford and the rural districts of Chester, Runcorn and Preston.

Group U comprises the most affluent of the suburban areas. The main group marked on the graph includes the Manchester dormitory areas of Wilmslow, Marple, Hazel Grove, Cheadle and Macclesfield RD. Merseyside's affluent fringe is represented by Formby, Neston and Wirral, and Preston's northern suburbs appear in the form of Fulwood UD. A small sub-group comprising Poulton-le-Fylde, Alsager and the rural districts of West Lancashire and Bucklow (south-west of Manchester) is included in U on the basis of high scores on population change, though its affluence level is comparable with group V. Right at the top of the affluence scale are Bowden and Hale, with rather lower scores on population change than the main body of group U. These represent the 'best' Manchester suburban areas, though it must be remembered that the use of complete local-authority areas hides certain other local peaks of affluence, such as the Prestbury area in Macclesfield RD.

Groups U and V are mapped as one category in Fig 33. In the southern part of the region they form a clear and continuous belt on the south side of the main urban-industrial complex. A similar though less distinct belt fringes Merseyside and the western edge of the industrial areas in central and western Lancashire.

A Regional Subdivision

The two views of the regional geography of economic health, based respectively on industrial and socio-economic criteria, have proved to be different in many respects, but they can be combined in a very general way. This has been attempted in Fig 34, where six major sub-regions are recognised and further subdivided. As in most regional classifications, the boundaries often represent zones of transition rather than sharp breaks in character, and no great significance should be attached to their exact position.

Sub-region I comprises Greater Manchester. It contains an inner core made up largely of the cities of Manchester and Salford, and three peripheral subdivisions. The least healthy areas from both the industrial and socio-economic points of view fall into the Pennine Fringe subdivision, which includes the textile towns south of Rossendale. The subdivision centred on Bolton and Bury is, in general, healthier than the Pennine Fringe from an industrial point of view, and marginally so in socio-economic terms. The City Core as a whole has a similar status to Bolton–Bury, but there are local areas which are very badly off. South Manchester comprises the conurbation's more affluent suburbs, as well as some of the healthier industrial areas.

Merseyside (II) divides into two on the basis of socio-economic criteria. The Core represents areas of relatively poor social structure, while the Periphery includes the more affluent inner and outer suburban areas. Both fall into the healthiest category on the basis of industrial criteria.

Central Lancashire (III) is divided into North and South. The North is in poor health on industrial rather than socio-economic grounds, while the South, which largely comprises the mining townships, looks generally poor on both sets of criteria. North-East Lancashire (IV) is also divided into two, to take into account the very poor industrial

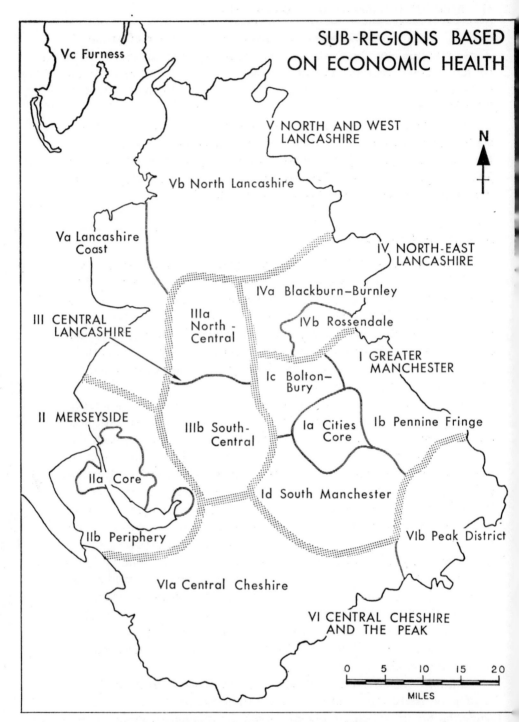

Fig 34. A sub-regional classification based on economic health. This map attempts a compromise between Figs 30 and 33.

situation in the Rossendale valley. Almost all the Blackburn–Burnley area looks poor on socio-economic grounds, but the unhappy industrial position of Nelson and Colne is compensated for by the rather healthier situation in lower parts of the valley.

Sub-regions V and VI comprise the peripheral, largely non-industrial, parts of the region. The Lancashire Coast is identified separately on the grounds of its healthy industrial position. In the south the Peak District is separated from Central Cheshire because of its poorer performance on the industrial criteria.

This sub-regional classification may be far from perfect as a summary of the regional geography of economic health. But it does appear to represent a reasonable compromise between the results of two rather complicated statistical analyses, and it does not greatly conflict with regional subdivisions in current use for planning and other purposes, arrived at on more conventional geographical grounds. It now remains to take a closer look at each sub-region.

References to this chapter are on page 244.

A View of the Sub-Regions

Descriptions of various subdivisions of the North West can be found in a number of existing publications.[1] In addition, the two conurbations are the subject of detailed enquiries which are still proceeding including two major land-use and transportation studies, the regional planning council is sponsoring an investigation of the potential of north-east Lancashire, and other parts of the region have been dissected in depth by various planning groups looking at sites for new towns or cities. Because of this, the sub-regional treatments here are very brief. They are confined to industrial development and related problems, and attempt to place some of the facts which have already emerged in a more local context.

I Greater Manchester

Greater Manchester, with its 2·5 million people, is a highly complex geographical entity. At its heart is Manchester itself, from which the nineteenth-century suburbs spread out to envelop a number of industrial satellites and dormitories. To the north are Bolton, Bury and Rochdale, their once tenuous links with the rest of the conurbation having solidified into virtually continuous built-up strips; to the east Oldham and the other Pennine-fringe towns are more closely connected with Manchester; to the west the peat mosses make a break in the outer urban ring, except in the mining area between Leigh and Worsley; to the south-west the inner Cheshire suburbs are separated from the Lancashire part of the conurbation by the open land along the Mersey; beyond are the outer middle-class suburbs.

For a long time the economy of Manchester and its neighbours was dominated by the textile industry. Most places did little but manufacture cotton, though some had paper mills, coal mines and dye works, and the textile-machinery and clothing industries were added in the nineteenth century. Two things eventually broke the extreme dependence on cotton and associated trades. One was the diversification of textile-machinery manufacture into other types of equipment, and the beginnings of electrical engineering; the other was the opening of the Manchester Ship Canal, which brought food industries, bulk processing and other new activities into the city on a large scale.

Most of the towns to the north and east of Manchester remained dominated by cotton, however, so that when the depression came they had little alternative to fall back on. For most of the 1930s unemployment in the spinning towns varied between 20 and 35 per cent, with rather lower figures in the more diversified Manchester-Salford area. The rapid population growth of the period before the First World War ceased, and the Oldham area actually lost 20,000 people between 1921 and 1939. Only the southern suburbs, largely within Cheshire, continued to increase their population. At the end of the 1920s the Bolton, Bury, Rochdale and Oldham area had 210,000 textile workers, making up almost 60 per cent of all insured employees, but by 1939 this had gone down to 170,000 with no compensating growth in other industries.[2]

Since the Second World War diversification has been easier. Despite post-war building restrictions, land shortages, IDC difficulties, and no government subsidies (except for the inclusion of the Oldham and Rochdale areas on the DATAC list for about a year), most places have been able to develop some replacement industries. The reoccupation of vacated mills has been of supreme importance. Generally, increased employment in the service sector has been needed as well as new manufacturing to offset the loss of jobs in textiles, and as Chapter 3 showed, there are many places where even this has not been enough.[3]

The present industrial structure of the sub-region and its four component parts is summarised in Table 16. In Bolton–Bury and the Pennine Fringe textiles is still the leading industrial group, with one-third and 40 per cent respectively of all manufacturing employment. But together these areas now have 50,000 engineering workers. The variety of industry in the Core, mainly Manchester, Salford and Trafford Park, is plain from the figures, as is the predominance of engineering and electrical goods in South Manchester. In the sub-region as a whole, the engineering group is now the clear leader.

The gradual diversification has not been accompanied by any dramatic changes in industrial location. In Merseyside substantial dispersal has taken place (as described in the next section), but in south-east Lancashire industry has always been scattered, if locally concentrated around the old cores of the industrial towns. In the

M

post-war period, when so much of Merseyside's dispersal has taken place, government policy has tended to perpetuate the existing location pattern in Greater Manchester by diverting industrial growth to other areas or into the vacated mills.

But some breaks have taken place in the traditional Victorian pattern, dependent as it was very largely on the locational needs of cotton mills. The first, and still the most important, was at Trafford Park—Britain's first and largest industrial estate, and one of Europe's

Table 16

THE INDUSTRIAL STRUCTURE OF GREATER MANCHESTER 1966

Industry	City Core	Bolton–Bury	Pennine Fringe	South Manchester	Sub-regional total
Engineering and electrical	91,000	18,000	32,000	27,000	168,000
Textiles	20,000	34,000	49,000	8,000	111,000
Clothing	33,000	5,000	5,000	8,000	51,000
Paper, printing and publishing	24,000	10,000	5,000	7,000	46,000
Food, drink and tobacco	22,000	4,000	5,000	11,000	42,000
Chemicals etc	27,000	3,000	2,000	4,000	36,000
Vehicles	7,000	10,000	9,000	5,000	31,000
Other manufacturing	56,000	18,000	17,000	7,000	98,000
Total	280,000	102,000	124,000	77,000	583,000

Source: Ministry of Labour. Note: the figures here and in Tables 17 and 18 are based on estimates of insured employees and are approximate only. The areas indicated correspond roughly with those shown in Fig 34.

greatest industrial complexes. Development started in 1897, three years after the opening of the Ship Canal, and its position adjoining Manchester docks made it an excellent location for new industry. One of the early arrivals was the Ford Motor Company, who left in 1929 only to return to the North West thirty years later and chose, rather symbolically, a Merseyside location. Present employment in Trafford Park's 200 or so factories is over 50,000; the leading industries include engineering (especially electrical machinery), foodstuffs and chemicals. The M62 has helped to ease the congested road access and the estate will continue to provide jobs for about 10 per cent of the conurbation's workers. But as it passes the seventieth anniversary of its inception Trafford Park may be losing its attraction for some industries, to whom a virgin site nearer Merseyside may appear to be a better proposition.

Other departures from the old location pattern were initiated in the 1930s, generally taking the form of dispersal from inner Manchester. But there was only one large planned development on the scale of Liverpool's industrial estates—at Wythenshawe, where Manchester Corporation built a large housing estate for its overspill population. More than 400 acres were set aside for industry, and present employment approaches 20,000. The industries are typically light and clean, in contrast to many of those in Trafford Park, and include electrical apparatus, clothing, plastics, food and drugs. Since the Second World War other smaller industrial estates have been established in various of Manchester's satellite towns, generally as an attempt on the part of the local authority to attract replacement industries. Despite the volume of overspill, and the shortage of industrial land in Manchester, there has been little co-ordination of population and employment dispersal around the city. This has meant that many people moving to overspill estates have retained their jobs in Manchester, their journeys to work adding to congestion on an already inadequate road system.

The results of the South-East Lancashire and North-East Cheshire (SELNEC) Transportation Study can be expected to tell much about the likely future development of this sub-region. Their latest estimates for the 1965-81 period are that population will rise, but lower activity rates are expected to reduce total employment by about 50,000; the loss in the manufacturing sector is put at 35,000. Estimates made for individual areas show Manchester and Salford losing 30,000 industrial jobs between them, continuing the present trends, with growth concentrated in a relatively small number of places, including Bolton, Oldham, Heywood, Middleton and some of the Cheshire towns.[4]

In general, the future expansion of manufacturing industry is likely to be on the periphery, with the emphasis remaining on the southern part of the conurbation. But the northern part can be expected to gain from the completion of the Lancashire–Yorkshire motorway, which runs from the existing stretch of the M62 at Worsley through what is left of the open land south of Bolton, Bury and Rochdale. Sites capable of industrial development near the motorway access points are already attracting interest, and new employment in this area would help the local employment situation, particularly in Rochdale and its small eastern neighbours.

The industrial future of Greater Manchester is very much bound up with regional planning strategy and the implementation of the Board of Trade's industrial-location policy. At present the sub-region is rather in the shadow of the Merseyside Development Area. But as the remaining sites in and around Merseyside are taken up the pressure for development can be expected to shift eastwards. The critical question is whether this will lead to accelerated growth in the Manchester area, or whether major urban expansion in south-central Lancashire will become the focus for new industrial development.[5]

II   Merseyside

About 1·5 million people live in the Merseyside sub-region, including the cities of Liverpool, Bootle and Birkenhead, and extending inland to Widnes and Runcorn. The Mersey estuary is the North West's natural trading outlet, and Liverpool is the second port in Britain in terms of tonnage handled. The rise of the port started well before the Industrial Revolution; trade with the West Indies brought the first sugar to Merseyside for refining in the middle of the seventeenth century, and other industries soon grew up to process imported raw materials. The growth of the Lancashire cotton industry found Liverpool perfectly placed to deal with the trade in raw cotton and the export of finished cloth, and as port activities expanded an important shipbuilding and ship-repairing industry grew up in Birkenhead.

But the depression of the 1930s exposed a basic weakness in Merseyside's economic structure. The docks and port-based industries were seriously affected by the contraction in world trade, and the area had few of the more prosperous engineering and metal industries to provide an element of stability. By 1932 Merseyside's unemployment had risen to almost 30 per cent, and in 1939, when the national figure had fallen to under 10 per cent, the Merseyside rate was still almost 20 per cent. For about five years at least 40 per cent of those employed in shipping or shipbuilding were out of work.

The seriousness of the local employment situation led the City of Liverpool to take action in an attempt to diversify the economy. An Act of Parliament in 1936 enabled Liverpool to acquire land, build factories and offer loans to attract new firms to the area, the only place given similar powers being Jarrow. This resulted in the large industrial estates at Aintree and Speke, to which the one at Kirkby was added later. The war assisted the process of diversification; in 1930 shipping, shipbuilding, transport and distribution had accounted for half the total jobs in the sub-region, but by 1947 this had been reduced to about one-third, while employment in engineering and metals increased from less than 23,000 to a little more than 43,000.[6] But a high degree of dependence on the port and associated industries remained, accompanied by above-average unemployment, and it became clear that outside help was needed to tackle these problems.

In 1949 the Merseyside Development Area was established, and the sub-region has been on the list of assisted areas ever since.

Subsidies have certainly helped Merseyside to attract new manufacturing concerns. The Department of Economic Affairs has estimated that new industry provided over 31,000 new jobs between 1953 and 1963, mostly in the food, engineering and vehicle groups, but against this was a loss of 13,100 in indigenous industry, much of it in ship-building.[7] Between 1953 and 1959 there was an overall increase of 21,000, largely from local expansion; but from 1959 to 1963 there was a net loss of 3,000 despite the massive introduction of new industry from outside, including Ford and Vauxhall. Since 1963 the build-up of the motor industry has accounted for more new jobs than firms subsequently diverted to Merseyside, and considerably more than other existing industry.

Just how successful has government policy been in tackling Merseyside's structural and employment problem? P. E. Lloyd[8] has shown that up to 1953 jobs provided by new entrants to the sub-region exceeded those lost by firms leaving, but that between 1954 and 1959 the reverse was true. The firms who left during the second half of the 1950s included some of the newer ones which had set up in the industrial estates and failed to adjust to local conditions. By the end of the 1950s the industrial structure had changed little, and until the arrival of the motor industry the developments which took place with Board of Trade assistance were too small to exert any far-reaching effects on the unemployment problem.

Even the impact of Ford and Vauxhall was not quite what the government intended. The 'snowball' effect, in terms of ancillary industrial development, has been less than was hoped for, and labour for the motor factories came from existing industry rather than from the hard-core unemployed. By 1965 Ford and Vauxhall had taken about 2,500 workers from existing engineering firms and 2,000 from the chemical and food industries, as well as 4,500 from transportation, distribution and construction,[9] and the supply of skilled labour on Merseyside has subsequently become very tight. As has already been mentioned, both the motor companies avoided taking on the long-term unemployed, but their arrival certainly provided a lubricant to inter-industry labour mobility by indirectly creating openings in other activities. The unemployment situation is now improving; the Merseyside figure is now about $1\frac{1}{2}$ times the national rate compared with a ratio of at least 2 during most of the post-war period. After twenty years of government help there are at last signs that Merseyside's employment problem is nearing solution.[10]

A rough indication of the present industrial structure is given by Table 17. This stresses the importance now attached to engineering and electrical goods, particularly on the northern side of the estuary. The electrical branch is especially well-established, with major factories of English Electric, Plessey and BICC among others. The food industries retain a prominent position in North Merseyside, and employ more than engineering south of the estuary; leading firms include Tate & Lyle, Huntley & Palmer, Bibby, Kraft, Cadbury, Van den Bergh & Jurgens (Stork Margarine) and Birds Eye. Most of the shipbuilding and marine engineering is accounted for by Cammell Laird at Birkenhead, and to the south are the big chemicals complexes

Table 17

THE INDUSTRIAL STRUCTURE OF MERSEYSIDE 1966

Industry	Northern part	Southern part	Runcorn/ Widnes	Sub-regional total
Engineering and electrical	58,500	5,700	3,500	67,700
Food, drink and tobacco	39,000	9,300	1,400	49,700
Chemicals etc	12,300	16,200	13,700	42,200
Vehicles	16,100	8,700	—	24,800
Shipbuilding	5,400	10,100	—	15,500
Other manufacturing	64,100	14,300	6,700	85,100
Total	195,400	64,300	25,300	285,000

Source: Ministry of Labour.

in the Bebbington–Bromborough area (soaps, detergents, edible oils and fats) and Ellesmere Port (petro-chemicals). Runcorn and Widnes, with their big ICI plants, are still very dependent on the heavy-chemicals industry. The northern part of the conurbation has much more industrial variety than the southern part, as the large number of employees in the other-manufacturing category indicates. The 1966 figures underestimate the present employment in vehicles, which now exceeds 30,000 almost all of which is concentrated on the eastern fringe of the conurbation.

The restructuring of Merseyside industry since the 1930s has been accompanied by important changes in industrial location. Originally most manufacturing was near the docks, where the raw material arrived, or in and around the centre of Liverpool, but most recent growth has been on the periphery. This dispersal has been permitted by the development of firms with less reliance on bulky imported materials, but even those needing a waterside site have been forced up the estuary. The trend started with the industrial estates at Aintree, Speke and Kirkby, which now provide almost one in five of Merseyside industrial jobs,[11] and continued after the war as the estates filled up and other peripheral sites were found. The recent industrial growth at Winsford, and the Runcorn and Skelmersdale New Towns, associated with Liverpool overspill, represent a second stage of more distant dispersal. How far this trend continues is dependent on many things, including which of a number of alternative strategies the city and region chooses as a basis for future economic and land-use planning.[12]

The main reason for industrial dispersal has been shortage of land within the conurbation. This has been one of Merseyside's major post-war problems. The three big industrial estates are virtually full, though there is scope for their extension, and the speed with which sites on the Board of Trade's estate at Knowsley have been taken up is indicative of the continuing scarcity of land. However, the allocation of additional areas for industrial development is a possibility, and in the long run extensive plots could become available as backland to the docks is redeveloped.

Despite the dispersal of industry, the docks remain of vital importance to Merseyside. As well as the Port of Liverpool at the mouth of the Mersey, there are docks at Birkenhead, Garston and Bromborough, and the Ship Canal, which comes under the Port of Manchester, begins at Eastham. A £35,000,000 extension to the northern end of Liverpool docks will be completed in 1971, with large marshalling yards to cope with the growing transportation of goods by container. This, together with modernisation of existing facilities, improvement in road communication with the docks, and hopefully a better labour situation following decasualisation, should ensure the port's continuing importance to the regional and national economy.

The industrial future of Merseyside in 1969 looks better than it has done for a long time. The persistence of unemployment a little above average is now being seen more as a reflection of Merseyside's distinctive social character than as an indication of serious weaknesses in the sub-regional economy. Nevertheless, the removal of development-area status in the near future is unlikely, though certainly not out of the question; even if it could be conclusively shown that the employment problem had been solved for good, the political repercussions of de-scheduling would be difficult for any government to face. The general industrial performance of Merseyside in recent years has been relatively good, and the structure of employment now compares very favourably with most other parts of the region. As has been suggested in previous chapters, the recent growth must be partly attributed to economic attractions other than government subsidies. What has been observed is encouraging, but it is still perhaps too early to claim that a viable industrial sub-region with an adequate built-in growth capacity has yet been created.

It must be faced that despite the evident success of newcomers like Ford and Vauxhall, other firms have not found Merseyside to their liking. Studies of the birth and death of industrial establishments have shown generally higher survival rates on the fringe as compared with the inner industrial areas, but with a high turnover of small and medium-sized plants at Kirkby making it look less successful than the other industrial estates.[13] Local interests are quick to suggest that in almost every case the reasons for factory closure did not include dissatisfaction with Merseyside as an industrial location,[14] but the fact remains that several major concerns, some relatively new, have not been able to stay in business. There is evidence that even the peripheral industrial areas have their drawbacks; one newcomer from the South states that 'the [Kirkby] industrial estate is aesthetically of low standard, the internal roads are inadequate and public transport facilities to the nearby residential areas [are] poor', and sees decreased efficiency and increased costs resulting from its move.[15] With the social-planning failures in the nearby housing estate, Kirkby as a whole stands as a depressing reminder of some of the worst mistakes of post-war planning in Britain.

It has been recently estimated, in connection with the Merseyside Area Landuse Transportation Study (MALTS) that manufacturing employment in the sub-region will increase by about 45,000 up to 1991.[16] This is of course dependent on the continuing efficiency and competitiveness of existing industry, as well as on the ability of the area to attract more new development. With or without subsidies, this sub-region is probably the best location in the North West for many industries, but it must be remembered that for firms sent in by the Board of Trade, Merseyside is at best a second choice. If existing newcomers and those which follow are to thrive, every effort must be made to prevent the difficulties some have found in Kirkby and elsewhere, and to provide conditions comparable with those in the more prosperous regions of Britain.

III Central Lancashire

This sub-region, as defined at the end of the previous chapter, readily divides into two on general geographical grounds as well as in terms of economic health. In the South-Central section, with most of the active coalfield, some of the region's worst socio-economic conditions are found, but there are considerable variations in industrial health. The North-Central division, including Preston, Leyland and Chorley, looks little better than the Pennine-fringe areas in the industrial dimension, with large losses in some activities offsetting growth in others.

South-Central Lancashire

This area contains a population of 600,000 living in St Helens, Wigan, Leigh and Warrington, in a mass of smaller industrial communities, and in Skelmersdale New Town. Its scattered and confused pattern of settlement provides a discontinuous urban connection between the edges of the two great conurbations.

Economic development has been closely connected with the exploitation of the south-western part of the Lancashire coalfield. At first the coal was exported, but the improvement of communications brought coal-using industries in, and by the end of the eighteenth century St Helens had metal refining, glass and chemical works. In the nineteenth century the westward movement of the cotton industry reached the Wigan area. The growing railway system and the needs of the coalfield led to the setting up of big railway works at Horwich and Newton-le-Willows; and to the south Warrington, close to the coalfield, the textile districts and the chemical towns, developed a variety of industries.

For the past fifty years the degree of specialisation in South-Central Lancashire has been a major regional problem. At the end of the 1920s coal mining and textiles accounted for almost 90 per cent of industrial employment in the Leigh area and 70 per cent around Wigan, and after the Second World War these proportions were still as high as two-thirds and one-half respectively.[17] Because the mills were relatively new and modern, contraction in textiles has been less serious than in many other parts of the region, but its effect has been exacerbated by heavy losses of employment in mining and railway engineering.

The problems of the mining areas were officially recognised in 1946 with the creation of the South Lancashire Development Area. It has been estimated that the fifteen years of government assistance brought about forty-five new factories employing 8,000 workers.[18] The most important developments included those of Heinz at Kitt Green, Turner Asbestos at Hindley Green, and Reed Corrugated Cases at Goose

Green. All these are on the edge of Wigan, which helps to explain its reasonably satisfactory industrial position compared with other nearby towns. The area was de-scheduled in 1960, and the growth of new industry has subsequently slowed down.[19]

At present South-Central Lancashire has three major industrial growth points, St Helens, Skelmersdale and Warrington. St Helens gained considerably from its rather fortunate inclusion in the old South Lancashire Development Area, it has its highly successful glass industry, and as part of the Merseyside Development Area it is now a very attractive location. Since its first factory went into production in 1964, Skelmersdale New Town has completed 1·5 million sq ft of industrial building employing almost 4,000 people, and a further 1 million are under construction or at the design stage.[20] Full development-area grants have helped to attract major projects by such firms as Dunlop, Vick International, Union Carbide, RCA and Courtaulds. Warrington's growth is more potential than realised, being tied up with the possibility of planned urban expansion at this focal point of regional communications (see next chapter).

The local economy has diversified considerably in recent years. Both glass manufacturing and the engineering and electrical industries now employ more than either textiles or mining. With the M6 and other planned road improvements, many parts of the area look attractive for industrial development, and even less fortunate communities, like Hindley where unemployment has reached 7 per cent at times, are within commuting distance of growth points. The economic problems of South-Central Lancashire should now be near solution. What will take much longer is its environmental rehabilitation; the area has serious derelict-land problems, and some of the worst housing and lowest affluence levels in the North West.

North-Central Lancashire

The northern part of Central Lancashire has a population of about 300,000. The largest town, Preston, was an important cotton-manufacturing centre in the nineteenth century, as well as a port for Lancashire coal and cotton goods and incoming raw materials. Diversification in Preston has been an effortless process compared with most other places in which cotton was important. It has always had other industries, including some closely tied to the port, and its general situation with good communications has been more attractive to new firms than the valleys to the east. In addition, the steady build-up of employment at Leyland Motors has provided many jobs for men within easy reach of Preston. But even so, industrial employment has dropped by about 2,500 since the early 1950s, though there are 10,000 additional jobs in the service sector. Increases in engineering and vehicles have been unable to compensate for the effect of closures in cotton, which recently included the large Tulketh Mill equipped with modern machinery.

In the Chorley area the situation has been far less satisfactory. At the beginning of the 1950s there were still 9,000 working in textiles, representing one in three of all the employed, and about 1,000 in mining; since then over 4,000 jobs in the mills have been lost, and the last colliery closed in 1967. Despite conditions as serious as in many parts of South-Central Lancashire, Chorley was excluded from the former development area, and very little replacement industry has been attracted. Bamber Bridge, south of Preston, has also suffered difficulties arising from extreme specialisation in textiles.

At present, vehicle manufacturing is the leading employer in North-Central Lancashire as a whole, with about one-third of the industrial workers compared with a quarter in textiles. Dependence on the mills has been reduced, but it has been replaced by dependence on a relatively small number of big firms. About one-fifth of all jobs (not only industrial) are provided by six employers: the British Aircraft Corporation, the English Electric locomotive works and Courtaulds man-made fibre plant in Preston, an ordnance factory making explosives near Chorley, the Atomic Energy Establishment at Salwick near Preston, and Leyland Motors. At present they provide a solid base for local employment, but they are, in various ways, more than usually reliant for their long-term security on government policy.[21]

The future economic development of this area will be determined by the outcome of the proposal for a new city in central Lancashire, discussed in the next chapter. Without such a major infusion of new growth it is difficult to see any rapid industrial expansion taking place here.

IV   North-East Lancashire

It is in parts of North-East Lancashire that the economic problems of the region as a whole are to be found in their most extreme form. The upper Calder, Darwen and Rossendale valleys are generally more isolated from the growth points of the present day than are the other textile towns, and some of the old intensive industrial specialisation still remains. Part of the sub-region has the doubtful distinction of being the only section of the textile districts to have been a development area, and since it lost this status in 1960 it has persistently been towards the darker end of the 'grey' areas spectrum. With a population of a little less than 0·5 million, the future of North-East Lancashire is a matter of great concern. What happens here can almost be regarded as the ultimate test of the feasibility of economic revival for areas with a similar industrial history and location.

The Calder–Darwen and Rossendale valleys are quite separate geographical entities. Almost nine-tenths of the total population is in the Calder–Darwen valley, centred on Blackburn and Burnley; the small towns squeezed into the Rossendale valley house just over 50,000.

Blackburn–Burnley

The row of towns which extend from Blackburn to Colne forms what used to be the great weaving belt of the Lancashire cotton industry. Modern industry began in the 1820s with the introduction of the power loom, and the cotton trade expanded rapidly with the assistance of local supplies of coal. Most of the other industrial development which took place during the nineteenth century was connected with textiles; calico printing became very important in Accrington and was largely responsible for the beginnings of paper manufacturing here and in Darwen and Burnley, a textile finishing trade emerged with chemical works to supply the dyes, and in the larger towns textile-machinery manufacturing grew up.

With its high degree of specialisation and the close linkages between textiles and other activities, North-East Lancashire was particularly vulnerable when the decline of cotton manufacturing came. Between 1929 and 1939 employment in textiles was reduced from almost 150,000—over two-thirds of the insured population—to less than 100,000.[22] As people started moving out of the cotton towns the population of the Calder–Darwen valley fell to 440,000 by 1939 compared with a peak of about 520,000 just before the First World War; today's figure is about 420,000. Wartime concentration and the collapse of the brief post-war textiles boom brought further contraction. In the 1930s it had been the coarse-weaving area centred on Blackburn which suffered most, but this time it was the fine-cloth towns at the eastern end of the valley. The loss of about 35,000 jobs in textiles between 1953 and 1967 left barely 45,000 in the whole of North-East Lancashire, less than one-third of the peak figure half a century ago. The total employed population now stands at just over 200,000, having dropped by 10,000 since the early 1950s.

The loss of something like 100,000 jobs in textiles in forty years clearly created a vast employment vacuum, but the industrial diversification of North-East Lancashire has been totally inadequate to produce the kind of economic readjustment needed to stabilise population, and it has been unplanned to the extent of being almost entirely fortuitous in its impact.

During the 1930s little new industry could be expected. Of about fifty new projects, only three were of any real size: an ordnance factory, Philips electric lamp works in Blackburn and the Prestige kitchenware plant in Burnley. Many of the remainder were small developments in footwear, clothing or fancy goods, generally in vacated mills, but there was also some diversification of existing industry, for example from textile engineering into domestic appliances and from wallpaper into paints. The war brought some dispersal of stategic activities to North-East Lancashire, including Joseph Lucas who moved into Burnley in 1941, and now employ more than 4,000 people in their area factories. A number of others remained when the war ended, and engineering employment was 10,000 above the pre-war figure in 1947.[24]

During the post-war textile boom little thought was given to diversification, and few new firms came in, but the subsequent collapse of the cotton trade and the expectation of serious unemployment led to the creation of the North-East Lancashire Development Area in 1953, covering the fine-weaving area of Burnley, Padiham, Nelson and Colne. Government assistance continued until 1960, but its impact was not very great when related to the extent of the problems caused by mill closures. Ten firms moved into North-East Lancashire and their present combined employment is still only about 5,600.[25] Only three of the new projects were large ones: Mullard at Simonstone near Padiham, and Belling and Michelin at Heasandford, Burnley. There was some locally-initiated development and abandoned mills continued to be converted,[26] but seven years of development-area status saw employment in all the engineering, electrical, vehicle and metal industries rise by only about 7,000, while 17,000 jobs were lost in textiles. Manufacturing employment as a whole went down by 13,000. High unemployment was avoided, but only by large-scale outward population migration. If extensive diversification was an aim of government policy, it was certainly not achieved; in 1960 half the industrial jobs and almost one-third of all jobs were still provided by the mills.

The cotton industry reorganisation scheme of 1959 was paradoxically followed almost immediately by the removal of development-area status in North-East Lancashire, as the 1960 Local Employment Act replaced earlier industrial-location policy. So at a time when the need for new employment became critical as mill closures were accelerated, government financial assistance was taken away. New firms have continued to come into North-East Lancashire, but none employing more than a few hundred workers. Since the 1959 Cotton Industry Act the textile industry in the area has lost a further 17,000 or so jobs; growth in the engineering, electrical, vehicle and metal industries has been less than half this figure. Present industrial employment is down by roughly 4,000 on the 1959 level.

Table 18

THE INDUSTRIAL STRUCTURE OF NORTH-EAST LANCASHIRE 1966

Industry	Blackburn area	Burnley area	Rossendale valley	Sub-regional total
Textiles	17,000	19,300	9,300	45,600
Engineering and electrical	22,100	11,500	1,000	34,600
Clothing, including footwear	3,700	2,100	5,400	11,200
Other manufacturing	24,100	13,000	2,100	39,200
Total	66,900	45,900	17,800	130,600

Source: Ministry of Labour.

The degree of specialisation which still persists is indicated in Table 18. Textiles are still the leading employer, but their share of industrial workers has now been reduced to one-third. The engineering and electrical group has overtaken textiles in the Blackburn area, but it has a long way to go in Burnley. The main engineering activities are textile machinery (employing about 8,000), radio apparatus (mainly Mullard), domestic appliances (Burco, Main Morley and Belling), and components for aircraft and motor vehicles (largely Lucas). The other-manufacturing category includes Prestige, Michelin tyres, the large Walpamur wallpaper and paint factories in Darwen, and about 5,000 employed in food industries.

In the Calder–Darwen valley the traditional specialisation is now greatest in the Burnley area, particularly in Nelson and Colne and it is here that the problems of industrial diversification and environmental rehabilitation are specially serious. By comparison, Blackburn, with its more varied employment, is reasonably prosperous.

The future prosperity of this area is perhaps more dependent on the outcome of regional-planning policy than that of any other part of the North West. It has recently been estimated that manufacturing employment in the whole of North-East Lancashire will fall by a further 20,000 by 1991, given present planning policy, with most of the loss occurring by 1975.[27] The proposed new city for Preston–Leyland–Chorley could stimulate growth in the Blackburn area, but might accelerate decline in the more isolated Calder valley, which is not very attractive as a location for new industry. Even with government financial inducements, and a serious attempt to integrate North-East Lancashire with some major development to the west, the economic regeneration of some towns would be difficult and costly. Whether such a course is feasible or indeed desirable is a question reserved for the final chapter.

Rossendale

By most criteria, the Rossendale valley is the most economically deprived part of the North West, as previous chapters have shown. The early industrial growth was based largely on cotton, and the development of the slipper and shoe industry in the latter part of the nineteenth century brought diversification earlier than in most of the other textile districts. At the time it provided a valuable new source of employment, but has generated little local growth in recent years. A specialisation in heavy cloths for industrial purposes and in the cotton-waste trade, less seriously affected by foreign competition than most other branches, has protected the Rossendale textile industry to some extent, but many mills have been closed and to add to the problems, there has been an almost complete lack of replacement industry. The economy has thus stagnated, and since the beginning of the 1930s Bacup, Haslingden and Rawtenstall have lost almost one-fifth of their population, amounting to about 12,000 people.

The present industrial structure (Table 18) shows the mills and footwear factories still accounting for four-fifths of manufacturing employment. This is almost two-thirds of all jobs. The two leading industries have lost 4,000 workers since the beginning of the 1950s, and the only growth of alternative employment has been about 600 jobs in engineering and metal industries. Even generous government subsidies would probably be unlikely to entice much new growth industry into these uninviting valleys.

V   North and West Lancashire

This area is of much less importance industrially than the sub-regions already considered. Employment in manufacturing amounts to only about 70,000, barely one-twentieth of the region's total. The

industry that does exist is concentrated very largely in the string of
coastal towns from Southport to Barrow.

The Lancashire Coast and North Lancashire

The Lancashire coast subdivision (Va in Fig 34) comprises the
Fylde and the Southport–Ormskirk lowland. The larger towns
originated as resorts and places of retirement, and industry developed
almost as an afterthought. In Southport, Lytham St Anne's and Blackpool, employment is still dominated by the service sector. Southport
is close enough to Merseyside not to need much local employment,
and what there is falls into the light engineering and consumer goods
categories typical of seaside towns. At Lytham St Anne's recent
developments, particularly in the aircraft industry, have given the town
one of the fastest employment growth rates in the region. Blackpool
has a good range of light industry, but its employment position is
closely tied up with the chequered history of the former aircraft
factory at Squires Gate which provided 11,000 jobs during the war.
The site is still being reoccupied after the closure of the Hawker
concern in 1957 put 4,250 out of work. Of the other towns, Ormskirk
has food and agricultural-machinery industries, Kirkham is a small
mill town, and Fleetwood has its harbour, its fishing fleet, varied small-
scale manufacturing, and an ICI chemical plant nearby.

The main problem of the coastal towns in recent years has been
unemployment at a level somewhat above the regional average.[28]
Seasonal shortages of work are to be expected at seaside resorts, but
some of the figures have been high enough to cause alarm, particularly
in Fleetwood where 8 per cent has been recorded. There has been
some talk of 'grey' area status and government assistance for the Fylde,
but the number of jobs needed is relatively small.

Most industry in North Lancashire is around Lancaster and Morecambe. Lancaster's industrial development started early, with the
processing of materials imported from the West Indies, to which was
added cotton manufacturing and later the production of oilcloth and
linoleum. This latter activity, now including vinyl-coated materials, is
the leading employer today, but the town retains a wide variety of
industries. Across the Lune estuary at Heysham are the Shell refinery
and an ICI agricultural-chemicals plant, and the site chosen for a
major nuclear power station. The Lancaster and Morecambe councils
have co-operated in developing a ninety-acre industrial estate at White
Lund, in an attempt to attract some new employment, but except for
the J. & P. Jacobs' clothing factory, expected to employ 500, little

interest has been shown in this site. How far the M6 and Lancaster's university may stimulate industrial development remains to be seen.

Furness

Most of the 22,000 industrial jobs in this subdivision are in or around Barrow-in-Furness. The fact that for most of the 1960s Furness has been the only part of the North West other than Merseyside to have development-area status gives this rather remote corner of Lancashire special importance.

Industrial development began with the opening of the Furness Railway in 1846, which gave Barrow a connection with the growing national network. Shipyards and iron and steel works were soon set up, with the railway company as the leading entrepreneur, and Barrow expanded rapidly as a heavy-industrial town and thriving port. In 1897 the leading shipyard was taken over by the firm which later became Vickers Armstrong, and as shipbuilding expanded Vickers gradually took on the paternalistic role formerly held by the railway company, in what was always very much an industrial company town.[29]

The vulnerability of the one-sided industrial structure showed up in the depression of the inter-war years.[30] Trouble came early in shipbuilding and to add to the town's difficulties the Furness Railway engineering works was closed when the company was taken over by LMS; population began to move away, and at present it is 10,000 below the 1921 peak of 74,000.

Since the war continuing efforts have been made to attract new industry to reduce the dependence on Vickers and eliminate relatively high female unemployment. In the late 1940s and the 1950s a number of new firms came in, often with Board of Trade guidance though not financial support. These included the Lister spinning concern, British Cellophane, the Glaxo antibiotic factory at Ulverston, and some clothing industries. Female labour was an important location factor in almost every case. In 1963 the closure of Barrow Ironworks raised unemployment in Furness temporarily to almost 6 per cent, and brought development-district status. This helped the expansion of some local activities but brought no immediate benefits in terms of new firms.[31] Recently the situation has looked more encouraging however, with the big new Bowater-Scott paper plant and Ferranti taking a Board of Trade advance factory, together with ambitious expansion planned by Lister.[32]

But extreme specialisation still remains. Vickers employ about

N

14,000 (7,500 in the shipyard and 6,500 in engineering)—almost two-thirds of all industrial workers. With one plant in a nationally declining industry and heavily dependent on government orders occupying such a dominant position, the local economy must continue to be insecure. The town has the advantage of a good female labour supply and under-used docking facilities, and long-overdue road improvements could improve its accessibility, but the enthusiasm of the railway company in the early days probably pushed Barrow into an economic role beyond that which its location justified. Post-war development has been largely a holding operation, and responsibility for the continued preservation of the *status quo* rests firmly with Vickers and the Board of Trade.

VI   Central Cheshire and the Peak District

To the south and south-east of the major Merseyside–Manchester industrial belt is the largely rural area of central Cheshire and the north-western Derbyshire uplands. Its scattered industrial towns together employ about 80,000 manufacturing workers.

In the east is the series of old textile towns which grew up in the Peak District valleys or at the edge of the plain where streams emerged from the hills. Glossop, New Mills, Hayfield and Chapel-en-le-Frith were involved in the early water-power phase of the cotton industry, but distance from the coalfield as steam power was introduced slowed down their growth. Gradually new industries developed, and the Ferodo factory at Chapel shows that a successful business with a national market can operate quite satisfactorily near the heart of the Peak District.

To the south, Macclesfield and Congleton grew up on the silk industry, and were locations for some of Britain's first water-powered textile mills. Macclesfield, like Glossop and New Mills, is now just within the Manchester commuter belt, and has attracted important new industries, particularly pharmaceuticals. As in Congleton, silk is no longer of any great importance, and other textiles and clothing industries have moved into many of the mills.

Most of the towns of mid-Cheshire owed their initial growth to the salt industry which survives in varied forms in Northwich, Winsford, Middlewich and Sandbach. Chemical manufacturing is still of local importance, as was shown in Chapter 2, but mid-Cheshire is now over-shadowed by the Ship Canal sites to the north. The effects of mining subsidence are clearly evident in the water-filled hollows or 'flashes', and in the strange angle of many of the buildings; the dereliction of land is a major problem.[33] In the Chester area, two major sources of industrial employment have grown up westwards in recent years, the Shotton steelworks and the Hawker Siddeley aircraft factory at Broughton, supplementing what is available within the city, but the service sector is far more important than manufacturing in Chester itself.

The major growth point in Central Cheshire is Winsford, the subject of a Town Development Act expansion scheme to take Liverpool overspill. Winsford's population has risen from less than 13,000 at the start of the 1960s to about 20,000 at present, and the latest plan involves an increase to 70,000 by 1986,[34] employment in manufacturing is expected to rise from about 4,000 to 16,000. With full development-area assistance, and barely ninety minutes from Birmingham by motorway, Winsford is proving to be a very attractive location for industry, and the obvious location for almost any major new development in mid-Cheshire. The growth generated here should ultimately spread out to neighbouring towns, at present in the economic shadow of Winsford.

At Crewe, to the south, employment has been fairly stable since the war. Growth at Rolls-Royce and elsewhere has been offset by losses at the railway works. Laid out in the 1840s as a company town beside the works, Crewe was for long entirely dependent on one industry with almost all its workers male, but it is now more diversified. The long-term possibility of large-scale urban expansion in south Cheshire (discussed in the next chapter) could make Crewe a very important focal point for industrial growth, but at the moment this seems to be some way off.

References to this chapter are on pages 244 to 246.

8

Industrial Development and Regional Planning

THE INCREASING IMPORTANCE attached to regional planning has been one of the most significant trends in the social and economic life of Britain during the 1960s. It arose from the realisation that solving the problems of the country's major regions, both the rapidly expanding ones and those less fortunate, requires more co-ordination of local planning. It was also a recognition of the fact that national problems centred around the rate of economic growth and the balance of payments have a regional component to them. Just as the unfortunate or lagging regions tend to hold back the national growth rate, so the expanding regions, where demand for the factors of production is greater, can act as inflation leaders, forcing up the price of labour and other resources and hence raising production costs. The solution of national problems thus involves the solution of regional ones.

Much controversy surrounds the subject of regional planning in Britain, as befits a movement in its infancy. At the one extreme there are those who oppose any form of planning, retaining a faith that the economy is best left to the free play of market forces. At the other extreme it is held that what passes for regional planning in Britain at the end of the 1960s is only a watered-down and impotent version of the real thing. On more technical matters such as the strategy of metropolitan expansion, the form of new towns and cities, and the stimulation of declining local economies, there is a similar range of views. On top of this is a continuing difficulty in resolving what some see as the conflicting aims of economic planning on the one hand and land-use planning on the other. Many of these issues, and how they are settled, have an important bearing on the future economic development of North West England.

Regional planning and industrial development are interrelated in very obvious ways. The regional planner's decisions about the future distribution of population and use of land will clearly influence the location and performance of industrial activity, and the existing structure, location, mobility and growth potential of the industrial economy act as a major constraint on what the planners may propose as a realistic strategy. An important purpose of regional planning is to reconcile conflicting economic and social objectives in a way which will optimise the well-being of the community at large. The first tentative steps in this direction in North West England are of special interest. How one of the world's first great specialised industrial regions attempts to complete its economic readjustment, while at the same time creating a worthwhile environment for its growing population, has significance well beyond the limits of the North West.

The Regional Problems

All the major problems facing the North West are of a specifically industrial nature, or closely connected with industry through their origin or solution. The first of the industrial problems relates to the nature of the regional economy as a whole. Productivity and incomes are below the national average, largely as a result of the numbers employed in textiles and clothing, with their relatively low output per worker and low wages. A structural predisposition towards a slow rate of economic growth still exists, despite the reduced importance of the declining industries (in particular textiles) and the development of new activities. If the regional growth rate is to be improved, further structural alteration is required. There must be a continuing shift of manpower and other resources into industries with greater output, higher wages, and better growth potential, and with good prospects of success in export markets. New firms of this kind have come to the region in recent years and existing ones have expanded, but more are needed, and they have to be sited and housed where they can function efficiently—too much of the region's industry faces the 1970s in locations and premises more suited to the needs of the 1870s. The complete economic revival of the North West, if it can be achieved, is dependent on the creation of an environment and service infrastructure conducive to a level of industrial efficiency and a rate of growth comparable with that of the more prosperous regions of Britain.

Secondly, there is the sub-regional industrial problem. In earlier chapters great emphasis was placed on variations within the North West in the structure and performance of the industrial economy. This was summarised in the discussion of the geography of economic health, in which it was made clear that many of the areas with industrial

problems are also socially deprived in various ways. Evening out
these sub-regional variations in prosperity is generally considered
to be a major planning objective, on both economic and social
grounds.

Industrial location is an important thread connecting these two
basic problems. The regeneration and restructuring of a region's
economy implies changes in location, which in its turn means the
selection of some sub-regions for development in preference to others;
the sub-regional allocation of industry inherited from the past is
not necessarily the one best suited to achieve regional-planning
objectives.

But industrial location and development cannot be considered in
isolation. In a regional-planning context they are inseparably bound
up with the future distribution of population. The number of people
in the North West is increasing steadily, and the problem of deciding
where they shall live has tended to dominate planning in recent years.
The latest population projection by the North West Economic
Planning Council[1] is a rise of 750,000 between 1964 and 1981. This
involves about 175,000 new households, and to the dwellings they will
require must be added the needs of people at present in shared
accommodation, as well as the replacement of sub-standard housing.
The region still has an enormous slum-clearance problem, about
400,000 houses, or a fifth of the nation's slums at the present time,
and many others which cannot be regarded as acceptable for much
longer. The worst conditions are in the cores of the two conurbations,
where urban renewal will continue to generate big overspill problems.
All this means finding room for and building a further 550,000 dwellings between 1968 and 1981, according to the planning council's
estimates.

The housing problem is only one part of the general need for
environmental improvement in most parts of the industrial North West.
By present-day standards the old cotton-manufacturing and mining
towns are obsolete as urban structures, as well as having many
domestic, commercial and industrial buildings unsuitable for their
present use. Redevelopment of central areas and improvement of the
road system are the top priorities; along with this is the need to
remove the air of drabness and decay which pervades so many of the
older industrial towns, as it is thought to repel new industry and
stimulate emigration of population in search of new jobs in a better
environment.

The reclamation of derelict land is an important part of environmental rehabilitation. The worst problems are in the Cheshire saltfield

with its subsidence, the chemical-manufacturing towns with their vast areas of waste tips, and coalmining areas with their familiar spoil heaps. Wigan Pier may be a Music Hall joke, but the great conical tip heaps of the 'Wigan Alps' are an unfortunate reality. There are 10,000 acres of derelict land in the industrial parts of the region; such an area could hold 100,000 houses at the fairly low density of ten to the acre, or provide space for factories employing 300,000 people assuming thirty jobs to the acre as a reasonable present-day expectation for the region. Not all the derelict areas are necessarily suitable for development, but these figures help to stress the seriousness of having land sterilised in this way.

The improvement of communications is another major regional problem. External connections are being made more efficient by the motorways (M6 and M62), by the electrification of railways to the south, by freightliner terminals, and by the development of container facilities along with the general modernisation of the docks. But internal movement between the main industrial areas is still archaic. This is particularly true of the Manchester–Merseyside route, where traffic can take $1\frac{1}{2}$ hours to grind along the East Lancashire Road, while in the United States comparable cities would be connected by a properly designed multi-lane freeway which could be travelled in half the time. There are plans for inter-city motorway connections, of course, but these and the necessary feeders to the docks are required urgently. Major new roads are also needed if the relative isolation of Furness and parts of north-east Lancashire is to be reduced.

Other problems also exist, relating to such matters as water supply, air pollution, the disposal of waste and industrial effluence, the development of recreational facilities, and the preservation of amenities such as attractive countryside. But it is future population distribution, environmental renewal and the development of efficient communications which are the major spheres of action most closely and immediately related to problems of the industrial economy.

Towards a Regional Planning Strategy

The Town and Country Planning Act of 1947 made planning essentially a local matter, in the hands of a great many separate bodies. Two complete counties, part of a third, and numerous county boroughs, gave the North West twenty-four independent planning authorities, preoccupied with their own internal problems within boundaries which often had no geographical or economic significance. Each authority was made responsible only to the national government in the form of the Ministry of Town and Country Planning, now the Ministry of Housing and Local Government. With overall control of planning in places with less than county-borough status, the county councils of Lancashire and Cheshire have been able to perform a co-ordinating function over fairly large areas. But responsibility for taking a truly regional view has been left to the central government in London, whose tentative commitment to regional planning is a fairly recent innovation.

It is not surprising, then, that most post-war planning has been of a largely piecemeal and unco-ordinated nature. The approach to urban renewal and population distribution has been largely pragmatic, with room for overspill found as and when required. In Liverpool's case people have been rehoused within the city limits, in major developments round the fringe, and more recently in new towns, while Manchester has arranged for the reception of varying numbers in about thirty neighbouring towns. Urban sprawl has been restricted by green belts, which, like the overspill schemes, have kept immediate problems at bay. But green belts tend to fossilise existing urban forms and their recreational function can be greatly exaggerated; their role in planning is now seriously open to question. In short, most of what has happened has been the result of short-term expediency and conventional solutions rather than part of an imaginative long-term regional-planning strategy.

Economic problems associated with local structural weaknesses and unemployment have been viewed in almost complete isolation from other planning matters. The Board of Trade's industrial-location policy has often been in open conflict with the planning policy of local authorities, as approved by the Ministry of Housing and Local Government. The refusal of IDCs at Winsford while the town was taking Manchester overspill in the early 1960s[2] is one of a number of instances which could be cited. The difficulty experienced by many towns outside the development areas in trying to attract new industry to stabilise population has been mentioned in a previous chapter.

By the early part of the 1960s it was becoming clear that a regional approach to planning in Britain was required urgently. The main stimulus came from the need to find room for greater population growth than had originally been expected. In the North West it was obvious that the overspill problems of Manchester and Merseyside could not be dealt with by the proliferation of small schemes (about half those promoted by Manchester to date involve less than 500 dwellings), and more ambitious solutions were sought. The major problem was that of deciding what general strategy urban expansion in the North West should follow. The three basic alternatives were: large scale expansion in south-central Lancashire between the two conurbations, long-range movements of population and employment into northern Lancashire and southern Cheshire, or some relaxation of the green belt around the cities to allow peripheral growth, mainly on the southern side of the two conurbations.[3]

In February 1965 the North West Economic Planning Council came into being. Like those established at the same time in other regions, it was given the task of assisting in the formulation of a regional plan, advising on the steps necessary to implement it, and looking at the regional implication of national economic policies. Along with the council, an economic planning board was set up, consisting of officials of the government departments most closely concerned with planning matters, under a chairman from the Department of Economic Affairs. There was some criticism on grounds that as purely advisory bodies with little financial backing the councils would be useless, but most observers saw the move as a step in the right direction.

Later the same year came the publication of *The North West: A Regional Study*. Prepared by a multi-departmental government research team, this was the first major factual survey of the region and its problems. Using a base date of 1964, it was estimated that by 1981 natural increase would raise the region's population by about 930,000, which a continuation of outward migration would reduce to just under 800,000 on the basis of past trends. The need to improve its housing stock was seen as the region's dominant problem. In reviewing the overall need for land for housing, it was felt that the four major existing proposals under the New Towns Act (Skelmersdale, Runcorn, Warrington and Leyland–Chorley), together with the smaller overspill schemes, would be enough to meet the needs of the two conurbations up to the mid-1970s or even until after 1981 if people continued to move out of the region. But outward pressures from Merseyside and Greater Manchester, in the form of both slum clearance overspill and voluntary migration, could produce a land shortage and in this case a new urban expansion scheme would be needed. The southern Cheshire or northern Staffordshire area was seen as a potential site for a large new town, perhaps taking overspill from Birmingham as well as from the North West, with construction beginning in the late 1970s. Once the future of Leyland–Chorley has been assured it might also be reasonable to think of further development in the north of the region, such as a completely independent urban complex centred on Lancaster. Among other tentative proposals was the possibility of major development on the western side of the Dee estuary, with the construction of a new road-crossing.

The question of further development between the conurbations was considered very briefly. The study took the view that to go much beyond existing new town and expansion schemes would be difficult, though the pressures for development here were recognised, as was the importance of planning the area as a whole. The idea of inducing movement back into the towns north and east of Manchester was rejected, and the statement that it would be unwise to plan for a reversal of well-established trends for people to move away from these towns brought sharp reaction from some local interests.[4]

Although *The North West Study* provided a much-needed survey of the region, it could be criticised from a number of points of view. In particular, it has little to say about the industrial problem areas, apart from references to unemployment. The critical matter of variations from place to place in industrial performance was reviewed only superficially at a broad sub-regional level, and its significance for regional-planning strategy was largely overlooked. A broader criticism made in many quarters was that, although the extent of the regional problems was set down, no clear guidelines for action were offered, and much of the responsibility was left to individual local authorities.[5] A regional plan was still a long way away.

The North West Study was referred to the economic planning council for consideration and in February 1966 the council produced its own preliminary ideas in *An Economic Planning Strategy for the North West Region*, now known as *Strategy I*. They thought it wrong to plan for continued outward migration from the region, and considered the implications of a possible additional population of something like 1 million by 1981. The need for at least two areas for major growth in addition to existing proposals was felt to be urgent, and the council followed *The North West Study* in recommending south Cheshire and north Lancashire. The former area, including Crewe, Sandbach and Nantwich, was seen to have a special attraction for engineering industries, wholesale distribution, and other activities dependent on motorway and fast main-line railway transport. The latter 'might be attractive (for instance) to science-based industries and office development', largely because of clean air, ample space, and good road communications; in both areas proximity to a university was also mentioned as an advantage. Again, the possibility of filling up vacant areas between Manchester and Liverpool was rejected.

The problem posed by the less prosperous parts of the region was not considered in any depth in *Strategy I*. Assurances were given that proposing some areas for major development did not mean that others would stagnate; areas like north-east Lancashire would not be neglected. On the general subject of industrial location, the council favoured a broad sub-regional approach to the problem areas, rather than siting industry in relation to local pockets of unemployment. Stress was placed on locating industry where it was most likely to succeed, but the possibility that such a policy could in fact lead to the neglect of areas like north-east Lancashire, and create great pressure for development between Manchester and Merseyside was not considered.

In June 1968 the council published its second major policy document—*Strategy II: The North West of the 1970s*. This differed considerably from both *Strategy I* and *The North West Study* in its emphasis, placing less stress on the need for room for population growth and more on industrial location and efficiency. In assessing future population, the lower natural-increase and household-formation projection of the Registrar General, and a return to the assumption of continued outward migration, led to the conclusion that the increase up to 1981 might now be no more than 750,000 people. The need to consider large-scale development in south Cheshire and north Lancashire was thus no longer regarded as urgent, though both proposals were retained as long-term possibilities. The council broadly supported the existing New Town strategy, rejecting once again piecemeal development on the edge of the region's older towns, and incursions into the green belt.

It was the attention to industrial matters which made *Strategy II* so important. The major conclusions include the following points:

1 The main influence on industrial location should be where it can operate most efficiently within a broad planning framework. If part of the price for this is longer journeys to work this has to be accepted, and is in any case in line with the trend for increased personal mobility.
2 In order to help parts of the region suffering from problems such as the decline of staple industries and falling employment opportunities, development-area assistance should be given to selected growth points to serve those areas.
3 Government policies should be such as to encourage the replacement of unsuitable and badly sited industrial premises by new ones, in a location where the firm can operate efficiently. At present, this can be prevented by the refusal of an IDC, which means that old location patterns tend to be perpetuated.

4   Transport facilities need to be improved, both to further industrial
    efficiency and to encourage labour mobility. The council put this
    as its first priority for investment in the region, above the housing
    programme which was placed second.

Strategy II thus contains a degree of economic realism which was
lacking in earlier statements, and *Strategy III*, promised for 1970, is
awaited with interest.

Before current policy and its economic implications are evaluated,
the main regional-development proposals may be summarised in a
sketch map (Fig 35). The broad strategy for urban development turns
out to be a compromise between filling-in the area between the
conurbations, and dispersal along the north–south axis of the M6.
The main motorway proposals tend to strengthen the region's existing
cruciform communications pattern, but with stress on east–west movement now that the M6 is completed.

Development during the 1970s will be focused on the four New
Towns. Skelmersdale is already well under way, with a population of
over 16,000 in mid-1968 including 5,000 in development-corporation
houses; the ultimate population will be 90,000, with employment
approaching 40,000. A start has also been made at Runcorn, where
eastward growth from the existing town will raise population from
30,000 to 75,000 by 1981, and ultimately to about 100,000. Both
Runcorn and Skelmersdale are taking population from Merseyside.
Large-scale expansion at Warrington was given ministerial approval
in April 1968, to provide room for further growth along the Merseyside to Manchester axis. About 40,000 people from Greater Manchester
will be rehoused here by 1981, and between now and 1991 the total
population of the Warrington area will have risen by 80,000 to over
200,000. Warrington New Town has some excellent industrial sites,
including Burtonwood Airbase and the ordnance factory at Risley.[6]

The largest of the New Town proposals, in central Lancashire, is
more truly a new city. The history of this scheme goes back to 1951,
when a settlement of 70,000 people from the congested parts of
Manchester, Wigan and Preston was suggested for the Chorley–
Leyland–Preston area in *The Preliminary Plan for Lancashire*. This
was not acted on, but in 1964 it was revived in the form of a proposal
for a new town of 150,000 people. In 1966 the Ministry of Housing
and Local Government appointed consultants to look into the idea,
and they concluded that it was certainly feasible. Their preliminary
sketches of the form the development might take show a new city
extending north from Chorley to take in Leyland and Preston, and

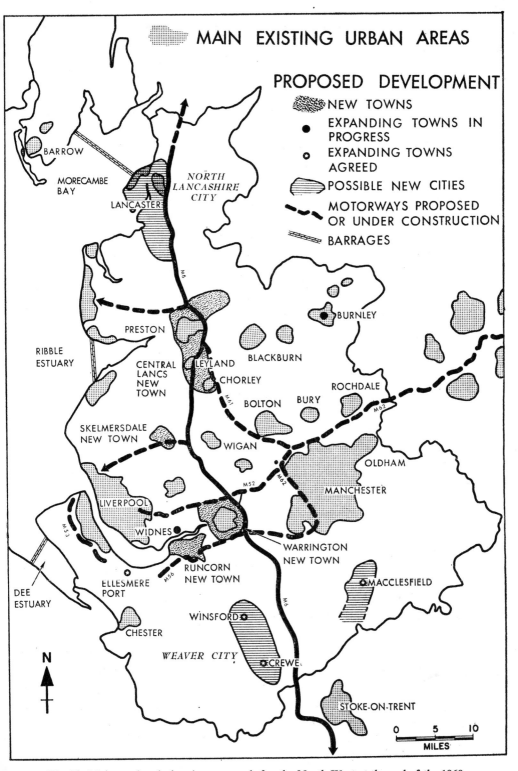

Fig 35. Major regional-planning proposals for the North West at the end of the 1960s.

then bending east up the Ribble valley. The population of the area as a whole could rise from about 250,000 to as much as 500,000 by 1991, with 150,000 coming in from elsewhere and the rest the result of natural increase. Expansion on this scale would require an additional 100,000 or so jobs.[7] The Central Lancashire city was given ministerial approval in December 1968.

Some of the town-expansion schemes are almost comparable in scale with New Towns. Winsford, the largest, will increase its population from 20,000 to 70,000 by 1986, to become central Cheshire's major employment centre with over 30,000 workers. Winsford began by receiving Manchester overspill at the beginning of the 1960s, but now all the intake is from Liverpool, which gives the town the advantage of development-area status. Almost 50,000 people will be rehoused in Winsford by the mid-1980s.[8] Crewe, with an agreement to take 14,000 from Manchester, is the other growth point in the area which some planners think could become a new city along the Weaver valley by the end of the century. Two schemes are shown in Fig 35 on the edge of the Merseyside conurbation—Ellesmere Port, which agreed in 1959 to take 20,000 people from Liverpool, and a more recent proposal of similar size for Widnes. To the south of Manchester a small expansion scheme is underway in Macclesfield, and major growth at Wilmslow is under consideration. Burnley's proposal to take an eventual 16,000 to 18,000 people from the region's conurbations and from Greater London stands as a symbol of the optimism with which north-east Lancashire can still view its future; progress will be watched with interest, not least by those who believe it would be difficult to entice people into the Calder valley from Blackburn, never mind from further afield.

Also shown diagramatically in Fig 35 are three estuary barrages which have been proposed. The Morecambe Bay barrage is the only one to be examined in any detail up to now; a favourable preliminary report commissioned by the government was completed at the beginning of 1967, and a full-scale feasibility study is now under way. As well as providing electric power and helping to relieve Manchester's water supply problem, the damming of Morecambe Bay could lead to a reclamation of land and the creation of new recreational facilities. Improved communications with Barrow-in-Furness via a barrage motorway could also result. This is a long-term proposal, unlikely to be completed until the 1980s if at all, but its impact on the region, especially if it was followed by barrages across the Ribble and Dee, could bring significant changes in the existing pattern of communications, settlement and industry.

An Appraisal of Current Policy

Any regional-planning strategy is bound to be a compromise since it must try to reconcile a mass of conflicting forces in the best interests of society as a whole. On the one hand there are strong economic pressures for development in certain areas, as businessmen seek the most favourable locations for their factories, and builders to try to satisfy people's residential preferences; on the other hand there exist opposing forces, physical, economic and political, which tend to restrict industrial or urban growth in certain directions. The resolution of these conflicts, in the form of a regional plan, must above all be realistic from an economic point of view. The development pattern which would result from allowing the free play of market forces can only be modified for social ends at a cost, and this is a realistic exercise only if society is able, and willing, to bear the cost.

The main regional constraints imposed on large-scale development at present are summarised in Fig 36. The physical restrictions—the existing built-up areas and the uplands—are perhaps the most powerful because they are also economic; a new city could be built in the Peak District or in what is now central Manchester, but only at enormous cost. The institutional constraints are generally more flexible; development on good agricultural land, the green belt, and areas of scenic attraction is restricted only because society says so, though in the case of the National Parks and areas of outstanding natural beauty their relief often acts as a physical-economic restriction as well. Other more local constraints include areas of lowland peat (in particular Chat Moss west of Manchester), derelict land, areas liable to mining subsidence, and the many square miles around Jodrell Bank telescope where development is strictly controlled for scientific reasons.[9]

The map emphasises the narrow range of choice for the location of major new urban development if all three constraints are obeyed. Only two extensive areas are left, central Lancashire, chosen for the Chorley–Leyland–Preston city, and central Cheshire with the Winsford and Crewe schemes and perhaps the future 'Weaver City'. The Skelmersdale, Runcorn and Warrington New Towns have been squeezed in only at the expense of some green belt and good agricultural land. But in general the existing proposals conform well to the major constraining factors.

The main attractive forces operating on industrial and urban development are considered to be the existing areas of relatively rapid economic growth and the major transportation facilities. Directions of the main pressures for development are suggested in Fig 36. The

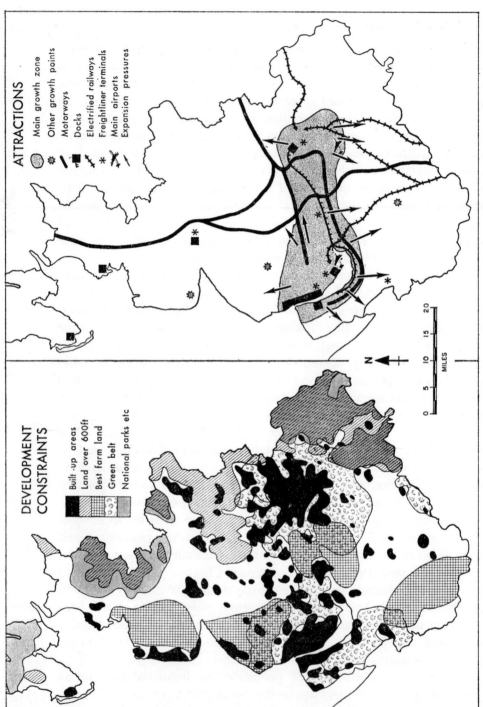

ATTRACTIONS

- Main growth zone
- Other growth points
- Motorways
- Docks
- Electrified railways
- Freightliner terminals
- Main airports
- Expansion pressures

DEVELOPMENT CONSTRAINTS

- Built-up areas
- Land over 600ft
- Best farm land
- Green belt
- National parks etc

N

0 5 10 15 20
MILES

Fig 36. The major factors restricting and promoting large-scale industrial and urban development at the end of the 1960s.

Mersey growth zone is without doubt the most favourable part of the region for industry, and it is here that new economic activity would concentrate in the absence of planning restrictions. The general advantages of the zone have been mentioned a number of times in previous chapters, but the good transport situation and the economies of agglomeration which firms often gain from a location in a major urban-industrial region may be stressed again. The proposed motorways across northern Cheshire and southern Lancashire will add to the importance of this zone as the focus of intra-regional east–west movement. The main expansion pressures generated in the growth zone are for the southward extension of the two conurbations, and for development in the intervening corridor towards the M6. Pressures for northward expansion are not as strong, but the Lancashire–Yorkshire motorway may increase the industrial potential of the area to the north of Manchester.

A comparison between the two maps in Fig 36 shows some of the difficulties facing the regional planner. The opposing constraints and attractions conflict to an extreme extent in the Merseyside to Manchester belt. It is here that the strongest pressures for industrial and urban expansion directly oppose two fervently-upheld institutional restrictions on development—the green belt and the best agricultural land. Up to now the constraints have tended to win the battle in this major regional zone of conflict; blinded by an almost instinctive fear of urban sprawl, the planners have largely failed to see the advantages of development between the two conurbations.

The Runcorn and Warrington New Towns are of course a concession to the pressures for development along the east–west axis; their combined population growth will be about 200,000 by the 1990s. But this certainly does not exhaust the capacity of the area between the conurbations. In 1964 it was estimated that the area might hold a further 0·5 million people by the year 2000, in addition to those accounted for by natural increase and existing overspill schemes.[10] *The North West Study* conceded the possibility of further growth in the area bounded roughly by Skelmersdale and Wigan in the north and the Ship Canal in the south, by 'allowing some further peripheral spread of the two conurbations or by the planned expansion of certain other towns in the area between them which lie near the line of the M6 and have shown that they can support successful industrial growth'. Some very fine industrial sites still exist along the Ship Canal, and the economic planning council in *Strategy II* stressed the need to take advantage of this. Failure to do so means the neglect of one of the region's major economic assets.

o

The problems facing large-scale development along the Merseyside to Manchester belt are considerable. Physical difficulties include the peat mosses of the Mersey valley, mining subsidence, the dereliction of large areas of land, and the scattered and outworn nature of much existing urban development. But the main constraints are institutional, and therefore more flexible. So far the inviolability of green belts and first-class agricultural land has been largely preserved, but they may soon have to give way to the needs of the regional economy, the performance of which is dependent on getting the right industries into the best possible locations. Planning for large-scale industrial and urban growth in this area would certainly not be easy, but there are a number of ways in which it could be done without endangering the environment of existing residents.[11] Indeed, a comprehensive plan for growth could assist in clearing up some of the mess left in the mining districts and in rehabilitating its towns, and if some of the smaller nineteenth-century settlements, with their mass of inferior houses, were eliminated completely they would be no great loss. Before the implementation of further plans for the dispersal of economic activity in the North West, including the Chorley–Leyland–Preston scheme, it would be wise to conduct a full-scale investigation of the development potential of the inter-conurbation belt. On purely economic grounds large-scale expansion here is probably the best long-run strategy. There are indications that an increasing number of planners are now looking in this direction: J. S. Miller, the Manchester city planning officer, has recently proposed the creation of a giant dispersed city extending from the Pennines to the sea through Manchester and Liverpool, with thousands of acres of new housing set in man-made forests on either side of the M6 and huge industrial plants along the new motorways and the Ship Canal.[12] But before such a policy of concentrated development in the Mersey growth zone can effectively replace the present strategy based on population and industrial dispersal, a fundamental reorganisation of local-government structure will probably be needed.

The proposal for a new city in northern Lancashire seems the most questionable of the dispersal ideas. The area's potential has been investigated by Lancashire County Council, who has concluded that up to 100,000 more people could eventually live here, including 65,000 newcomers, probably from the conurbations.[13] There is no doubt that an exciting new city could be created in this very attractive environment, but it is much less certain that industry could be brought in without substantial government subsidy. The joint Lancaster–Morecambe industrial estate has attracted little interest, and the

economic planning council's original references to the growth of
'science-based' industries and office development seem extremely
optimistic. The supposed advantages of clean air, ample space, attractive scenery and the motorway may well be offset by the additional
cost which firms would incur in this relatively isolated location away
from the country's main industrial districts, and the advantages to
industry of proximity to the University of Lancaster can easily be
exaggerated.[14] The impact of the Morecambe Bay barrage, if it is ever
built, could change the situation, but at the moment the north
Lancashire city looks a very doubtful economic proposition.

The Weaver city proposal for southern Cheshire is more sensible.
Winsford is doing well industrially with government assistance, Crewe
is certainly an attractive location for engineering, and some of the
nearby towns have shown significant post-war growth as was indicated
in Chapter 3. Cheshire County Council has developed the notion of a
linear city on a Northwich–Winsford–Crewe axis, though Sylvester &
Rodgers had earlier suggested the expansion of Crewe in the direction
of Sandbach and Alsager.[15] A major new growth point somewhere
here could perform a number of functions: it could attract industry
and population from the congested West Midlands conurbation as well
as from Manchester and Merseyside, and it might help to revitalise
the rather stagnant economy of the Potteries. If the strategy of
dispersal continues, southern Cheshire is likely to be able to develop
industry more easily than other peripheral parts of the region.

Another possibility in Cheshire is growth along the eastern edge of
the plains in the vicinity of Macclesfield. The county council has
estimated that up to 66,000 more people might be accommodated by
1986 on land 'ripe for early development', and a southward extension
towards Congleton might provide room for another 45,000 to 75,000
by early in the twenty-first century;[16] this would not interfere with the
green belt, the major constraints being the hills to the east and Jodrell
Bank's protected area to the west. As a compromise between the
existing pressures for southward growth from Manchester towards
Macclesfield, and the desire to restrict the expansion of the conurbation, this proposal has considerable merit. The successful diversification of the old silk-manufacturing town suggests that it is a reasonably
attractive location for new industry.

Another tentative proposal yet to be looked into in detail is for a
new urban area on the Welsh side of the Dee estuary, to take Liverpool
overspill. Connected with Merseyside by a new motorway across the
estuary, a Deeside town or city could relieve some of the pressure for
residential development in the Wirral green belt. Large-scale industrial

development, perhaps connected with the proposed barrage, is a long-term possibility; some of the existing advantages of the Mersey estuary might be recreated here.

In many respects the central Lancashire city based on Preston, Leyland and Chorley is an attractive proposal and the economic planning council feels that it should go ahead as a matter of urgency. It would make a major contribution towards solving the Manchester and Merseyside overspill problems and help to pull industrial growth northwards along the line of the motorway. The city can be expected to revitalise one of the region's industrial problem areas, and it should also benefit the old mining district centred on Wigan to the south as well as some of the mill towns to the east. However, distance from the region's main growth zone raises doubts about the area's capacity to attract the industry necessary to support population growth at the rate envisaged, even with development-area status.

Skelmersdale, much nearer Liverpool, has succeeded with government assistance, but apart from the proposed Viyella plant at Chorley new industry has shown little interest in the area north of Wigan. The industrial aspects of the central-Lancashire proposal are the subject of a special study commissioned by the Department of Economic Affairs, the object being to find out which new industrial activities would complement those already in the area and its surroundings and produce a complex capable of generating relatively fast growth.[17] This approach is a welcome if belated departure from the previous policy of leaving the industrial structure of the New Towns very largely to chance.

The decision on the central Lancashire city was postponed for some time pending an evaluation of its impact on north-east Lancashire. The original proposal caused some alarm in the Darwen and Calder valleys, on the grounds that it would divert any new industry destined for the cotton towns, whose decline would thus be accelerated. The consultants' report suggests that the new city would speed up migration from north-east Lancashire, and would stimulate the growth sectors of its industry while possibly adding to the difficulties of the declining sectors. What growth there is would in general take place in the Blackburn area. The main hope for some benefit to Burnley, Nelson and Colne appears to be a fast road link to new jobs in central Lancashire.[18] But the more commuting there is into the new city, the more industry it has to attract. There is some merit in an alternative plan for the city, which would take it from Preston to Blackburn instead of south to Chorley; this would capitalise on Blackburn's good industrial performance in recent years, and make use of its central-area facilities. This plan also has the political attraction that it would give north-east Lancashire a stake in the new city; the main drawback is that the city would be further separated from the Mersey growth zone.

It is interesting that the problems of the region's expanding conurbations, projected into central Lancashire in a massive overspill scheme, should come home to roost in north-east Lancashire. It is almost as if the natural growth tendencies of the second-half of the twentieth century are bound to adversely affect the old cotton towns, whatever planning strategy is selected. The problems of the Calder–Darwen valley, Rossendale and the Pennine-fringe mill towns to the south have been referred to often enough in previous chapters to require no repetition here. The question of their future is of vital significance in the development of regional strategy.

The basic issue is whether these places should be subsidised to assist their economic revival, or whether their decline should be allowed to continue. The choice between spending more money and incurring political unpopularity is never easy, and it is perhaps not surprising that the government has assiduously avoided a decision one way or the other. The Board of Trade, in the implementation of its industrial-location policy, has done little to assist the growth of new employment, except for Burnley and district's few years as a development area. For some time the calls for a clearer national policy towards these areas, and those like them in other regions, have been muted by anticipation of the report of the Hunt Committee looking into the problems of the so-called intermediate or 'grey' areas.[19] But the continuing delay in publishing the committee's findings, still not available at the beginning of 1969, adds to the suspicion that the government is not yet ready to face a full policy review capable of incorporating the recommendations of Sir Joseph Hunt and his colleagues. At the time of writing it is widely expected that the committee will suggest limited financial aid, short of full development-area grants, to selected growth points in 'grey' areas like north-east Lancashire. Finding the money to implement such a scheme without an overall increase in the cost of industrial-development policy would imply some reduction in the support given to certain of the existing development areas. Recent improvements in the employment situation on Merseyside while the problems of the old cotton towns remain might justify the removal of Merseyside's development-area status, particularly if this could release funds to assist the 'grey' areas. However, local interests can be expected to protect Merseyside's present privileged position fiercely, and any proposal to substantially alter existing development-area policy will clearly be

accompanied by much political intrigue. It is to be hoped that whatever policy finally emerges from the Hunt Committee's review, it will
be based on objective economic and regional planning considerations
rather than representing the all too familiar compromise between conflicting local political pressures (see pp 235–6).

The mill towns have vociferous champions in their own councils,
MPs and LAMIDA, but there are signs that the truth about their very
limited industrial potential is gradually being appreciated. One regional
study in 1964 concluded that 'the decline of the economic base of these
valley areas must mean increasing migration from them, and a considerable daily journey to work to Manchester and Central Lancashire
is inevitable'.[20] The economic planning council's policy, as reflected in
its evidence to the Hunt Committee and in *Strategy II*, is for selected
growth points to have development-area assistance, while people will
be encouraged by better roads to commute to where the jobs are. A
detailed strategy must await results of the study of north-east Lancashire's potential and its place in regional development, which the
council is sponsoring.

At the moment, however, it is difficult to avoid the conclusion that
many of the valley mill towns have had their day. With a few exceptions, they lost their economic *raison d'être* when the cotton trade
collapsed. Hopefully, they will retain most of their existing industry
when the reorganisation in textiles is complete, and they may even
attract a few new firms, but it would be quite wrong to push industry
into these relatively isolated places when the region has much better
locations to offer. The Yorkshire and Humberside Economic Planning
Council has recently told Todmorden, in the upper Calder valley, that
it admires local efforts to attract new industry, but cannot foresee any
major development in a location unfavourable to modern economic
activity.[21] It may not be long before the facts of economic life are put
to similar places in the North West with equal bluntness.

Some of the mill towns may be able to stabilise population by
becoming more residential in character; with the old dirt and debris
removed, a small town on the edge of the Pennines could be an
attractive place to live. This gradual change in function would depend
on car ownership and swift road connections with the growing centres
of employment—a north-east Lancashire motorway could almost put
a Colne resident within half an hour of a job in Preston.

It is in connection with the declining cotton and coal-mining towns
that the Board of Trade industrial-location policy has been criticised
most bitterly in the North West. LAMIDA have argued for some time
that in these towns 'government policy has patently militated against

the achievement of a satisfactory rate of economic growth and a rise in prosperity equal to that of the country generally'; when firms wish to expand 'the industrial development certificate is often granted with considerable reluctance by the Board of Trade and after the most frustrating delays'.[22] It seems quite wrong that any difficulty should be put in the way of firms willing to build modern factories in these towns, and it is certainly true that the areas of poorest industrial health, as defined in Chapter 6, have gained virtually nothing from post-war industrial-location policy. But to give development-area status to these so-called 'grey' areas would be a mistake; the relatively slow rate of economic growth in the North West is not improved by indefinitely subsidising industry in numerous high-cost locations, which in a free market would be marginal or unprofitable. All these towns have the right to expect is the uninhibited growth of indigenous industry and of any firms who freely wish to move there, together with the assurance of jobs in growth areas within commuting distance.

The rights and wrongs of industrial-location policy in Britain could be debated at length, but this is the place for summary comments only. If the financial support of the country's declining industrial areas is accepted as a sensible use of the nation's resources, and even this is questioned by believers in the free market, then the claims of Lancashire cotton and coal towns have been very great. The degree of their difficulties was shown in Chapter 6; only the official insistence that the need for help can be adequately measured by statistical unemployment has justified their exclusion from the development areas. As it is, most of the public investment arising from implementing industrial-location policy has been channelled into Merseyside, which is far better placed to look after itself than are the towns of the Pennine fringes.

The stimulation of industrial development in and around Merseyside since the war is probably one of the best things which could have happened to the North West. This is partly because an uncertain local-employment situation has been improved; but much more important is the fact that new industry has been permitted, and encouraged, in an area which has proved to be conducive to the success of major growth industries. The Board of Trade, in rigidly applying the unemployment criterion, has thus assisted a natural growth zone while restricting development in less attractive locations on the region's eastern periphery. There is some irony in the thought that this much-maligned body may turn out to have done the right thing, if (on the face of it) for the wrong reasons.

The general conclusion is that much post-war planning policy in the North West, as in Britain as a whole, has lacked a realistic attitude towards industrial location and development. Some current proposals are based on untested assumptions, regarding the mobility of industry and its capacity to succeed in certain areas, which could well turn out to be completely unfounded. One of the main difficulties is that the kind of planning which has emerged in Britain has been understandably preoccupied with environmental improvement and the preservation of amenity—with clearing up the chaos produced by nineteenth-century *laisser-faire* and preventing it from happening again. In the process, the possibilities for positive economic planning have been largely overlooked. Few people would deny the importance of the preservation of the countryside, areas of great natural beauty and recreational facilities, and no-one questions the need to create an attractive, healthy and exciting environment for the growing urban population. There are many instances in which economic freedom can reasonably be curtailed in the interests of amenity, just as the artificial support of industrial development in some areas where it is needed for social reasons seems a legitimate field for government action. But a first priority must always be the efficient functioning of the economic system, local, regional and national. Without a viable economy social planning becomes meaningless. It is to be hoped that as the theory and practice of regional planning in Britain continues to develop it will take on a more positive economic role, with the encouragement of technical and locational efficiency as a major industrial objective.

A Vision of the Future

What kind of industrial region will emerge in North West England during the remainder of this century? Present planning strategy, as summarised in Fig 35, gives a clue to this, but much depends on the uncertainties of national economic and political developments. On the economic side the general progress of this region, like any other, is dependent on the maintenance of national prosperity, which in these days of balance of payments crises is never sure. It is also dependent on the continuing ability of manufacturers in the North West to sell their goods, particularly in foreign markets. Of critical importance is the region's continuing capacity to provide good locations for the growth industries. In the nineteenth century the world wanted cotton goods, which could be produced nowhere cheaper than in Lancashire; today new industries making new products are prospering in certain parts of the North West, and by the end of the century the region's ability to accommodate entirely new growth industries will no doubt have been tested.

On the political side there are a number of imponderables which could greatly affect national prosperity and the comparative economic advantage of the North West. These include possible entry into the Common Market, Britain's trading relationships with EFTA partners and the Commonwealth, and policy towards the importation of cheap goods, such as textiles, from the developing countries.

Despite these unknowns, the optimistic regional planner could probably make some broad predictions and, as the 1960s end, his vision of the future might be something like this. The central Lancashire city is started, and its carefully-planned industrial complex developed with government assistance creates a virulent growth point; its revitalising effect spreads into the old cotton towns to the east. Industrial land in and around Merseyside is quickly used up, pressure for further development in the area between the conurbations grows, and Warrington New Town is a great success. A comprehensive plan is produced for the whole of the Merseyside to Manchester belt, with provision for substantial industrial growth and a million new residents in a city of revolutionary form. By the 1990s an extended urban region is emerging in the Manchester–Liverpool–Preston triangle, with a prosperous economy based on the production of advanced electronic equipment and automated industrial plant, vehicle manufacturing, and a closely-integrated chemicals–textiles–paper complex. The peripheral parts of the region are connected with this new Lancastrian megalopolis by fast motorways and commuter mono-rail services, and the cleaning up of the old Pennine-fringe industrial towns turns some of them into middle-class residential areas. Limited peripheral industrial development takes place; the Weaver city in northern Cheshire is started as a Birmingham overspill project as land in the West Midlands is used up, and barrage schemes in Morecambe Bay and the Dee Estuary are attracting new industry to waterside sites by the 1990s. Motorways and express rail-freight services connect the North West with the regions to the east and south, and beneath or across the English Channel to the rest of the United States of Europe.

Such a vision would not necessarily please every planner. Some would change matters of detail, but probably few would now question the inevitability of a major urban-industrial agglomeration based on the existing growth zone. Given imaginative planning, the final submergence of nineteenth-century chaos beneath a multi-nucleated city-region designed for the twenty-first century is physically feasible and economically realistic.

But before this kind of dream can become reality certain prerequisites must be met. The first is for a more positive and purposeful approach to the whole question of regional planning in Britain. There is an urgent need for some kind of national economic and land-use plan, into which regional plans can be fitted, for without closer guidance on the part each region can expect to play in the national economic system, prediction of such vital matters as inter-regional population migration and industrial movement will remain guesses.

Just as regional plans have little meaning outside the context of a national plan, so individual town and city plans need the guiding framework of an agreed regional strategy. More than four years after the setting up of the economic planning council, the North West seems little nearer the regional plan mentioned in the council's terms of reference. *The North West Study*, *Strategy I* and *Strategy II* all quite rightly disclaimed any pretentions of being regional plans, but development still goes on. New Towns are being planned, town maps revised, and overspill schemes agreed; if a true regional plan ever appears there is a danger that it will be nothing more than a formal recognition of what has already been proposed by a large number of different planning agencies.

This raises the question of the usefulness of the regional-planning machinery (if such it may be termed) set up in 1965. The economic planning councils have performed valuable advisory functions, and offer an outlet for an independent view of regional problems, but their lack of power strictly limits what they can achieve. If the idea is really to produce and implement a regional plan, it is difficult to see how this can be done without a regional authority with executive powers. This is closely bound up with the urgent need for the reorganisation of the archaic local-government structure in Britain. If the Maud Commission investigating this problem proposes some form of regional government, and if it is implemented with greater speed and enthusiasm than past changes in local-government structure, this would be an important move in the right direction.

Another difficulty facing the economic planning councils is their lack of resources to finance research. In *Strategy II* it was forcefully stated that more research staff is badly needed if any discernible headway is to be made.[23] Information on many subjects is urgently required; among the problems raised in *Strategy II* were population mobility, travel-to-work habits, and the best places for industry to be located—all vital matters in deciding where new development should take place. The general inadequacy of much official statistical data at a regional and local level will be apparent from earlier parts of this book, and a regional data bank in which large volumes of information could be stored in a computer system to which government departments and research groups could have rapid access seems a first priority.[24] Such a system would encourage the use of more sophisticated research techniques than many of those in current use.

If these prerequisites are not met, successful regional planning is unlikely. All that can be expected is a series of largely unrelated decisions dictated by expediency and based on inadequate knowledge. In this event the end of the century might find the cities of the North West as outdated and congested as ever, the intervening areas filled with a jungle of unco-ordinated piecemeal development, badly located New Towns failing to attract industry, and the old mill towns in the last stages of their slow and painful decay. Time alone will show whether this or the other vision becomes reality.

Epilogue

As this book goes to press, two long-awaited reports have recently appeared, the contents of which are of considerable importance to industrial development in the North West. The first is the Textile Council's major study of the Lancashire spinning, weaving and finishing industry.[25] The report estimates that the increasing rate of re-equipment will reduce the number of companies in the industry from 375 in 1968 to 120-150 by 1975, and that employment will have been reduced to about 55,000 during this period. The main recommendations are for greater protection from foreign competition, and for further mill re-equipment and rationalisation of production. A 15 per cent tariff on cotton textile imports from the Commonwealth is called for, though the replacement of the present quota system by a tariff would be difficult politically. There is a growing feeling that some government assistance of this kind will be needed if the industry is to satisfactorily complete its reorganisation, and remain a viable element in the economy of the traditional textile-manufacturing districts.

The second report is that of the Hunt Committee set up to investigate the problems of the intermediate or 'grey' areas.[26] The committee agree that the rate of economic growth in the North West outside the existing development areas is a matter for concern. Their major recommendations are for building grants of 25 per cent to assist new industrial developments within the region, and for help in such fields as manpower training, the improvement of the service infrastructure and the reclamation of derelict land. It is also suggested that growth zones should be identified within the region, and that industrial estates should be established at key points. The most controversial recommendation is the descheduling of the Merseyside Development Area.

Merseyside would then join the rest of the region (except Furness, in the Northern Development Area) in having an 'intermediate' status between the development areas and regions without any industrial subsidies. However, one member of the committee dissented on this recommendation, on the grounds that the descheduling of Merseyside would not divert industry into the problem areas, like north-east Lancashire, but would deprive the region as a whole of some new industry.[27]

The main recommendations of the Hunt Committee have been promptly rejected by the government. Merseyside is to retain development-area status, and it appears that additional assistance is to be confined to north-east Lancashire.[28] Merseyside should thus continue to be the major focal point for industrial development in the North West, at least until the construction of the new city in the Preston–Leyland–Chorley area gets underway. But the 1970s may well see Merseyside's development incentives transferred to the new city, or perhaps to some project of similar size in the area between the two conurbations. As far as the region as a whole is concerned, it may not matter much where the assistance goes within the Liverpool–Manchester–Preston triangle, as long as there is one major growth area capable of competing with other parts of Britain, and Europe, as a location for new industrial development.

References to this chapter are on pages 246 and 247.

Acknowledgments

MY FIRST DEBT of gratitude is to the large number of people in North West England who helped in various ways during the preparation of this book. Statistics and other information have been provided by the regional offices of the Ministry of Labour, Board of Trade, Ministry of Housing & Local Government, Department of Economic Affairs, and by many local planning authorities including Cheshire County Council, Lancashire County Council, and the Cities of Manchester and Liverpool. The individuals concerned are too numerous to mention by name, but they will be able to judge the extent of my indebtedness to them by the time they put at my disposal. Representatives of many firms have been good enough to answer letters and circulars and I am grateful to them all, particularly those who provided information and photographs which have been used in the text. Special mention must be made of the assistance given by the Lancashire & Merseyside Industrial Development Association, whose director, Mr E. G. W. Allen, made much useful information available to me, and kindly read certain chapters in draft form.

This project was begun at the University of Manchester, where I learned much from the conversation and fellowship of colleagues in the School of Geography. Peter Lloyd and Peter Dicken have helped in a variety of ways, and the writings of T. W. Freeman and Brian Rodgers (University of Keele) have been a constant source of stimulation.

Much of the research on which this book is based was done while on the staff of the Geography Department at Southern Illinois University. Working on North West England from the United States has been made easy by the excellent facilities and support provided by the University. This included research assistance, contributions towards two trans-Atlantic fares, and grants to cover certain secretarial and other expenses. Of particular benefit has been the co-operation of the Data Processing and Computing Centre, who programmed various statistical problems and made available as much computer time as was needed. The illustrations in the book were drawn in the Cartographic

Laboratory, Southern Illinois University, under the supervision of
Dan Irwin and Tso-Hwa Lee, to both of whom I am very grateful
indeed.

The completion of this project would have been very difficult without two generous grants from the Penrose Fund of the American
Philosophical Society. This enabled me to spend six months working
in Manchester in 1968 without any other commitments, and helped
to meet other research expenditure.

Finally I would like to thank my wife Margaret for a critical review
of the manuscript and for her general support, my son Michael for
allowing me time off from more important pursuits to write the book,
and my daughter Tracey for delaying her arrival until the job was
done.

Notes and References

CHAPTER 1
An Introduction to the North West. Page 13.

1 For a much fuller geographical introduction to the region, see Freeman, T. W., Rodgers, H. B., & Kinvig, R. H. *Lancashire, Cheshire and the Isle of Man.* Nelson, 1966 (henceforth cited as Freeman & Rodgers). See also Carter, C. F. (editor) *Manchester and its Region.* Manchester University Press, 1962, especially chapters 1–4 and 10–12; and Smith, W. (editor) *A Scientific Survey of Merseyside.* Liverpool University Press, 1953.

2 A much more detailed account of the industrial development of the region will be found in Freeman & Rodgers, *op cit,* chapters 3, 4 and 5. Parts of this section are based on Freeman & Rodgers' account.

3 *Ibid,* p 67.

4 For a vivid description of the region in the first throes of the Industrial Revolution, see Aikin, J. *A Description of the Country from Thirty to Forty Miles Round Manchester,* 1795, reprinted by David & Charles in 1968.

5 See Freeman & Rodgers, *op cit,* pp 59–61.

6 Rodgers, H. B. 'The Lancashire Cotton Industry in 1840', *Transactions and Papers,* Institute of British Geographers, Vol 28, 1960, pp 135–53.

7 *The Sunday Times,* 29 Aug 1965. The figures are: Lancashire 4·1 betting shops per 10,000 people; Cheshire 2·4.

8 See The Registrar General *Statistical Review of England and Wales 1965,* Part 1, Medical Tables. HMSO, 1967.

9 For more detailed maps of the 1951–61 period see Rodgers, H. B., 'Recent Industrial Changes in North-West England and their Economic and Social Consequences', *Problems of Applied Geography* II (*Geographica Polonica* 3), 1964, pp 221–6.

10 *Ibid,* p 226.

11 See Smith, D. M. 'Recent Changes in the Regional Pattern of British Industry', *Tijdschrift voor Economische en Sociale Geografie,* Vol 56, 1965, pp 133–45.

12 *The National Plan.* HMSO, 1965, p 88.

13 Lancashire and Merseyside Industrial Development Association (LAMIDA) *Twenty Second Annual Report,* 1968, p 32. Figures for previous years give the same impression.

14 There is a fairly close relationship at a regional level, if not locally,

239

between unemployment and the amount of inward or outward migration. See Oliver, F. 'Interregional Migration and Unemployment 1951–61', *Journal*, Royal Statistical Society, Series A, Vol 127 Part I, 1964, p 46; and Thirlwall, A. P. 'Migration and Regional Unemployment: Some Lessons for Regional Planning', *Westminster Bank Review*, Nov 1966, pp 34–8.

15 For further details, see Coates, B. E. & Rawstron, E. M. 'Regional Variations in Incomes', *Westminster Bank Review*, Feb 1966, pp 1–19. See also *idem* 'Opportunity and Affluence', *Geography*, Vol 51, 1966, pp 1–15; and Holmans, A. E. 'Inter-Regional Differences in Levels of Income: Are there "Two Nations" or One?', in Wilson, T. (editor) *Papers on Regional Development*. Blackwell, 1965, pp 1–19.

16 *Ministry of Labour Gazette*, Feb 1968.

17 Metcalf, D. & Cowling K. 'Regional Wage Inflation in the United Kingdom', *District Bank Review*, June 1967, p 48. The relationship between income and unemployment is examined further in Pullen, M. J., 'Unemployment and Regional Income Per Head', *The Manchester School of Economic and Social Studies*, Vol XXXIV, 1966, pp 15–40.

18 *Family Expenditure Survey*. HMSO, 1967.

19 North West Economic Planning Council *Strategy II: The North West of the 1970s*. HMSO, 1968, pp 36 and 75–8.

CHAPTER 2

The Regional Pattern of Industrial Activity. Page 41.

1 Department of Economic Affairs *The North West: A Regional Study*. HMSO, 1965, p 34.

2 For further details, see Thomas, W. J. & Perkins, R. J. 'Land Utilisation and Agriculture in the North West', in *Manchester and its Region*, pp 156–70.

3 These areas are defined in LAMIDA *Lancashire and Merseyside*. Industrial Report No 8, 1952, pp 15–6.

4 See Pullen, M. J. & Williams B. R. 'The Structure of Industry in Lancashire', in *Manchester and its Region*, p 152 (Fig 21).

5 *Strategy II*, p 11.

6 *Abstract of Regional Statistics, 1966*. HMSO, 1967.

7 Eversley, D. 'Shades of Prosperity', *New Society*, 4 Jan 1968, p 8.

CHAPTER 3

Recent Changes in the Regional Pattern of Industry. Page 78.

1 *The North West Study*, p 25.

2 *Ibid*, p 41, Fig 18.

3 *Ibid*, pp 37–8.

4 See for example LAMIDA *The Development of Lancashire and Merseyside—Past, Present and Future*. 1963; LAMIDA *The North West Region—Development Prospects and Needs*. 1964; and Allen, E. G. W.

'Post-War Industrial Development in Lancashire and Merseyside', *Journal* Manchester Statistical Society, 1964, pp 1–29.

5 Rodgers, 'Recent Industrial Changes in North West England . . .', pp 211–28.

6 *The North West Study*, pp 32–3.

7 The problems of measuring industrial diversification in this way are considered more fully in Conkling, E. C. 'South Wales: A Case Study in Industrial Diversification', *Economic Geography*, Vol 39, 1963, pp 258–72; and *Idem*, 'The Measurement of Diversification', in Manners, G. (editor) *South Wales in the Sixties*. Pergamon Press, 1964, pp 161–83.

8 The *weighted mean centre* of industrial employment in North West England, based on exchange area data, was at national grid reference point 36921·40460 in 1953, and had shifted to 36758·40415 by 1965. This represented a movement of almost two miles. The *weighted standard distance* from the respective mean centre was 21·0 miles in 1953 and 21·9 miles in 1965, indicating very little change in the degree of dispersal of employment. For an explanation of these measures, see Bachi, R. 'Standard Distance and Related Measures for Spatial Analysis' *Papers and Proceedings*, Regional Science Association, Vol 10, 1963, pp 83–134.

9 Figures from LAMIDA (conversions) and the Board of Trade (new building).

10 Rodgers, *op cit*, p 218, Fig 1.

11 *Ibid*, pp 217 and 219.

12 LAMIDA *Annual Reports*, years ending March 1966, 1967 and 1968. The chemical industries accounted for 76 of 688 industrial enquiries in the three years, compared with 227 in engineering and electrical, and 111 in miscellaneous manufacturing.

CHAPTER 4

Explaining Recent Trends. Page 106.

1 For a partial attempt to construct such a model for this region, see Smith, D. M. 'Industrial Location and Regional Development: Some Recent Trends in North West England', *Environment*, Vol 1, 1969.

2 This section is based largely on Smith, D. M. *Industrial Location and Regional Planning in the North West*. Report prepared for the Industrial Working Party, South-East Lancashire and North-East Cheshire Traffic Survey. School of Geography, University of Manchester, 1966 (mimeo).

3 *Ibid*, p 6.

4 *The North West Study*, pp 31–4.

5 Smith, *op cit*, p 17.

6 LAMIDA *Twenty Second Annual Report*. 1968, p 29.

7 Allen, *op cit*, p 20.

8 *Board of Trade Journal*. 28 Oct 1966, p 1049.

9 Full Particulars of Development Area assistance will be found in official publications, such as the Board of Trade's *Room to Expand* booklets.

P

10 LAMIDA *Annual Reports*. 1964–68, Appendixes.

11 Speech by the President of the Board of Trade at Buxton, 1 Aug 1967, reported in LAMIDA *Newsletter No 24*, Sept 1967, p 4.

12 LAMIDA *The Decline of the Cotton and Coal Mining Industries of Lancashire*. 1967, p 11.

13 *Ibid*, pp 26–7.

14 LAMIDA *Twenty Second Annual Report*. 1968, p 7.

15 Board of Trade *The Movement of Manufacturing Industry in the United Kingdom 1945–65*. HMSO, 1968, p 17.

16 Much of the information used in this section was kindly provided by Mr C. F. Chapman of LAMIDA, who bears no responsibility for the way the material has been used or interpreted.

17 Information from Manchester City Planning Office.

18 LAMIDA *Twentieth Annual Report*. 1966, p 35.

19 LAMIDA *Buyers Guide to Industry in the North West*. 1968, pp 503–25. For other information in this section the author is indebted to Mr K. Dickens and Mr C. F. Chapman of LAMIDA.

20 This and the Ferranti information is from *The Sunday Times*, 4 Feb 1968.

21 Holt, R. A. *The Changing Industrial Geography of the Cotton Areas of Lancashire, 1951–1961: A Study of Mill Conversion and Employment structure*. Unpublished MA Thesis, University of Manchester, 1964. This work contains the most thorough survey of mill conversions to date, and has much valuable information on the subject. Three of Holt's maps are reproduced in Freeman & Rodgers, *op cit*, pp 136, 146 and 148.

22 LAMIDA *Closure and Reoccupation of Cotton Mills*. 1967 (mimeo).

23 Freeman & Rodgers, *op cit*, p 145; Allen, *op cit*, p 23.

24 Holt, *op cit*, Tables 30, 34 and 35.

25 Freeman & Rodgers, *loc cit*, where a number of other pertinent comments on mill conversion will be found.

26 LAMIDA *An Industrial Policy for the North West*. 1966 (mimeo) p 5; *Newsletter No 26*, March 1968, p 2; *Twenty Second Annual Report*. 1968, pp 6–7.

27 Miles, C. *Lancashire Textiles: A Case Study of Industrial Change*. National Institute of Economic and Social Research, Occasional Papers XXIII. Cambridge University Press, 1968, p 110.

28 LAMIDA *Twenty First Annual Report*. 1967, p 9; *Newsletter No 23*, June 1967, p 5.

29 The Merseyside labour situation is considered more fully in Department of Economic Affairs *The Problems of Merseyside*. HMSO, 1965, pp 21–7. See also the Merseyside social and economic survey *Merseyside in the 1960s*, Longman, 1969, Chapters 9 and 10.

30 Salt, J. 'The Impact of the Ford and Vauxhall Plants on the Employment Situation of Merseyside, 1962–1965', *Tijdschrift voor Economische en Sociale Geografie*, Vol 58, 1967, pp 255–64.

31 Taylor, J. 'Estimating Labour Reserves: A Study of the Furness Sub-Region' *The Manchester School of Economic and Social Studies*, Vol XXXIV, 1966, pp 197–209.

32 Personal communication with the author, June 1968.
33 *Ministry of Labour Gazette*, Feb 1968. The figures refer to Oct 1967.
34 Board of Trade *The Movement of Manufacturing Industry . . .*, p 40.
35 Based on information compiled with help from the Board of Trade.
36 LAMIDA *Annual Reports*. 1966–8.

CHAPTER 5
The Critical Industries. Page 141.

1 Robson, R. *The Cotton Industry in Britain*. Macmillan, 1957.
2 Miles, *op cit*.
3 *Ibid*, p 24.
4 Rodgers, H. B. 'The Changing Geography of the Lancashire Cotton Industry', *Economic Geography*, Vol 38, 1962, pp 301–3. See also Freeman & Rodgers, *op cit*, pp 123–6.
5 Miles, *op cit*, p 40.
6 *Ibid*, pp 19–20.
7 The provisions and operation of the Act are described in detail by Miles: *Ibid*, pp 46–78; and 'Contraction in Cotton: Some Comments on the 1959 Cotton Industry Act', *District Bank Review*, June 1965, pp 19–38.
8 Miles, *Lancashire Textiles*, p 56.
9 This account is based on Rodgers, *op cit*, pp 305–7.
10 All the points in this paragraph are discussed more fully in Miles, *op cit*, pp 66–78.
11 *Ibid*, pp 84–8.
12 Another study, of the 1940–60 period, arrived at a similar conclusion. See Wallwork, K. L. 'The Cotton Industry in North West England: 1941–61', *Geography*, Vol 47, 1962, pp 246–7.
13 Further particulars of trends in the various districts will be found in LAMIDA *The Decline of the Cotton and Coal Mining Industries . . .*, pp 11–22; and in Freeman & Rodgers, *op cit*, pp 125–8.
14 Miles, *op cit*, p 51.
15 Textile Council *Cotton and Allied Textiles—A Report on Present Performance and Future Prospects*, 1969. This study urges a 15 per cent tariff on imports from the Commonwealth.
16 *The Guardian*, 30 Apr 1968.
17 Full particulars of closures between 1950 and 1967 will be found in LAMIDA *op cit*, pp 40–3.
18 *Coal News*, Apr 1968, p 6.
19 Freeman & Rodgers, *op cit*, pp 133–5.
20 *White Paper on Fuel Policy*. HMSO, 1968.
21 See Freeman & Rodgers, *op cit*, pp 142–3.
22 North, G. 'Industrial Development in the Rossendale Valley', *Journal*, Manchester Geographical Society, Vol LVIII, 1961–2, p 28.
23 *The Financial Times*, 8 Apr 1968.
24 Information kindly provided by the Ford Motor Co Ltd, along with certain other facts in this section.

25   LAMIDA *Nineteenth Annual Report*. 1965, pp 27–9.
26   *Merseyside: An Industrial and Commercial Review*. Pyramid Press, 1967, p 32.
27   Salt, *op cit*, p 263.
28   Labour recruitment is considered fully in Salt, *op cit*, pp 255–64.
29   *Ministry of Labour Gazette*, Feb 1968.
30   *The Financial Times*, 8 Apr 1968.
31   In October 1967 the average weekly wage for men 21 and over in the paper group was £24 11s 7d, compared with £23 8s 9d in vehicles and £21 7s 11d in all manufacturing. *Ministry of Labour Gazette*, Feb 1968.
32   Freeman & Rodgers, *op cit*, p 144.
33   *The Financial Times*, 8 Apr 1968.
34   Freeman & Rodgers, *op cit*, pp 141–2.

CHAPTER 6

The Regional Geography of Economic Health. Page 171.

1   Parts of the analysis which follows are based on Smith, D. M. 'Identifying the "Grey" Areas: A Multivariate Approach', *Regional Studies*, Vol 2, 1968, pp 183–93.
2   Hunt, Sir Joseph *The Intermediate Areas*. Report of a Committee under the Chairmanship of Sir Joseph Hunt. HMSO, 1968.
3   The correlation coefficients upon which these comments are based are reproduced in Smith, *op cit*, Table 1.
4   See Thompson, J. H. et al 'Towards a Geography of Economic Health: The Case of New York State', *Annals*, Association of American Geographers, Vol 52, 1962; Bell, W. H. & Stevenson, D. W. 'An Index of Economic Health for Ontario Counties and Districts', *Ontario Economic Review*, Vol 2, 1964; and Berry, B. J. L. 'Identification of Declining Regions: An Empirical Study of the Dimensions of Rural Poverty', in Thoman, R. S. & Wood, W. D. (editors) *Areas of Economic Stress in Canada*, Queen's University Press, Kingston, Ontario, 1965.
5   The communalities for the original fourteen variables, which show how far they contribute to the two factors, are listed in Smith, *op cit*.

CHAPTER 7

A View of the Sub-Regions. Page 192.

1   The best sub-regional descriptions are in Freeman & Rodgers, *op cit*, Chapters 7–10. See also the British Association handbooks *Manchester and its Region* and *A Scientific Survey of Merseyside*. The two conurbations are described at length in Freeman, T. W. *The Conurbations of Britain*. Manchester University Press, revised edition, 1966, Chapters 4 and 5.
2   Conditions in the inter-war years are described in detail in two of a series of publications by the Lancashire Industrial Develop Associ-

ation, now LAMIDA: *The South East Lancashire Area and parts of Cheshire and Derbyshire.* Industrial Report No 4, 1949; and *The Spinning Area.* Industrial Report No 5, 1950.

3   The experiences of each of the main textile areas are outlined in LAMIDA *The Decline of the Cotton and Coal Mining Industries . . .*, pp 15–18.

4   Information on the progress of the SELNEC survey was kindly supplied by Mr Gillespie and Mr Dunstan, Cheshire County Planning Office.

5   The industrial future of the Manchester area is discussed in more detail in Manchester City Planning Office *Manchester and its Region.* 1969.

6   These figures are from LAMIDA *Merseyside.* Industrial Report No 3, 1949, where much additional background on the inter-war period will be found.

7   Department of Economic Affairs *The Problems of Merseyside*, pp 13–20.

8   Lloyd, P. E. 'Industrial Changes in the Merseyside Development Area 1949–1959' *Town Planning Review*, Vol 35, 1965, pp 285–98.

9   Salt, *op cit*, pp 259–60.

10 This and other matters relating to the recent industrial development of Merseyside are considered in much more detail in articles by Lloyd, P. E. and by Cunningham, N. J. in the forthcoming survey *Merseyside in the 1960s.*

11 The role of the industrial estates, in particular Kirkby, is examined fully by Gentleman, H. *Ibid.*

12 See Amos, F. J. C. 'Alternative Plans for Sub-Regional Problems' *Regional Studies*, Vol 1, 1967, pp 135–46.

13 Lloyd, *op cit*, pp 293–7. See also *idem*, in *Merseyside in the 1960s.*

14 LAMIDA *Seventeenth Annual Report.* 1963, p 31.

15 Personal communication with the author, June 1968.

16 Masser, F. J. *Economic Base Study: Review of Population and Employment Trends.* Traffic Research Corporation 1967 (mimeo).

17 LAMIDA *The Coal/Chemical Area.* Industrial Report No 6, 1950. This contains a detailed account of the area's inter-war problems. See also Freeman & Rodgers, *op cit*, pp 213–8, for an excellent summary of the coalfield and its problems.

18 South Lancashire Development Committee *Industry in South Lancashire.* Burrows, undated, p 9.

19 LAMIDA attribute this to the shortage of existing premises in which development can take place. See LAMIDA *The Decline of the Cotton and Coal Mining Industries . . .*, p 19.

20 Skelmersdale Development Corporation *New Town Progress at 31st March 1968.*

21 Ministry of Housing and Local Government *Central Lancashire— Study for a City* (Robert Matthew, Johnson-Marshall & Partners). HMSO, 1967, p 14.

22 LAMIDA *The Weaving Area.* Industrial Report No 2, 1948, p 10.

23 See Wallwork, K. L. *Aspects of the Modern Economic Geography of the Calder-Darwen Valley.* Unpublished MA thesis, University of Manchester, 1955, passim.

24 LAMIDA *op cit*. pp 12 and 17.
25 *Central Lancashire New Town Proposal: Impact on North East Lancashire* (Robert Matthew, Johnson-Marshall & Partners; Economic Consultants Ltd) Advance Copy of Consultants' Appraisal, 1967, p 69.
26 See the discussion of industrial readjustment in the Calder-Darwen valley in Wallwork, K. L. 'The Cotton Industry in North West England' *op cit*, pp 247–54.
27 *Impact on North East Lancashire*, p 83.
28 This is examined in detail in LAMIDA *The Problems of Seasonal Unemployment and Labour Supply in the Coastal Towns of Lancashire,* 1965. Excellent profiles of the resorts will be found in Freeman & Rodgers, *op cit*, pp 238–45.
29 For a detailed account of the growth of Barrow, see Hammersley, A. D. *The Urban Geography of Barrow-in-Furness*. Unpublished MA thesis, University of Manchester, 1965.
30 The problems of the inter-war years are described in detail in LAMIDA *The Furness Area*. Industrial Report No 1, 1948.
31 LAMIDA *Nineteenth Annual Report*. 1965, p 41; *Fourteenth Annual Report*. 1960, p 21.
32 Some of the problems involved in getting new employment into the Furness area are considered more fully in Grime, E. K. & Starkie, D. N. M. 'New Jobs for Old: An Impact Study of a new Factory in Furness', *Regional Studies*, Vol 2, 1968.
33 See Wallwork, K. L. 'Subsidence in the Mid-Cheshire Industrial Area', *Geographical Journal*, Vol 122, 1956, pp 40–53.
34 Shankland, Cox & Associates *Expansion of Winsford*. Consultants' master plan, 1967. The background to the expansion proposal, and its early progress is described in Rodgers, H. B. *Overspill in Winsford*. University of Keele, 1964.

CHAPTER 8

Industrial Development and Regional Planning. Page 212.

1 *Strategy II*, pp 24–7.
2 See letter from C. G. T. Tomlinson, Chairman of Winsford UDC, *The Times*, 29 Oct 1963.
3 These alternative strategies were set down in more detail in *Regional Shopping Centres: A Planning Report on North West England*. Dept of Town and Country Planning, University of Manchester, 1964, pp 81–97.
4 The study group's proposals are summarised in *The North West Study*, pp 108–12. For some of the local reaction, see for example LAMIDA *Newsletter No 17*, Dec 1965.
5 See for example a report prepared by J. Miller, Manchester City Planning Officer, reviewed in *The Daily Telegraph*, 30 Oct 1965.
6 For full particulars of the Warrington proposals, see Ministry of Housing and Local Government *Expansion of Warrington* (Austin-Smith/Salmon/Lord Partnership). HMSO, 1966. The land area finally

designated differs slightly from that recommended by the consultants in their report.

7 See *Central Lancashire: Study for a City*.

8 See *Expansion of Winsford*.

9 For a more detailed account of the factors restricting or promoting large-scale development, see *Regional Shopping Centres*, pp 62–74, and Figs 4·2 and 4·3.

10 *Ibid*, p 77.

11 Some alternatives are illustrated in Reynolds, J. P. 'The South Lancashire Project', *Town Planning Review*, Vol 37, 1966, pp 102–16.

12 Paper presented to the Town and Country Planning Association Summer School, Manchester, Sept 1968.

13 *Strategy II*, pp 54–6.

14 These points were made following the publication of *Strategy I* in 1966, in Smith, D. M. *Industrial Location and Regional Planning in the North West*, p 12.

15 Sylvester D. & Rodgers, H. B. *Crewe—A Geographic, Economic and Demographic Study of the Town in relation to S.E. Cheshire*. Borough of Crewe, 1965.

16 Cheshire County Planning Office. *Macclesfield Sub-Region Feasibility Study for Urban Expansion*. Cheshire CC, 1967.

17 Economic Consultants Limited *Industrial Complex Study*, to be published in 1969.

18 See *Impact on North East Lancashire* for full details. The case for such a road has been accepted by the Ministry of Transport.

19 Report of the Hunt Committee.

20 *Regional Shopping Centres*, p 79.

21 Yorkshire and Humberside Economic Planning Council *Halifax and the Calder Valley—An Area Study*. HMSO, 1968.

22 LAMIDA *The Decline of the Coal and Cotton Industries of Lancashire . . .*, pp 26–7.

23 *Strategy II*, p 67.

24 This idea is developed further in Lloyd, P. E. & Dicken, P. 'The Data Bank in Regional Studies of Industry', *Town Planning Review*, Vol 38, 1968, pp 304–16.

25 Textile Council *Cotton and Allied Textiles—A Report on Present Performance and Future Prospects*. 1969.

26 *The Intermediate Areas*. Report of a Committee under the Chairmanship of Sir Joseph Hunt. 1969.

27 *Ibid*, Note of Dissent by Professor A. J. Brown, pp 159–60.

28 *The Times*, 25 April 1969, reporting a statement by the Secretary of State for Economic Affairs.

Bibliography

This list is selective and concentrates on the literature of the past twenty years. Only the most important sources on pre-war industrial development are included.

BOOKS

Aikin, J. *A Description of the Country from Thirty to Forty Miles Round Manchester.* 1795, reprinted by David & Charles, 1968

Allison, J. E. *The Mersey Estuary.* Liverpool University Press, 1949

Barker, T. C. & Harris, J. R. *A Merseyside Town in the Industrial Revolution: St Helens, 1750–1900.* Liverpool University Press, 1954

Carter, C. F. (editor) *Manchester and its Region.* British Association Handbook, Manchester University Press, 1962

Chaloner, W. H. *The Social and Economic Development of Crewe.* Manchester University Press, 1950

Chapman, S. J. *The Lancashire Cotton Industry—A Study in Economic Development.* Manchester University Press, 1904

Dilke, M. S. *Field Excursions in North West England.* Rivington, 1965

Edwards, K. C. *The Peak District.* New Naturalist, 1962

Fogarty, M. P. *Prospects of the Industrial Areas of Great Britain.* Nuffield College Social Reconstruction Survey, 1945

Freeman, T. W. *The Conurbations of Britain.* Manchester University Press, revised edition, 1966

Freeman, T. W., Rodgers, H. B. & Kinvig, R. H. *Lancashire, Cheshire and the Isle of Man.* Nelson, 1966

Green, L. P. *Provincial Metropolis: The Future of Local Government in South-East Lancashire.* Allen & Unwin, 1959

Hardie, D. W. F. *A History of the Chemical Industry in Widnes.* ICI, 1950

Lawton, R. (editor) *Merseyside in the 1960s.* Longman, 1969

Marshall, J. D. *Furness and the Industrial Revolution.* Barrow-in-Furness Library and Museum Committee, 1958

Miles, C. *Lancashire Textiles: A Case Study of Industrial Change.* National Institute of Economic and Social Research, Occasional Papers XXIII, Cambridge University Press, 1968

Millward, R. *The Making of the English Landscape: Lancashire.* Hodder & Stoughton, 1955

Moser, C. A. & Scott, W. *British Towns.* Oliver & Boyd, 1961

Mounfield, P. R. & Ortolani, M. *Lombardia e Lancashire*. Memorie di Geografia Economica e Antropica, Nuova Serie, Vol 3. Instituto di Geografie dell Universita Napoli, 1963

Parkinson, C. N. *The Rise of the Port of Liverpool*. Liverpool University Press, 1952

Robson, R. *The Cotton Industry in Britain*. Macmillan, 1957

Smith, W. *A Physical Survey of Merseyside*. Liverpool University Press, 1946

An Economic Geography of Great Britain. Methuen, 1948

(editor) *A Scientific Survey of Merseyside*. Liverpool University Press, 1953

Tippett, L. H. C., *A Portrait of the Lancashire Textile Industry*. Oxford University Press, 1969

Tupling, G. H. *The Economic History of Rossendale*. Manchester University Press, 1927

Wilson, T. (editor) *Papers on Regional Development*. Journal of Industrial Economics, Supplement II, Blackwell, 1965

GOVERNMENT PUBLICATIONS

Board of Trade *Working Party Report: Cotton*. HMSO, 1946

Reorganisation of the Cotton Industry. HMSO, 1959

The Movement of Manufacturing Industry in the United Kingdom 1945–65. HMSO, 1968.

Department of Economic Affairs *The National Plan*, HMSO, 1965

The North West: A Regional Study. HMSO, 1965

The Problems of Merseyside. HMSO, 1965

Hunt, Sir Joseph, *The Intermediate Areas*. Report of the Committee under the Chairmanship of Sir Joseph Hunt. HMSO, 1969.

Local Government Commission *North Western General Review Area*. HMSO, 1965

South-East Lancashire and Merseyside Special Review Areas. HMSO, 1965

Ministry of Fuel and Power *Regional Survey of the North West Coalfield*. HMSO, 1949

Ministry of Housing and Local Government *Expansion of Warrington*. HMSO, 1966

Central Lancashire—Study for a City. HMSO, 1967

Central Lancashire New Town Proposal: Impact on North-East Lancashire. HMSO, 1968

North West Economic Planning Council *An Economic Planning Strategy for the North West*. 1966 (mimeo), now known as *Strategy I*.

Strategy II: The North West of the 1970s. HMSO, 1968

Registrar General *Census of England and Wales 1961*. HMSO, various volumes

Sample Census 1966. HMSO, various volumes

Statistical Review of England and Wales 1965. HMSO, 1967

Abstract of Regional Statistics 1966. HMSO, 1967

Yorkshire and Humberside Economic Planning Council *Halifax and the Calder Valley—An Area Study*. HMSO, 1968

REPORTS AND PAMPHLETS

Chadwick, C. F. & Medhurst, D. F. *Housing Needs and Land Availability in the Southeast Lancashire Conurbation*. Town and Country Planning Association, 1962

Cheshire County Planning Office *Macclesfield Sub-Region Feasibility Study for Urban Expansion*. Cheshire CC, 1967

Economic Consultants Ltd *Industrial Complex Study*. 1969

Economist Intelligence Unit *A Study of the Prospects for the Economic Development of North-East Lancashire*. 1959

Financial Times *The North West—A Financial Times Survey*. 8 Apr 1968

Gresswell, R. K. & Lawton, R. *British Landscape through Maps: Merseyside. Geographical Association*, 1964

Lancashire Industrial Development Association (now LAMIDA) *The Furness Area*. Industrial Report No 1, 1948
   The Weaving Area. Industrial Report No 2, 1948
   Merseyside. Industrial Report No 3, 1949
   The South East Lancashire Area and parts of Cheshire and Derbyshire. Industrial Report No 4, 1949
   The Spinning Area. Industrial Report No 5, 1950
   The Coal/Chemical Area. Industrial Report No 6, 1950
   The Lancashire Coast Area. Industrial Report No 7, 1951
   Lancashire and Merseyside. Industrial Report No 8, 1952

Lancashire and Merseyside Industrial Development Association *(LAMIDA) Distribution of Industry Policy*. Research Memorandum No 2, 1953
   Shipbuilding in Lancashire and Merseyside. Research Memorandum No 4, 1954
   The Occupation of Cotton Mills for Other Industries. 1961 (mimeo)
   The Problem of Migration from North East Lancashire. 1962 (mimeo)
   The Labour Position in the Furness Area. 1962 (mimeo)
   The Problem of Migration from the Furness Area. 1962 (mimeo)
   The Development of Lancashire and Merseyside—Past, Present and Future. 1963
   The North West Region—Development Prospects and Needs. 1964
   The Problems of Seasonal Unemployment and Labour Supply in the Coastal Towns of Lancashire. 1965 (mimeo)
   An Industrial Policy for the North West. 1966 (mimeo)
   The Decline of the Cotton and Coal Mining Industries of Lancashire. 1967
   Closure and Reoccupation of Cotton Mills. 1967 (mimeo)
   Buyers Guide to Industry in the North West. 1968
   Annual Reports. 1959–68
   Newsletters. Various dates (mimeo)

Lancashire County Planning Office *A Preliminary Plan for Lancashire*. Lancashire CC, 1950

Future Development of Central Mid-Lancashire (with particular reference to the Chorley-Leyland Area). 1965

Manchester City Planning Office *Manchester and its Region.* 1969

Masser, F. I. *Economic Base Study: Review of Population and Employment Trends.* Report for Merseyside Area Landuse Transportation Study. Traffic Research Corporation, 1967 (mimeo)

Rodgers, H. B. *Overspill in Winsford.* University of Keele, 1964

Shankland, Cox & Associates *Expansion of Winsford.* Consultant's master plan, 1967

Smith, D. M. *Industrial Location and Regional Planning in the North West.* Report prepared for the Industrial Working Party, South-East Lancashire and North-East Cheshire Traffic Survey. School of Geography, University of Manchester, 1966 (mimeo)

Sylvester, D. & Rodgers, H. B. *Crewe—A Geographic, Economic and Demographic Study of the Town in relation to S.E. Cheshire.* Borough of Crewe, 1965 (mimeo)

Textile Council *Cotton and Allied Textiles—A Report on Present Performance and Future Prospects.* 1969

Town and Country Planning Association *Papers and Report of Conferences on Planning in the North West.* 1962

University of Manchester, Economics Research Section *An Industrial Survey of the Lancashire Area.* HMSO, 1932
Readjustment in Lancashire. Manchester University Press, 1936

University of Manchester, Department of Town and Country Planning *Regional Shopping Centres: A Planning Report on North West England.* 1964
Part Two: A Retail Shopping Model. 1966

ARTICLES

Allen, E. G. W. 'Industrial Development in the North West', *District Bank Review*, Sept 1961
'Post-War Industrial Development in Lancashire and Merseyside', *Journal*, Manchester Statistical Society, 1964

Amos, F. J. C. 'Alternative Plans for Sub-Regional Problems', *Regional Studies*, Vol 1, 1967

Barker, J. C. 'Lancashire Coal, Cheshire Salt, and the Rise of Liverpool', *Transactions*, Historical Society of Lancashire and Cheshire, Vol 103, 1951

Bor, W. G. & Shankland, C. G. L. 'Renaissance of a City: A Study in the Re-development of Liverpool', *Journal*, Town Planning Institute, Jan 1965

Bowden, P. K. 'The Limestone Quarrying Industry of North Derbyshire', *Geographical Journal*, Vol 129, 1963

Coates, B. E. & Rawstron, E. M. 'Regional Variations in Incomes', *Westminster Bank Review*, Feb 1966

Cullingworth, J. B. 'Overspill in South East Lancashire—The Salford-Worsley Scheme', *Town Planning Review*, Vol 30, 1959–60

Estall, R. C. 'Industrial Changes in Lancashire and Merseyside', *Geography*, Vol 46, 1962

Ferguson, J. 'History of the Heavy Chemical Industry on Merseyside', *Advancement of Science*, Vol 2, 1954

Gibson, G. 'Distribution of Industry in the North-West Region', *Transactions*, Manchester Statistical Society, 1947–8

Gibson, J. R. 'The Paper Industry of North West England', *The Paper-Maker and British Paper Trade Journal*, monthly issues Sept 1958 to Jan 1959

+ Gittus, E. 'Migration in Lancashire and Cheshire: A Sample Analysis of the National Register', *Town Planning Review*, Vol 32, 1961–2

Gregory, S. 'Some Aspects of Water Resource Development in Relation to Lancashire', *Problems of Applied Geography II (Geographica Polonica 3)*, PWN (Polish Scientific Publishers), 1964

Grime, E. K. & Starkie, D. N. M. 'New Jobs for Old: An Impact Study of a New Factory in Furness', *Regional Studies*, Vol 2, 1968

Hall, P. 'Which Barrage in the North West?', *New Society*, 10 Dec 1964

Jackson, J. N. 'Industrial Surveys within a Declining Town', *Town Planning Review*, Vol 31, 1960–61

Jewkes, J. 'The Localisation of the Cotton Industry', *Economic History*, Vol 2, 1930

Lawton, R. 'The Population of Lancashire in the Mid-Nineteenth Century', *Transactions*, Historical Society of Lancashire and Cheshire, Vol 107, 1955

'Population Trends in Lancashire and Cheshire from 1801', *Transactions*, Historical Society of Lancashire and Cheshire, Vol 114, 1962

Lloyd, P. E. 'Industrial Changes in the Merseyside Development Area 1949–1959', *Town Planning Review*, Vol 35, 1964–5

Lloyd, P. E. & Dicken, P. 'The Data Bank in Regional Studies of Industry', *Town Planning Review*, Vol 38, 1967–8

McLoughlin, J. B. 'Planning and Administration in Metropolitan Manchester', *Town Planning Review*, Vol 35, 1964–5

Metcalf, D. & Cowling, K. 'Regional Wage Inflation in the United Kingdom', *District Bank Review*, June 1967

Miles, C. 'Contraction in Cotton: Some Comments on the 1959 Cotton Industry Act', *District Bank Review*, June 1965

'Should the Cotton Industry be Protected?', *District Bank Review*, June 1966

Musson, A. E. & Robinson, E. 'The Origins of Engineering in Lancashire', *Journal of Economic History*, Vol 20, 1960

Nairn, J. 'New Towns in the Pennines East of Manchester', *Architectural Review*, Sept 1964

North, G. 'Industrial Development in the Rossendale Valley', *Journal*, Manchester Geographical Society, Vol 58, 1962

'Lancastria', in Mitchell, J. (editor) *Great Britain: Regional Essays*. Cambridge University Press, 1962

Ogden, H. W. 'The Geographical Basis of the Lancashire Cotton Industry', *Journal*, Manchester Geographical Society, Vol 43, 1927

Oliver, F. 'Interregional Migration and Unemployment 1951–61', *Journal* + Royal Statistical Society, Series A, Vol 127 Part I, 1964

Ormerod, A. 'The Prospects of the British Cotton Industry', *Yorkshire Bulletin of Economic and Social Research*, Vol 15, 1963

Patmore, J. A. 'The Railway Network of Merseyside', *Transactions and Papers*, Institute of British Geographers, Vol 29, 1961
'The Railway Network of the Manchester Conurbation', *Transactions and Papers*, Institute of British Geographers, Vol 34, 1964

Pearce, D. W. & Herrington, R. R. 'Economic Aspects of the Morecambe Bay Barrage', *District Bank Review*, June 1965

Pickett, K. G. 'Aspects of Migration in North West England 1960–61', + *Town Planning Review*, Vol 38, 1967–8

Pilkington, W. G. 'Cotton Under Scrutiny', *District Bank Review*, Dec 1959

Pullen, M. J. 'Unemployment and Regional Income Per Head', *The Manchester School of Economic and Social Studies*, Vol 34, 1966

Rawstron, E. M. & Coates, B. E. 'Opportunity and Affluence', *Geography*, Vol 51, 1966

Reynolds, J. P. 'Shopping in the North West', *Town Planning Review*, Vol 34, 1963–4
'The South Lancashire Project', *Town Planning Review*, Vol 37, 1966–7

Rodgers, H. B. 'Industrial Lancashire and the British Cotton Industry', *Przeglad Geograficzny*, Vol 30, 1958
'Employment and Journey to Work in an Overspill Community', (ie Worsley), *Sociological Review*, Vol 17, 1959
'The Lancashire Cotton Industry in 1840', *Transactions and Papers*, Institute of British Geographers, Vol 28, 1960
'The Suburban Growth of Victorian Manchester', *Journal*, Manchester Geographical Society, Vol 58, 1961–2
'The Changing Geography of the Lancashire Cotton Industry', *Economic Geography*, Vol 38, 1962
'Recent Industrial Changes in North West England and their Economic and Social Consequences', *Problems of Applied Geography* II (*Geographica Polonica* 3), PWN (Polish Scientific Publishers), 1964

Salt, J. 'The Impact of the Ford and Vauxhall Plants on the Employment Situation of Merseyside, 1962–1965', *Tijdschrift voor Economische en Sociale Geografie*, Vol 58, 1967

Shankland, G. et al 'The Central Area of Liverpool', *Town Planning Review*, Vol 35, 1964–5

Smith, D. M. 'Recent Changes in the Regional Pattern of British Industry', *Tidjschrift voor Economische en Sociale Georgafie*, Vol 56, 1965
'Identifying the "Grey" Areas: A Multivariate Approach', *Regional Studies*, Vol 2, 1968
'Industrial Location and Regional Development: Some Recent Trends in North West England', *Environment*, Vol 1, 1969

Smith, W. 'Trends in the Distribution of the Lancashire Cotton Industry', *Geography*, Vol 26, 1941

Taylor, J. 'Estimating Labour Reserves: A Study of the Furness Sub-Region', *The Manchester School of Economic and Social Studies*, Vol 34, 1966

+ Thirlwell, A. P. 'Migration and Regional Unemployment: Some Lessons for Regional Planning', *Westminster Bank Review*, Nov 1966

Tupling, G. H. 'The Early Metal Trades and the beginning of Engineering in Lancashire', *Transactions*, Lancashire and Cheshire Antiquarian Society, Vol 61, 1949

Turner, H. A. & Smith, R. 'The Slump in the Cotton Industry 1952, *Bulletin*, Oxford University Institute of Statistics, Vol 15, 1953

Turton, B. J. 'Horwich: The Historical Geography of a Lancashire Industrial Town', *Transactions*, Lancashire and Cheshire Antiquarian Society, Vol 72, 1962

Vitkovitch, B. 'The United Kingdom Cotton Industry 1936–1954', *Journal of Industrial Economics*, Vol 3, 1955

Wallwork, K. L. 'Subsidence in the Mid-Cheshire Industrial Area', *Geographical Journal*, Vol 122, 1956
'The Mid-Cheshire Salt Industry', *Geography*, Vol 43, 1959
'Some Problems of Subsidence and Land Use in the Mid Cheshire Industrial Area', *Geographical Journal*, Vol 126, 1960
'Land Use Problems and the Evolution of Industrial Landscapes', *Geography*, Vol 45, 1960
'The Cotton Industry in North West England: 1941–1961', *Geography*, Vol 47, 1962

Wright, H. Myles 'National and Regional Planning', *Town and Country Planning Summer School*, 1962

SELECTED THESES (unpublished)

Dicken, P. *The Location of the Clothing Industries in the Manchester Conurbation*. MA Thesis, University of Manchester, 1968

Hammersley, A. D. *The Urban Geography of Barrow-in-Furness*. MA Thesis, University of Manchester, 1965

Holt, R. A. *The Changing Industrial Geography of the Cotton Areas of Lancashire, 1951–1961: A Study of Mill Conversion and Employment Structure*. MA Thesis, University of Manchester, 1964

Lloyd, P. E. *The Post-War Industrial Geography of Merseyside*. MA Thesis, University of Manchester, 1965

Wallwork, K. L. *Aspects of the Modern Economic Geography of the Calder-Darwen Valley*. MA Thesis, University of Manchester, 1955

APPENDIX A

Notes on Sources of Data and Methods of Statistical Analysis

1 *Census Statistics used in Chapter 1*

All the figures from the *Sample Census 1966* and some from the *1961 Census* are based on a ten-per-cent sample. They are subject to some bias, as well as to sampling errors which can be considerable in local-authority areas with a small population. The geographical patterns revealed by mapping census statistics are partially determined by the areas of different size and shape for which the figures are compiled. In general, large areas and those with large populations are unlikely to show the extreme values for social and economic measures which may occur in smaller areas with less varied character. In mapping the census figures in Chapter 1, local-authority area boundaries are omitted, and some generalisation has been necessary to ensure clarity of reproduction.

2 *Correlation between certain socio-economic variables referred to in Chapter 1*

Product moment correlation coefficients calculated from data for the 177 local-authority areas are as follows:

Variable	1	2	3	4	5	6	7	8	9
1	1·00								
2	0·27	1·00							
3	−0·61	−0·20	1·00						
4	0·55	−0·22	0·88	1·00					
5	0·49	0.25	−0·75	−0·84	1·00				
6	0·40	0·07	−0·60	−0·46	0·40	1·00			
7	0·48	0·13	−0·63	−0·51	0·49	0·77	1·00		
8	−0·61	−0·22	0·80	0·82	−0·70	−0·49	−0·57	1·00	
9	−0·58	−0·20	0·81	0·84	−0·66	−0·41	−0·46	0·92	1·00

The variables are:

1 Death rate index, 1965 (national rate = 100).
2 Infant mortality, 1965 (‰ of live births).
3 Persons over 25 leaving school at 15 or later, 1961 (‰ of total).

4   Professional workers etc, 1966 (‰ of working males).
5   Semi-skilled and unskilled manual workers, 1966 (‰ of working males).
6   Dwellings with rateable value less than £30, 1966 (‰ of total).
7   Households without a fixed bath, 1966 (‰ of total).
8   Number of motor cars, 1966 (per 1,000 households).
9   Households with two or more cars, 1966 (‰ of total).

The correlation coefficient varies from 1·00, indicating a perfect positive linear relationship, to −1·00, indicating a perfect inverse relationship between two variables. A coefficient of around 0·00 indicates a random relationship. The method of calculation is explained in any statistics textbook.

3   The Ministry of Labour Estimates of Insured Employees

These annual figures are based on a one-in-four sample of national insurance cards exchanged in the quarter-year beginning in June, and on returns made by employers of five or more workers. Because of sampling, and the varying completeness of the employers' returns, the estimates are subject to errors, which can be considerable for small figures and in areas with a small number of workers. The Ministry provides the following information on the margin of error (either way) due to sampling:

Size of category (eg industry in an area)	Poor coverage of employers returns	Average coverage of employers returns
1,000,000	3,500 error	1,400 error
100,000	1,100 ,,	440 ,,
10,000	350 ,,	140 ,,
1,000	110 ,,	40 ,,
100	35 ,,	14 ,,

Other problems arising from the way in which the estimates are made include the omission of most civil servants, and employers or self-employed. In figures for employment-exchange areas the number working in activities with a large proportion of self-employed, such as farming, can be substantially under-estimated.

The descriptions of the industrial structure of the region as a whole in Chapter 2 are based on the Ministry's regional estimates for 1967. The more detailed analysis of location and structure, which required much more processing of data, is based on figures for 1965 from the *Employment Records II* for the ninety-five employment-exchange areas which give the closest approximation to the North West Standard Region. Because of the greater under-estimation in the exchange area figures, their sum will be less than the regional total employment.

4   The Coefficient of Localisation

This is calculated by comparing the percentage distribution by areas of a given industry with that of all industry. Put formally it is given by:

$$C_1 = \tfrac{1}{2} \sum_{i=1}^{N} \left| \frac{100\ X_i}{X_t} - \frac{100\ Y_i}{Y_t} \right|$$

where X_i is the number employed in a given industry X in the ith areal
   subdivision, or employment-exchange area
X_t is total regional employment in industry
Y_i is employment in all industry in area i
Y_t is total regional employment in all industry.

The vertical brackets indicate the absolute value of the expression within, ie the difference between the two percentages irrespective of sign. Instead of taking half the sum of the deviations ignoring their sign, the sum of either the positive deviations or the negative deviations can be used. (This and similar coefficients are discussed more fully in Isard, W. *Methods of Regional Analysis.* MIT Press, 1960, pp 249–79.)

5 Identifying 'One Industry' and 'Two Industry' Areas

The figures used were percentages of total industrial employees in each of five major industrial groups, for each exchange area. It was assumed that in a 'one industry' town the 'ideal', or expected percentage distribution, would be 100 per cent in one group and nil in the others, in a 'two industry' town it would be 50 per cent in one industry 50 per cent in a second, and nil in the rest. In a 'three industry' town the percentages would be 33·3, 33·3, 33·3, 0 and 0, in a 'four industry' town 25, 25, 25, 25 and 0, and in the final category, indicating an even share of all industries, each should score 20 per cent. For each exchange area the actual percentage distribution in the five industrial categories, in rank order, was compared with these 'ideal' structures, and the difference measured by summing the squares of the deviations of actual from ideal. The ideal structure which the actual structure most closely resembled provided the classificatory description for the area in question, ie, if it most closely resembled the 100, 0, 0, 0, 0 distribution it was classed as a 'one industry' town, with the industry identified as the largest of its five groups. Areas found to resemble another pattern more closely than the 'one' or 'two industry' ideals were considered to be diversified. (This method is explained more fully in Haggett, P. *Locational Analysis in Human Geography.* Arnold, 1965, pp 220–1.)

6 The Coefficient of Specialisation and Index of Structural Change

The coefficient of specialisation compares the percentage distribution of industrial employees among given branches of industry (in this case Orders of the SIC) in any area with the regional employment structure. A big deviation from the regional structure gives a large coefficient of specialisation, and vice versa. The formal expression can be written:

$$C_s = \tfrac{1}{2} \sum_{i=1}^{N} \left| \frac{100\ X_i}{X_t} - \frac{100\ Y_i}{Y_t} \right|$$

where X_i is the number of workers in industrial category i in an exchange area X

X_t is total industrial employment in area X

Y_i is regional employment in industry i

Y_t is total regional industrial employment

Thus the deviations of the exchange-area percentages from the regional percentage are summed irrespective of sign for all the N industrial categories, and the result halved, to give a coefficient ranging from 0 to 100 (cf note 4).

The index of structural change is calculated in the same way, except that X_i and X_t are figures for an individual industry and all industry respectively in any area at the base year (1953), and Y_i and Y_t are the same figures for some subsequent year (1965).

7   *The Delimitation of Industrial Sub-Regions in Chapter 2*

The twelve-unit subdivision in Figure 10 was built up in three stages. First, figures for percentage employment were examined for four major industrial groups—engineering and metals; textiles and clothing; chemicals, glass and ceramics; and mining and quarrying. This made possible the identification of sub-regional core areas, based on the criterion of one standard deviation above the exchange-area mean percentage employment in any group. Secondly, some adjoining areas were added to these cores, on the grounds of a clear commitment to the industrial group in question, and certain districts in which textiles and engineering are of comparable importance were recognised tentatively. Finally, the exact boundaries between sub-regions were established by two measures of the overall structural similarity of adjoining exchange areas at the fourteen industrial subdivisions level, namely, a cross-boundary index of similarity (as explained in the previous note), and a cross-boundary correlation analysis using Spearman's rank coefficient. (More sophisticated statistical methods for grouping areas, such as the one based on factor analysis used in Chapter 6, were rejected because of the relatively low correlations between the percentage-employment figures for individual industries: a factor analysis revealed a first factor which accounted for only 12 per cent of the variance, and a second accounting for 11 per cent.)

8   *The use of Ministry of Labour Employment Figures in Chapter 3*

Changes in the method of compiling the annual estimates mean that 1953 is the earliest year which can be used as a base for comparison with more recent figures. The 1959 revision of the Standard Industrial Classification requires some adjustments to earlier figures, and all the 1953 estimates used in this chapter have been adjusted, where necessary, by the method recommended by the Ministry of Labour. Because of errors which cannot be eliminated, individual employment-exchange areas are considered only with respect to the main sectors of the economy, and estimates of changes in employment at the Order level of the SIC are compiled only at the regional level. In order to identify the growth and declining industries as clearly as possible, some calculations have been made for changes in broad subdivisions of certain Orders, and as these are regional figures they can be accepted with a reasonable degree of confidence. However, detailed comparison at a Minimum List Heading level of the SIC was deemed inadvisable, even for the region as a whole. It should be noted that the revision of the SIC has necessitated the combination of Orders VI and IX for comparative purposes, to produce an 'engineering and metal goods' category.

9 *The Industrial Change Model used to test the Structural Hypothesis in Chapter 4*

The comparative change in employment in any area is the actual change related to regional change. Thus in the North West between 1953 and 1964 the regional change was minus 6·4 per cent, so any area which did better than this had a positive comparative change, even if the actual change was negative. Comparative change (COMPAR) and compositional change (COMPOS) are given by:

$$\text{COMPAR} = Y_{ta} - X_{ta} \frac{Y_{tr}}{X_{tr}}$$

$$\text{COMPOS} = \sum_{i=1}^{N} \left(X_{ia} \frac{Y_{ir}}{X_{ir}} \right) - X_{ta} \frac{Y_{tr}}{X_{tr}}$$

where X_{ia} is employment at base year in industry i in area a
    X_{ta} is employment at base year in all industry in area a
    X_{ir} is employment at base year in industry i in the region
    X_{tr} is employment in all industry in the region
    Y_{ia}, Y_{ta}, Y_{ir} and Y_{tr} are the same variables for the later year.

Competitive change (COMPET) is given by:

    COMPET = COMPAR minus COMPOS

(For further details on this method, see Fuchs, V. R. 'The Determinants of the Redistribution of Manufacturing in the United States since 1929', *Review of Economics and Statistics*, Vol 44, 1962, pp 167–8).

The number of industries (N) is in this case nineteen. These are Orders II to XVI of the SIC, with VI and IX combined, and with some internal sub-division necessitated by the very different rates of change of different branches of certain Orders. Mining has been subdivided into coal and other mining and quarrying; railway engineering has been separated from the other vehicle industries, textiles has been divided into cotton etc, textile finishing, and other textiles; and the footwear industry has been separated from other clothing.

10 *Survey of Firms Completing a New Industrial-Building Project in 1967*

A postal survey was conducted in May 1968, with a questionnaire sent to 202 manufacturing firms. This represented all firms with completed developments in 1967 known to the Board of Trade. There were 89 replies (a response rate of almost 45 per cent) of which 27 provided no information and, of the remaining 62, some did not answer the whole questionnaire. The results are thus based on a sample which is not random, though not markedly biased in terms of size of project, location and type of industry. They must therefore be treated with some reservations as to how truly representative they are.

11 *The Factor Analysis and Grouping Procedures used in Chapter 6 to identify the Geography of Economic Health*

Each of the two sets of data used comprised an m x n order matrix, where n is the number of observations and m the number of variables. For the industrial data n = 95, ie the number of exchange areas, and for the socio-economic data n = 177 (local-authority areas). In both cases m = 14; for technical reasons a larger number of variables would have been preferred, but the choice was restricted by data available. The two sets of data were subjected to multiple-factor analysis, with the principal factors rotated according to the normal varimax criteria. This is the rotation generally used in this kind of analysis; it tends to produce relatively high factor loadings on a relatively small number of variables, and facilitates the indentification of the factors. The loadings on the first two rotated factors were used to compute each area's factor scores. For any area i on any factor k the score (f) is given by:

$$f_{ik} = \sum_{j=1}^{m} a_{jk} z_{ij}$$

where j is one of m variables, a represents the factor loading,and z the original observation in the standard form (zero mean and unit standard deviation) as used in the factor analysis.

The final classifications were produced by application of a stepwise grouping procedure. Areas were grouped together according to proximity (or similarity) in the two-dimensional statistical space produced by a plot of scores on the first two factors. The two closest (most similar) areas were grouped first, and replaced by their mean centre. Then the next two closest, and so on, until a convenient level of aggregation had been reached. In the case of both sets of data, the procedure was stopped when six major independent groups of areas had emerged. Then minor groups and outlying individual areas were allocated to their nearest major group.

These procedures are explained more fully in the following:

Berry, B. J. L. 'A Method for Deriving Multi-Factor Uniform Regions', *Przeglad Geogroficzny*, Vol 33, 1961, pp 263–82

Berry, B. J. L. 'Grouping and Regionalisation: An Approach to the Problem using Multi-Variate Analysis', in Garrison, W. L. & Marble, D. F. (editors) *Quantitative Geography: Part I Economic and Cultural Topics*. Dept of Geography, Northwestern University, 1967, pp 219–51

Berry, B. J. L. 'A Synthesis of Formal and Functional Regions, in Berry, B. J. L. & Marble, D. F. (editors) *Spatial Analysis: A Reader in Statistical Geography*. Prentice Hall, 1968, pp 419–28

Hagood, M. J. et al, 'An Examination of the use of Factor Analysis in the Problem of Sub-Regional Delineation', *Rural Sociology*, Vol 6, 1941, pp 216–33

APPENDIX B

Key to Employment-Exchange Areas

1	Accrington	33	Golborne	65	Preston
2	Altrincham	34	Grange-over-Sands	66	Prestwich
3	Aston-in-Makerfield	35	Great Harwood	67	Radcliffe
4	Ashton-under-Lyne	36	Haslingden	68	Ramsbottom
5	Atherton	37	Heywood	69	Rawtenstall
6	Bacup	38	Hindley	70	Rochdale
7	Bamber Bridge	39	Horwich	71	Royton
8	Barrow-in-Furness	40	Hoylake	72	Runcorn
9	Bebington	41	Hyde	73	St Anne's
10	Birkenhead	42	Irlam	74	St Helens
11	Blackburn	43	Kirkham	75	Saddleworth
12	Blackpool	44	Lancaster	76	Salford
13	Bolton	45	Leigh	77	Sandbach
14	Burnley	46	Leyland	78	Shaw
15	Bury	47	Littleborough	79	Southport
16	Buxton	48	Liverpool	80	Stalybridge
17	Chapel-en-le-Frith	49	Macclesfield	81	Standish
18	Chester	50	Manchester	82	Stockport
19	Chorley	51	Marple	83	Stretford
20	Clitheroe	52	Middleton	84	Swinton
21	Colne	53	Middlewich	85	Thornton
22	Congleton	54	Morecambe	86	Ulverston
23	Crewe	55	Mossley	87	Upholland
24	Dalton-in-Furness	56	Nantwich	88	Walkden
25	Darwen	57	Nelson	89	Wallasey
26	Denton	58	Neston	90	Warrington
27	Earlstown	59	New Mills	91	Westhoughton
28	Eccles	60	Northwich	92	Widnes
29	Ellesmere Port	61	Oldham	93	Wigan
30	Farnworth	62	Ormskirk	94	Wilmslow
31	Fleetwood	63	Padiham	95	Winsford
32	Glossop	64	Prescot		

These are the Ministry of Labour employment-exchange areas as defined in 1968, except for the amalgamation of Lytham and St Anne's (necessary for the comparison with previous years), and the omission of Skelmersdale created in 1965. The areas are identified by numbers in Fig 5, Chapter 2.

APPENDIX C

Key to Local Authority Areas

Cheshire
1   Birkenhead CB
2   Chester CB
3   Stockport CB
4   Wallasey CB
5   Alderley Edge UD
6   Alsager UD
7   Altrincham MB
8   Bebington MB
9   Bollington UD
10 Bowdon UD
11 Bredbury and
    Romiley UD
12 Cheadle and
    Gatley UD
13 Congleton MB
14 Crewe MB
15 Dunkinfield MB
16 Ellesmere Port MB
17 Hale UD
18 Hazel Grove and
    Bramhall UD
19 Hoylake UD
20 Hyde MB
21 Knutsford UD
22 Longdendale UD
23 Lymm UD
24 Macclesfield MB
25 Marple UD
26 Middlewich UD
27 Nantwich UD
28 Neston UD
29 Northwich UD
30 Runcorn UD
31 Sale MB
32 Sandbach UD
33 Stalybridge MB
34 Wilmslow UD
35 Winsford UD
36 Wirral UD
37 Bucklow RD
38 Chester RD
39 Congleton RD
40 Disley RD
41 Macclesfield RD

42 Nantwich RD
43 Northwich RD
44 Runcorn RD
45 Tarvin RD
46 Tintwistle RD

Lancashire
47 Barrow-in-Furness
    CB
48 Blackburn CB
49 Blackpool CB
50 Bolton CB
51 Bootle CB
52 Burnley CB
53 Bury CB
54 Liverpool CB
55 Manchester CB
56 Oldham CB
57 Preston CB
58 Rochdale CB
59 St Helens CB
60 Salford CB
61 Southport CB
62 Warrington CB
63 Wigan CB
64 Abram UD
65 Accrington MB
66 Adlington UD
67 Ashton-in-Makerfield
    UD
68 Aston-under-Lyne MB
69 Aspull UD
70 Atherton UD
71 Audenshaw UD
72 Bacup MB
73 Barrowford UD
74 Billinge and
    Winstanley UD
75 Blackrod UD
76 Brierfield UD
77 Carnforth UD
78 Chadderton UD
79 Chorley MB
80 Church UD
81 Clayton-le-Moors UD

82   Clitheroe MB
83   Colne MB
84   Crompton UD
85   Crosby MB
86   Dalton-in-Furness UD
87   Darwen MB
88   Denton UD
89   Droylsden UD
90   Eccles MB
91   Failsworth UD
92   Farnworth MB
93   Formby UD
95   Fulwood UD
96   Golborne UD
97   Grange-over-Sands UD
98   Great Harwood UD
99   Haslingden MB
100 Haydock UD
101 Heywood MB
102 Hindley UD
103 Horwich UD
104 Huyton-with-Roby
     UD
105 Ince-in-Makerfield
     UD
106 Irlam UD
107 Kearsley UD
108 Kirkby UD
109 Kirkham UD
110 Lancaster MB
111 Lees UD
112 Leigh MB
113 Leyland UD
114 Litherland UD
115 Littleborough UD
116 Little Lever UD
117 Longridge UD
118 Lytham St Anne's
     MB
119 Middleton MB
120 Milnrow UD
121 Morecambe and
     Heysham MB
122 Mossley MB
123 Nelson MB

124 Newton-le-Willows UD
125 Ormskirk UD
126 Orrell UD
127 Oswaldtwistle UD
128 Padiham UD
129 Poulton-le-Fylde UD
130 Preesall UD
131 Prescot UD
132 Prestwich MB
133 Radcliffe MB
134 Rainford UD
135 Ramsbottom UD
136 Rawtenstall MB
137 Rishton UD
138 Royton UD
139 Skelmersdale UD
140 Standish-with-Langtree UD
141 Stretford MB

142 Swinton and Pendlebury MB
143 Thornton Cleveleys UD
144 Tottington UD
145 Trawden UD
146 Turton UD
147 Tyldesley UD
148 Ulverston UD
149 Up Holland UD
150 Urmston UD
151 Walton-le-Dale UD
152 Wardle UD
153 Westhoughton UD
154 Whitworth UD
156 Widnes MB
157 Withnell UD
158 Worsley UD
159 Blackburn RD

160 Burnley RD
161 Chorley RD
162 Clitheroe RD
163 Fylde RD
164 Garstang RD
165 Lancaster RD
166 Lunesdale RD
167 North Lonsdale RD
168 Preston RD
169 Warrington RD
170 West Lancashire RD
171 Whiston RD
172 Wigan RD

Derbyshire
173 Buxton MB
174 Glossop MB
175 New Mills UD
176 Whaley Bridge UD
177 Chapel-en-le-Frith RD

Index

References to plates are in italics